Semantics for Counting and Measuring

The use of numerals in counting differs quite dramatically across languages. Some languages grammaticalize a contrast between count nouns (*three cats*; *three books*) and 'non-count' or mass nouns (*milk*; *mud*), marking this distinction in different ways. Others use a system of numeral classifiers, while yet others use a combination of both. This book draws attention to the contrast between counting and measuring, and shows that it is central to our understanding of how we use numerical expressions, classifiers and count nouns in different languages. It reviews some of the more recent major linguistic results in the semantics of numerals, counting and measuring and theories of the mass/count distinction, and presents the author's new research on the topic. The book draws heavily on crosslinguistic research, and presents in-depth case studies of the mass/count distinction and counting and measuring in a number of typologically unrelated languages. It also includes chapters on classifier constructions and on adjectival uses of measure phrases.

SUSAN ROTHSTEIN is a professor in the Department of English Literature and Linguistics at the Faculty of Humanities at Bar-Ilan University. She has written more than fifty articles and is the author of two previous books, *Predicates and Their Subjects* (2001) and *Structuring Events* (2004), as well as editor or co-editor of several others.

T0384782

KEY TOPICS IN SEMANTICS AND PRAGMATICS

'Key Topics in Semantics and Pragmatics' focuses on the main topics of
study in semantics and pragmatics today. It consists of accessible yet
challenging accounts of the most important issues, concepts and
phenomena to consider when examining meaning in language. Some
topics have been the subject of semantic and pragmatic study for many
years, and are re-examined in this series in light of new developments in
the field; others are issues of growing importance that have not so far
been given a sustained treatment. Written by leading experts and
designed to bridge the gap between textbooks and primary literature,
the books in this series can either be used on courses and seminars, or as
one-stop, succinct guides to a particular topic for individual students and
researchers. Each book includes useful suggestions for further reading,
discussion questions and a helpful glossary.

Already published in the series:

Meaning and Humour by Andrew Goatly

Metaphor by L. David Ritchie

Imperatives by Mark Jary and Mikhail Kissine

Modification by Marcin Morzycki

Semantics for Counting and Measuring by Susan Rothstein

Forthcoming titles:

Game-Theoretic Pragmatics by Anton Benz

Pragmatics and the Philosophy of Language by Mitchell Green

Distributivity by George Tsoulas and Eytan Zweig

Implicature by Jacques Moeschler and Sandrine Zufferey

Experimental Pragmatics by Ira Noveck

Irony by Joana Garmendia

Semantics and Pragmatics in Sign Languages by Kathryn Davidson

Propositional Logic by Allen Hazen and Jeffrey Pelletier

Semantics for Counting and Measuring

SUSAN ROTHSTEIN

CAMBRIDGE
UNIVERSITY PRESS

CAMBRIDGE
UNIVERSITY PRESS

University Printing House, Cambridge CB2 8BS, United Kingdom

One Liberty Plaza, 20th Floor, New York, NY 10006, USA

477 Williamstown Road, Port Melbourne, VIC 3207, Australia

314-321, 3rd Floor, Plot 3, Splendor Forum, Jasola District Centre, New Delhi - 110025, India

79 Anson Road, #06-04/06, Singapore 079906

Cambridge University Press is part of the University of Cambridge.

It furthers the University's mission by disseminating knowledge in the pursuit of education, learning and research at the highest international levels of excellence.

www.cambridge.org
Information on this title: www.cambridge.org/9780521171823
DOI: 10.1017/9780511734830

First published 2017
First paperback edition 2019

A catalogue record for this publication is available from the British Library

ISBN   978-1-107-00127-5   Hardback
ISBN   978-0-521-17182-3   Paperback

A quantity therefore is called a multitude if it is countable and it is called a magnitude if it is measurable.

Aristotle, *Metaphysics* 13.1020a10

Contents

Acknowledgements

This book explores the interplay between theoretical and crosslinguistic semantics. I first thought of writing this book in 2010, but of course the work that made it possible to think up the project had started long before that.

My first and foremost debt of gratitude is to those who have worked with me and allowed me to work with them on the different languages discussed in this book. Keren Khrizman, Fred Landman, Xuping Li, Suzi Lima, Roberta Pires de Oliveira, and Brigitta Schvarcz have all been close collaborators for much of the last nine years. It has been enormously exciting to explore the topic of counting and measuring in depth with them in different languages, and it is they who made this whole project possible. I see the book as a stage in the collaborations, and look forward to continuing them. Other collaborators and students who have also been closely involved and whom I want to thank include Noa Epstein-Naveh, Chen Gafni, Maria Gepner, Christine Hnout, Adina Moshavi and Alessandro Treves. I owe a huge thank you to my informants for Hebrew, in particular Michal Drori, Henia Gal, Lior Laks and Alex Rothstein Landman. The starting point for this project was my 2009 study of Hebrew pseudopartitives, which appears here as part of Chapter 3, and without their generosity in discussing the data with me, the project would never have gotten off the ground. Thanks also to Geneviève Blanchard for discussing the French data with me.

I have presented different parts of this work at many different conferences and colloquia over the last nine years – far more than I can list – and had many, many conversations with colleagues all over the world. I thank all those whose comments and observations contributed to the book, especially Lisa Cheng, Edit Doron, Brenda Laca and Barbara Partee. A few events stick out especially. The first time any material included in this book was presented in public was at the workshop that Edit Doron organized in 2006 in honour of Anita Mittwoch's 80th birthday. Maria José Foltran invited me to the Formal

Linguistics Workshop in Curitiba in 2008, which is where I first met
Roberta. In 2012, Angelika Kratzer suggested that I invite Suzi Lima to
give a colloquium in Israel, so that she and I could talk about Yudja,
and we have been talking ever since. Vladimir Borschev, Hana Filip
and Barbara Partee found ways to come regularly to Israel and take
part in the (no-budget) annual workshops that I have organized since
2010 at Bar-Ilan, where they, my students, my Israeli colleagues and
I have been able to discuss, among other things, many of the issues
raised in this book. In December 2015, Bridget, Fred, Keren, Suzi and
I gave a joint paper at the Amsterdam Colloquium. Work on that
paper was a lot of fun, and it clarified many issues, making me
rewrite Chapters 8 and 9 of the book. Jurģis Šķilters asked me to co-
direct the 11th Symposium of Cognition, Logic and Communication
and accompanying Winter School at the University of Latvia,
in December of 2015, and the topic we chose was 'Number:
Cognitive, Semantic and Crosslinguistic Approaches'. The event
took place just before I sat down to do the final revisions on the
book, and I cannot imagine a better preparation for the revision
process. Jurģis, together with Hana Filip, Scott Grimm, Dan Hyde,
Fred Landman and Suzi Lima, as well as the other participants,
created an atmosphere of intense intellectual interaction which
both broadened my perspective on the whole topic, and allowed me
to focus on the particular area covered in this book.

The research in this book was funded in part by Israel Science
Foundation Grants 851/10 and 1345/13, and I thank the Foundation
for their support. The major writing and rewriting was done in 2015,
when I was able to use a Humboldt Research Award to take leave from
my university responsibilities and work on the book. I thank the
Humboldt Foundation, Gerhard Jäger who sponsored me, Tübingen
University for their hospitality, and my colleagues at Bar-Ilan who
generously and uncomplainingly made it possible for me to take an
extended leave.

Helen Barton has been a supportive, encouraging and patient editor
at Cambridge University Press. She originally invited me to write
a different book, which I didn't want to do, but accepted this project
instead with enthusiasm. She said all the right things at various
crucial points, which kept me working, even when it was clear that
I had seriously underestimated how long the whole writing process
would take. Thank you, Helen! Thank you also to Leigh Mueller, who
did a wonderful job as copy-editor.

Brigitta Schvarcz helped enormously with the editing, bibliography
and formatting, while Alex Rothstein Landman and Fred Landman

took care of the index, for which I am deeply grateful. Keren Khrizman found the quote at the beginning of Chapter 5, and Fred Landman reminded me of the quote at the beginning of Chapter 2. Xuping Li gave me the Envoi.

Living with Fred has created a synergy between the professional and the personal that has grounded this project. We have been talking about count and mass, measuring and counting, and, of course, about glasses of wine, for many, many years. We don't agree about everything, but many of the ideas in the book are ideas we have developed together or in parallel; some of them are as much his as mine. All the analyses have grown, developed and been sharpened and polished through discussions with him (including the parts he disagrees with). He read, criticized and commented on the entire manuscript and it is immeasurably better for it. Thanking him, which I do, is thanking him for a partnership and a life-style of which this book is only one element.

My daughter Alex has been there all along. She and I discovered the original facts about Hebrew pseudopartitives when we were cooking together one evening in 2009 and talking about how much water to add to the soup. She has kept me company the whole way, providing judgements and cups of tea, as well as (vegan) cookies for the annual workshops, commenting on the ideas and the data, letting me explain what I was doing and expressing her support and encouragement in many different ways. She now has her own home, and at the moment we are not even in the same country, but the support and encouragement continue. I really appreciate it.

Ronya (the cat) has also been there, on my lap and on the keyboard (in fact, she is here as I type this). She has put in many typos, deleted several sections and been thoroughly involved in the whole process.

Forty years ago, I was interviewed by the late Sybil Wolfram for a place at Lady Margaret Hall to read Philosophy. At the interview, she asked me how many things there were in her study. Later, as her student, I reminded her of this, and she apologized for 'asking me something so difficult at an interview'. But I didn't think she needed to apologize. I had been incredibly happy to find out that someone else was interested in what counted as 'one', and very excited to be able to talk about it.

I still feel that way.

Abbreviations

±C	±Count
±M	±Measure
2	second person
3	third person
ACC	accusative
ATT	attributive
AUX	auxiliary
Cl	classifier
COMP	comparative
COP	copula
CS	construct state form
CSP	construct state phrase
DEF	definite
F	feminine
FG	free genitive
GEN	genitive
IMPFV	imperfective
INDEF	indefinite
INST	instrumental
M	masculine
MOD	modifier
NOM	nominative
NU	natural unit
OBJ	object
PART	sentence-final particle
PFV	perfective marker
PL	plural
PRS	present
PST	past
RED	reduplication
SG	singular

1   Introduction

'You've hit the nail on the head my boy,' the devil replied. 'The thing that makes numbers so devilish is precisely that they *are* simple.'
Hans Magnus Enzenberger, *The Number Devil*

1.1   INTRODUCTION

This book is about the semantic interpretation of numerical expressions, and in particular of cardinal numerals. Cardinal numerals are used in different ways. They denote numbers in counting sequences such as *one, two, three . . . ninety-nine*. They are used alone in answer to questions such as *How many N are there?*, they are used to make statements such as *Two and two are four* and they are used in complex linguistic expressions, such as *two cats, two kilos of flour, two glasses of wine* and so on. So it is not enough to talk about the meaning of cardinal numerals out of context – we need to examine the different ways in which these meanings are incorporated into language. This book investigates this topic. It focuses on two basic operations which make use of cardinal numbers, counting and measuring, and investigates how these operations are expressed grammatically.

Numbers are abstract objects used in counting and in mathematical operations. *Numerals* or *numericals* are the expressions denoting these objects. The word *two* and the symbol *2* both denote the same abstract object, as do the complex expressions 2^1, 1+1, 4–2 and so on. I will use the term *numeral* or *numeral expression* to refer to any of the sample expressions in the previous sentence, and use *numerical* for numeral expressions phrased in words. So *two* and *2* are both numeral expressions, but only *two* is a numerical expression. *Two* is a cardinal numerical, but when the context does not require further elaboration, I will call it, and expressions like it, simply 'numericals'.

In addition to cardinal numericals, there are other semantically more complex numerical expressions which incorporate cardinal

1

numbers into their interpretation. These include the ordinals, such as *first, second, third*; expressions which are apparently equivalent to cardinals such as *dozen* and *score*; approximatives such as *hundreds, thousands, dozens* and *scores*; numerical adverbials such as *twice*, which means 'two times'; complex expressions such as *two-square* (2^2) or *two plus two*; fractions such as *one-half* and *one-third* (½ and ⅓); as well as decimal expressions such as *twenty-two point two* (22.2), and percentages, such as *twenty per cent* (20%). There are also 'quasi-numerical' expressions such as *double* and *triple* which mean 'multiply by 2'/ 'multiply by 3', *pair* and so on. Each of these different kinds of numerical expressions has its own syntactic and semantic properties. For the most part, I shall focus in this book on cardinal numerals, not because the others are unimportant or uninteresting, but because the whole topic of numerals is far too big a subject to be treated in one book. (Chapter 2 will, however, explore some complex numerical expressions – in particular, ordinals and approximatives.)

As already noted, numerals appear in different linguistic contexts. These contexts can be classified in terms of the kind of quantity operation they involve. So, in addition to counting sequences such as *one, two, three*, they can be used to express the result of counting, as in *I have two cats*, and in statements which express the result of measuring, such as *This bag of flour weighs two kilos*. They are used in mathematical statements where properties are ascribed to numbers, as in *Two plus two is four* or *Two is the only even prime number*. They are also used as labels, as in telephone numbers, numbers for bus lines and metro lines, identity numbers and so on, as in *Bus 4 will take you to the train station*. This last use, among others, is discussed at length in Wiese (2003). I shall be concerned in this book with the first three uses – counting and measuring and mathematical statements, and I shall argue that a grammar of numerals must distinguish between all three uses. For example, in (1), *two* is an argument and seems to be naming an abstract object. The sentence itself predicates a particular property of that object, that of being the smallest prime number.

(1)   Two is the smallest prime number.

In (2), in contrast, *two* gives a property of certain pluralities of cats, namely those which are made up out of two individual cats, or consist of two atomic cats.

(2)   I have two cats.

(3) illustrates numerals used with classifiers in measuring contexts. Intuitively, (3) contrasts with (2) because there are no two

individuable litres of orange juice which can be identified as the atomic parts out of which the whole is constructed.

(3)   There are two litres of orange juice in this punch.

A central thesis of this book is that counting and measuring are two very different semantic operations, despite the fact that they both use numerical expressions. Counting is putting individual entities in one-to-one correspondence with the natural numbers and this involves individuating the entities which are to be counted, while measuring involves assigning to a body (plurality or substance) an overall value on a dimensional scale which is calibrated in certain units. *I have two cats* requires locating individual cats and assigning each one a number in order, while *There are two litres of orange juice in this punch* assigns a value *two litres* as the overall quantity of orange juice in the punch on the volume dimension, without identifying individual litre-units. A single measuring operation can easily give a number of different values, depending on the unit of measurement: *two litres of juice* or *two thousand millilitres of juice* or *sixty-seven-point-six US fluid ounces of juice* are all results of the same measure operation and they use the same dimensional scale, though in each case the unit of calibration is different. Distinguishing between counting and measuring is compli-cated by the existence of expressions which are ambiguous. While *two cats* clearly is a counting expression and *two litres of orange juice* involves measuring, *two glasses of juice* can denote a plurality of two glasses filled with juice or juice which is equal to that contained in two glasses. In the first case, illustrated in (4a), *two* is used in a counting operation which involves individuating glasses full of juice and counting them, while (4b) illustrates a measuring use, in which *glasses* is used as a unit term analogous to *litre*, and no individuation of parts of the juice is required.[1]

(4)   a The waiter brought us two glasses of juice.
         b The cook added two glasses of juice to the punch.

A lot of this book will be devoted to exploring the linguistic differ-ences between counting and measuring. While they have always been distinguished, most linguists have tended to try and reduce one to the other. Commonly, it has been assumed that measuring can be reduced to counting, since measuring can be analysed as imposing a unit structure on some stuff and then counting the number of units involved. Thus Gil (2013) in the *World Atlas of Language Structures*

---

[1] In fact there are more than these two uses, as we will discuss in Chapter 8.

Online (ch. 55) says explicitly that expressions like **glass** *of N* and **pound** *of N* are often called 'mensural numeral classifiers', and that they 'provide nouns of low countability with a unit of measure by means of which they may then be counted', while Lyons (1977) suggests that 'a mensural classifier is one which individuates in terms of quantity' (p. 463). Less common has been the attempt to analyse counting as a form of measuring. In this approach, the natural units of individuation replace the explicit units mentioned in measure expressions. The most explicit account of this is Krifka (1989, 1995), who analyses *four cows* as denoting a sum of cows whose value is four on a scale calibrated in terms of natural units.

The position I shall argue for in this book is that in a significant number of languages, from different typological families, counting cannot be reduced to measuring, nor can measuring be reduced to counting. Counting and measuring are two different operations, expressed, usually, through different syntactic structures, and numericals are interpreted differently in each case. The examples in (4) play a crucial role in constructing this argument, since we will see that in a number of languages, the two different interpretations of these classifier constructions are associated with two different syntactic structures. In the counting examples like (4a), the numerical is adjectival, giving a property of the plurality in the denotation of the plural N; while in measuring contexts like (4b), the numerical combines with the measure unit to form a complex predicate. I shall suggest that the measure/counting contrast is fundamental in language, and that we can use it to throw new light on the contrast between mass nouns and count nouns. Specifically, I shall argue that, independent of any particular theory of mass and count nouns, the following generalization holds: mass nouns denote entities which can be measured, while count nouns denote sums of individuals which can be counted. In fact, I shall suggest, this may well be at the root of the mass/count distinction. This generalization will allow us to solve a number of puzzles about the mass/count contrast, and, in particular, the question of what makes nouns like *furniture, literature* and *rice* mass when they so obviously denote stuff which comes in individuable units. It will also give insight into the parallels and contrasts between so-called 'mass/count languages' like English and 'classifier languages' like Mandarin Chinese.

This book has a number of goals. It aims to review some of the major more recent linguistic results in the semantics of numericals, in counting and measuring and in theories of the mass/count distinction. But I also want to report on some of my own work on the topic, and on the research of some of the people I have collaborated with. I will not try to hide my own views on, for example, the semantic properties of numerals, or on the basis of the mass/count contrast. I have used my own theory of the mass/count distinction to work out semantic interpretations (since they must be worked out in some particular theory). However, I have tried to keep a lot of the discussion in theory-neutral terms, and many of the results about numerals, counting and measuring are independent of my theory of mass/count. The main goal of the book is to draw attention to the contrast between counting and measuring, and to argue that it needs to be central to any attempt to understand the use of numerical expressions, classifiers and count nouns in different languages.

The book draws heavily on crosslinguistic research, but I do not pretend to give a crosslinguistic survey of numerical phenomena or of counting and measuring expressions crosslinguistically. Instead, I present, in depth, studies of counting and measuring in a number of typologically unrelated languages. Much (though not all) of the crosslinguistic data come from research that I have been directly or indirectly involved in, and focuses on Arabic, Brazilian Portuguese, Dutch, English, French, Hungarian, Mandarin Chinese, Modern Hebrew, Russian and Yudja. This choice of languages is serendipitous: I discuss these particular languages because I had (in most cases) collaborators and students who were willing to work with me on these languages, and I had in all cases direct or indirect access to native informants. I thus had access to data which allowed a quite detailed exploration of counting and measuring crosslinguistically. I have been encouraged by the degree to which this research has yielded interesting results. In fact, one of the goals of the book is to show just how fruitful parallel crosslinguistic research into a single topic can be. What should come out clearly from this book is that the count-measure contrast is expressed in languages from different language families in different ways, depending on the morphosyntactic properties of the particular language, but that, beyond the differences, there are some fundamental structural commonalities at both syntactic and semantic levels. My hope is that this book will encourage the in-depth study of these phenomena in more and more languages, and that our general understanding of the semantics of numerals, counting and measuring will increase and be enriched. This hope is reflected in the suggestions for further research at the end of each chapter, which frequently encourage readers to explore the syntax and semantics of specific constructions in any language that they have access to.

I want to stress that the morphosyntactic devices described in this book that are used to mark contrasts between counting and measuring, mass and count nouns, individuated and non-individuated sets in the languages under discussion are in no way presumed to be exhaustive, and I have specifically tried to make generalizations in terms of patterns and not parameterization. I make no claims about universals, and my aim is to describe both the commonalities and the variation in an (I hope) balanced way.

The book is intended for a wide readership and not only for people with a strong background in formal semantics. This reflects my belief that understanding how numbers are used semantically is an essential part of understanding language and languages, and my conviction that these issues should be understood by as wide a range of linguists as possible. I have tried to keep semantic formulae to a minimum, and I have kept my model extensional, so that the formulae will be as straightforward and readable as possible. I have explained the meaning of the formulae used in English, so that the arguments will be accessible to people with no training in formal semantics at all. These readers are invited to skip the derivations if they look too scary. However, for those who do want to understand how the compositional interpretation takes place, and to see how parallel compositional processes occur crosslinguistically on the basis of different syntactic structures, the derivations should not be skipped. The kind of introduction found in any introductory semantics textbook is necessary to follow the derivations, but should also be sufficient. Those with a stronger background in formal semantics who want to add intensionality (where relevant) are invited to do so.

There are many topics which this book does not discuss. Central among them is the syntax and semantics of comparatives in the adjectival domain, as in *Jan is taller/older/cleverer than Kim*. Comparatives like these obviously involve comparison of measurements and as such are directly related to the topic of the book. However, adjectival comparatives constitute a huge topic and there was no way I could discuss them; so I have restricted myself strictly to measurement in the nominal domain. Other topics that I say little or nothing about include the derivational morphology of number systems, number as a morphological feature, the semantics of plurality, and crosslinguistic variation in the way in which singularity vs non-singularity is expressed. In contrast to adjectival comparative constructions, these issues do all interact directly with numerical expressions in the nominal domain, and at various points I do make reference to these issues, and direct the reader to selected relevant literature. I also (with regret) do not discuss the fascinating topic of number systems and of the various ways that different languages and cultures construct number systems.

1.2 OVERVIEW OF THE BOOK

The book is divided conceptually into three parts. Chapters 2 and 3 look at the semantics of numerals, and numerals in counting and measuring contexts. Chapters 4 to 7 focus on the mass/count distinction and its connection to counting and measuring. Chapters 8, 9 and 10 discuss classifiers and measure heads in counting and measuring contexts. Chapter 11 offers a brief conclusion. Chapter by chapter, we proceed as follows. Chapter 2 presents a semantic theory of cardinals, and thus provides a framework for the rest of the book. I adopt the traditional view that simple numerals are ambiguous between names of abstract entities (as in *Two is a prime number*) and predicates of pluralities (as in *two cats*). I work this out in a theory of predication based on Chierchia (1984) and Chierchia & Turner (1988). Chapter 3 presents evidence that counting and measuring are two different operations, drawing on data from a number of languages including English, Modern Hebrew, Hungarian and Mandarin Chinese. We show that, in these languages, in counting expressions such as *three cats* and *three glasses of water* (on its counting reading), numerals are interpreted as nominal modifiers, while in *three kilos of flour* and *three glasses of water* (on its measure reading), numerals denote abstract entities and are of the same type as numerals used in arithmetical expressions. Chapters 4 and 5 are devoted to a discussion of numerals and the mass/count distinction. Chapter 4 reviews semantic accounts of the mass/count distinction, including Link (1983), Gillon (1992), Chierchia (1998a), Chierchia (2010), Krifka (1989, 1995), Rothstein (2010) and Landman (2011a, 2016). We see that the contrast between mass and count nouns cannot be reduced to an ontological distinction between 'stuff' and 'individuals', nor can it be reduced to vagueness, or a distinction between expressions denoting sets of stable atoms and those denoting sets of non-stable atoms. We propose instead that countability is a grammatical property, and that the mass/count distinction reflects the distinction between nouns which lexically encode countability and those which don't. Chapter 5 discusses in depth the problem posed by *furniture* nouns which are crucial in any analysis of the mass/count contrast. These so-called 'object mass nouns' have the syntax of mass nouns, but denote sets of individuable atomic entities, as was shown experimentally in Barner & Snedeker (2005). We show, using crosslinguistic data, that object mass nouns support the hypothesis that mass morphosyntax is associated with measuring, while count morphosyntax is associated with counting. Chapter 6 is the heart of the crosslinguistic discussion, and explores how the mass/count and the measuring/counting contrast are related to each other crosslinguistically, especially in classifier languages. Chapter 7 is really a very long footnote on the much-vexed question of the Universal Grinder, and is included for completeness. Chapter 8 looks at classifiers, in languages like English, and at the contrast between English noun classifiers and Mandarin functional heads. Chapter 9 discusses measures. Chapter 10 examines the contrast between measure predicates in pseudopartitives, such as *two inches of wire*, and measure expressions as attributive modifiers, such as *two-inch wire*. In Chapter 11, I allow myself to muse briefly on what I think the extended study may have shown and to draw the reader's attention to what I take to be the next big questions. Each chapter (except for this one) ends with some questions and suggestions for further research. These are intended for the most part either to encourage crosslinguistic comparisons or to draw the reader's attention to interesting questions and issues which I have not had time to discuss in this book. Most of the questions will probably take a Ph.D. thesis to explore properly.

2 Numericals and How They Work

Fool: The reason why the seven stars are no more than seven is
a pretty reason.
King Lear: Because they are not eight?
Fool: Yes, indeed: thou wouldst make a good fool.
William Shakespeare, *King Lear*, I.5

2.1 CARDINAL NUMBERS – SOME BACKGROUND

This chapter discusses basic uses of number words, or *numericals*, in language. I shall use *numerical* as a general term for words whose meaning directly involves reference to a particular number. Numericals include, first and foremost, the *cardinal numericals* such as *one*, *two* and *twenty-two*, used in neutral counting sequences and in counting expressions like *two cows* and *four cats*. These are often called *numerals* or *cardinal numerals* (Comrie 2011, Hammarström 2010). However, since *numeral* naturally includes words like *two* and symbols such as *2*, I shall use the term *numerical* as a term denoting specifically words with interpretations based on numbers. Numericals include not only the cardinals, but also those words whose interpretation is derived from cardinal interpretations. These include ordinal numericals, such as *first*, *second*, *third*; fractions, such as *one-half* and *one-third* (½ and ⅓); decimal expressions such as *twenty-two-point-two* (22.2); and percentage expressions such as *twenty per cent* (20%). Numericals also include the nominal synonyms for cardinal numericals, such as *dozen* and *score*; approximators, or approximative classifiers, which are derived from cardinals and their nominal synonyms, such as *hundreds*, *thousands*, *dozens* and *scores*; numerical adverbials such as *twice*; and complex numerical expressions such as *two-square* or *two plus two*. There are other derived numerical expressions such as *double* and *triple*, *pair*, *triplet* and so on. Each of these different kinds of numerical expressions has its own syntactic and semantic properties, and each deserves at least a chapter or an article which explores its particular properties. In this book, I will be primarily concerned with cardinal numericals in counting and measuring contexts. This chapter, though, presents a general introduction to the semantics of numericals, focusing on the cardinals, but extending the discussion to some other types of numericals, in particular approximative classifiers and ordinals.

The purpose of this chapter is to discuss how cardinal numericals, words denoting numbers, are used in language, with English as the primary source of examples. I am not going to review the variety of numeral systems or the variations in properties of numeral systems crosslinguistically. This has been discussed extensively in Comrie (2011), Corbett (2000), Gil (2013), Hammarström (2010), Hanke (2010), Hurford (1987) and many others. I am also going to sidestep discussion of what numbers actually are, which is a question for the philosophy of mathematics. It is not necessary for a native speaker to have a theory or an opinion about what numbers are in order to use them in language, and the question under discussion here is not the philosophical question: 'What are numbers?', but the semantic question: 'How can we model the denotations of numericals so as to account for their grammatical and linguistic behaviour?' (For a relatively non-technical discussion of the basis of the concept of number, see Wiese 2003.)

The chapter begins with a review of some properties of cardinal numbers, their form and distribution. In Section 2.2, I will argue that cardinal numericals are ambiguous between predicates denoting properties of pluralities and arguments denoting abstract objects (numbers). In Section 2.3, I will give an analysis of numbers in the framework of property theory (Chierchia 1984, 1985; Chierchia & Turner 1988), and I will argue that cardinal numericals are best treated as property expressions with both a nominal and an adjectival realization. In Section 2.4, I will discuss alternative approaches, in particular Hofweber (2005) and Ionin & Matushansky (2006), showing how the data ultimately support the property-based account. Section 2.5 looks briefly at some non-cardinal numerical expressions.

Most of this chapter will be based on English data, because the aim is to give an in-depth analysis of the mapping between syntax and semantics in the numerical system of one language. The analysis of the English data should thus be seen as a case study of the morphosyntax and semantics of one numerical system. There is no reason to assume that it is representative, though some properties of the system are very obviously common to other languages. I am tacitly assuming that property theory can be used to model a semantics for numericals crosslinguistically (until evidence shows the contrary), but I also assume that the mapping between semantics and syntax may be very different in different languages. Be that as it may, a semantic analysis of numericals in other languages will raise similar issues and questions to the ones discussed here. For every system, we will need to ask: what are the simple and what are the complex numerical expressions; how are complex numerical expressions constructed and what arithmetical constructive processes do they reflect; do these expressions reflect these arithmetical processes directly in their structure; and are these complex expressions constructed in the lexicon or the syntax?

We start with some definitions which will allow us to clarify the issues. *Cardinal numericals* are words (or phrases) which denote the cardinal numbers. These are the numbers which Frege (1884) treated as equivalence classes, sets of equinumerous sets. Under this approach, the numerical denoting n denotes the equivalence class of sets with n members.

Cardinal numericals can be replaced by a string of figures. I use italicized numerals as symbols equivalent to the numericals, and I use non-italicized Arabic figures to represent the denotations of cardinals. So *two* or *2* both denote the number 2, and *two hundred and twenty-two* and *222* both denote the number 222. Cardinal numericals can be simple or complex. Simple cardinals are single, free morphemes which denote a number. Complex numericals can be analysed into subparts whose meanings are combined compositionally, using multiplication and addition.[1] This composition can be morphological or syntactic. For example, *six* is a simple numerical expression denoting the number 6, *sixteen* and *sixty* are single words, but are complex since they are composed out of the meaning of *six* and the suffixes *–teen* and *–ty*. Since both *–teen* and *–ty* are bound morphemes, it is plausible to assume that *sixteen* and *sixty* and numericals like them are composed in the lexicon. *Six hundred* and *six hundred and six* are complex numerical expressions or phrases composed in the syntax, for reasons that we will discuss below. A complex numerical may involve both morphological operations and syntactic operations as in *six hundred and sixty*. And while it seems clear that numericals like *sixty* are composed in the lexicon while *six hundred* is composed in the

---

[1] The use of subtraction in composing complex cardinal numericals is rare but Hammarström (2010) cites some examples. Division is even rarer.

syntax, it may not always be clear what kind of operation is involved. I analyse *sixty-six* as a single word, composed in the lexicon from *sixty* and *six*, but Ionin & Matushansky (2006) argue that it is composed in the syntax, from the lexical items *sixty* and *six*.

Simplicity and complexity of numerical expressions must be distinguished from arithmetical simplicity/complexity and from the question of whether numbers are simple or complex. Note first that, following Peano (1889), all cardinals are constructed in the same way, recursively, by using the successor function. Starting with 0, each of the natural numbers can be obtained in order, via the successor function, by adding 1 to the previous number. 1 is 0+1, 2 is 0+1+1 and so on. From this point of view, all numbers above 0 can be considered equally simple, or, alternatively, increasingly complex, since the cardinality of a number indicates how often the successor function has been applied to derive it. Distinct from the question of whether numbers are simple or complex objects, we can talk of arithmetical simplicity. Arithmetically simple objects like 3 and 5 are numbers expressed in single figures, while arithmetically complex objects are numbers expressed by strings of figures or by strings of figures and symbols. When the object is a string of figures, the interpretation of the strings involves either addition or multiplication or both. When the object is a string of figures and symbols, the symbols determine explicitly which operations are required for interpretation. So *six* denotes the arithmetically simple object 6, while *sixty-six* denotes the arithmetically complex object 66, which is equivalent to $6 \times 10^1 + 6$. Numerical simplicity is a linguistic property, and is distinct from arithmetical simplicity. They may correlate, but need not do so. In English, the numerals *one* to *twelve* are morphologically simple, but the numbers 11 and 12 denoted by *eleven and twelve* are normally represented as arithmetically complex: $1 \times 10^1 + 1$ and $1 \times 10^1 + 2$ respectively.[2]

Complex numerical expressions (as well as complex arithmetical expressions) are necessary in any language which aims to be able to enumerate the infinite series of cardinal numerals.[3] The enumeration

---

[2] *Eleven* and *twelve* and their correlates in other Germanic languages are considered historically to be morphologically complex (Dantzig 1954), derived from proto-Germanic *ain-lif* and *twa-lif* 'one-left [over from ten]' and 'two-left [over from ten]'. However, in terms of semantic interpretation, they can be considered morphologically simple since words are interpreted holistically, as opposed to, say, *twenty-two* or *fourteen*, or the Hebrew for 11, *axat-esrey*, literally 'one-ten'.

[3] Jorge Luis Borges in his story *Funes, the Memorious* describes an attempt to develop a non-recursive system for naming numbers. 'He told me that in 1886 he had

of any infinite series requires a recursive system, and numericals are no exception. Arithmetical writing systems allow infinite enumerations by using a system of bases, the most common being base ten, in which increasing powers of ten are assigned a different column in the sequence. A system for enumerating an infinite sequence of numericals in language uses lexical powers, which parallel arithmetical powers, but which are expressed lexically instead of through their position in a sequence. English counts using base ten, meaning that (most of) the lexical powers used are names for powers of ten and cardinal numericals above twelve are expressed lexically in terms of powers of ten – more precisely, $n \times 10^m + n'$. The linguistic system thus more or less matches the common arithmetical system. For numericals up to *ninety-nine*, only 10^1 is used, and numericals are constructed lexically. There are two bound morphemes for 10^1, which are allomorphs of *ten*, namely -*teen* used in the sequence *thirteen* to *nineteen*, and -*ty* used in the sequence naming the decades *twenty* to *ninety*. The numericals *three* to *nine* combine with -*teen*, and $n + teen$ is semantically interpreted as the result of adding the denotation of *n* to 10^1. Thus, *fourteen* denotes the number $10^1 + 4$. The interpretation of $n + ty$ is the result of multiplying *n* with 10^1, and *forty* denotes 4×10^1. Numericals from *twenty* to *ninety-nine* (with the exception of the round decades) involve both multiplication and addition, for example *sixty-two* denotes the result of multiplying 6 and 10^1 and then adding 2 to the result. Note that these lexical operations involve allomorphs of the names for some of the cardinals. There is an allomorph of *three*, namely *thir-* which is used in *thirteen* ($= 10^1 + 3$)

invented a numbering system original with himself, and that within a very few days he had passed the twenty-four thousand mark. He had not written it down, for anything he thought, even once, remained ineradicably within him. His original motivation, I think, was his irritation that the thirty-three Uruguayan patriots should require two figures and three words, rather than a single figure, a single word. He then applied this mad principle to the other numbers. In place of seven thousand thirteen (7013) he would say, for instance "Máximo Pérez"; instead of seven thousand fourteen (1714) "the railroad"; other numbers were "Luis Melián Lafinur", "Olimar", "sulfur", "clubs", "the whale", "gas", "a stewpot", "Napoleon", "Agustín de Vedia". Instead of five hundred (500), he said "nine." Every word had a particular figure attached to it, a sort of marker; the latter ones were extremely complicated ... I tried to explain to Funes that his rhapsody of unconnected words was exactly the opposite of a number *system*. I told him that when one said "365", one said "three hundreds, six tens and five ones", a breakdown impossible with the "numbers" *Nigger Timoteo* or *a ponchoful of meat*. Funes either could not or would not understand me': Jorge Luis Borges, Funes, His Memory. In Collected Fictions, translated by Andrew Hurley. New York: Penguin Books, 1999.

and *thirty* (= 3×10^1), while *twen-*, an allomorph of *two*, occurs only in combination with *-ty*, in *twenty* (= 2×10^1). In higher numbers, where the composition is syntactic and not lexical, these allomorphs are not used. Thus we have *two hundred* and *three hundred* using *two* and *three* and not *twen-* and *thir-*.

The infinite counting sequence is facilitated by incorporating names for powers above ten into the language, making it possible to count in terms of multiples of these powers. Since English is a base ten language, lexical powers are commonly names for powers of ten, although not all powers of ten have lexical names. English uses *hundred* (10^2), *thousand* (10^3), *million* (10^6), *billion* (10^9 in the USA and 10^{12} in the UK). *Myriad* denotes the number 10^4, but is rarely used except in contemporary English in translations. There is no lexical item for 10^5, 10^7 or 10^8. The choice of which powers to lexicalize differs from language to language, for example in Mandarin, 10^4 (= 10,000) is lexicalized as *wan*, and used in constructing complex numbers, thus 1,400,000 is expressed as *yi-bai-sishi-wan*, or 'one hundred forty [times] ten-thousand'.

Lexical powers above 10^1 in English are free morphemes. They are completely productive, unlike *-ty* which is only used in the fixed lexical forms in the sequence *twenty* through *ninety*.[4] *Ten hundred* can be used as a possible alternate for *one/a thousand*, while *twenty-five hundred* is a common alternate for *two-thousand five hundred*. Numerical expressions using these lexical powers, however, are syntactically complex. As we will discuss below in more detail, the power-word must combine with another cardinal, or with the indefinite determiner *a*, as shown in (1a). Using the bare singular is infelicitous, as in (1b):

(1)   a   a hundred, one hundred, three hundred, twenty-five hundred, *hundred

       b   … ninety-eight, ninety-nine, *(a/one) hundred, *(a/one) hundred and one

Note that there is crosslinguistic variation in how these complex expressions are constructed even within a small range of quite closely related languages. For example, English *two hundred* is paralleled by Dutch *twee honderd* – in each case, the power terms is in the singular. However, 100 in Dutch is expressed usually by the bare *honderd*, while in English a determiner or numerical expression is necessary.

---

[4] *Pace* J. R. R. Tolkien who opens *The Lord of the Rings* with a celebration of Bilbo Baggins' eleventy-first (i.e., 111th) birthday.

In French, 100 is expressed by the bare *cent*, analogous to Dutch *honderd*, but, unlike in Dutch, 200 is *deux cents* with plural agreement on the lexical power (at least in the written orthography).

Lexical powers are only partially determined by the arithmetical base of the language. As we have already seen, in English, only some of the powers of ten will be expressed lexically. But in addition to the base ten powers which are expressed lexically, English has a number of lexical powers which are not powers of 10. *A dozen* is 12^1 and *a gross* is 12^2, while *a score* is 20^1. These have exactly the same syntactic properties as the lexical powers of ten. They can be used to construct complex expressions for exact counting as in *three dozen eggs, three score and ten years, three hundred score and ten* and so on. As we will see in Section 2.4, both the base ten powers as well as *score* and *dozen* can be used as approximative classifiers as in *hundreds of N, thousands of N, dozens of N, scores of N*.

Syntactic constraints on forming complex cardinals are clearly language-specific, especially with respect to word order and whether or not the conjunction expressing additivity is explicit. In contemporary English, a bound allomorph of *ten* is always word final, as in (2a,b). From *twenty* to *ninety-nine*, the largest number is mentioned first, as in (2c). When lexical powers are used, the power is preceded by the multiplier, which itself can be complex. The highest lexical power is mentioned first, and the last lexical power is followed by an explicit *and* (2d,e). In archaic English, the unit may precede the expression of the decade, but then an explicit additive marker is required (2f).

(2) a thir-teen; four-teen
   b twen-ty; thir-ty; for-ty
   c twenty-one; ninety-five
   d one hundred and twenty-two; three thousand and one two hundred thousand and one
   e three thousand two hundred and one
   f one-and-thirty; four-and-twenty

German and Dutch pattern like archaic English. The examples in (3) are from Dutch:

(3) a twee-en-twintig
      two and twenty (= 22)
   b honderd twee-en-twintig
      hundred two and twenty (= 122)
   c honderd en twee
      hundred and two = (102)

2.2 *CARDINAL NUMBERS AS PROPERTIES*

2.2.1 Distribution of Cardinals

Cardinals occur in a number of different environments, as the examples in (4) show:

(4) a Six is bigger than two.
     b one cat, three girls, four boys, six hamsters, eighteen stairs

In (4a), the numericals look like arguments, and in (4b), they look like either determiners or adjectives. Note that the noun in (4b) is plural when the numerical is greater than *one*, but there is much crosslinguistic variation with respect to agreement. For example, in Standard Arabic, the cardinal numericals for three to ten are followed by a noun in the plural, while numericals from eleven upward are followed by a noun in the singular.

There has been much debate as to whether the cardinal in (4b) is an adjective or a determiner. In first-order predicate logic, cardinal numbers were treated as enriched indefinite determiners, and the meaning of the sentence 'Two cats are in the barn' was given as in (5), with the contribution of *two* represented syncategorematically. (5a) gives the 'at least' reading of *two* in predicate logic, and expresses the statement 'there are two non-identical individuals who are cats and are in the barn, but there may be more'. The addition of the universal clause in (5b) gives the 'exactly two' reading: 'there are two non-identical individuals who are cats and are in the barn, and any cat in the barn is either one of them or the other':

(5) a $\exists x \exists y [CAT(x) \land CAT(y) \land \neg x{=}y \land$ IN THE BARN(x) $\land$ IN THE BARN(y)]
     b $\exists x \exists y [CAT(x) \land CAT(y) \land \neg x{=}y \land$ IN THE BARN(x) $\land$ IN THE BARN(y) $\land \forall z [CAT(z) \land$ IN THE BARN(z) $\rightarrow z{=}x \lor z{=}y]]$

Formal semantics, and with it the search for compositional interpretations, led to cardinal numericals often being treated as determiners, as in Barwise & Cooper (1981), Keenan & Faltz (1984) and, much more recently, Hofweber (2005). Nominal expressions like *eighteen stairs* and *six cats* are DPs (Determiner Phrases) denoting generalized quantifiers. On this approach *four* and *eighteen* have a semantic interpretation analogous to *every* and *some*, and denote relations between sets. This is illustrated in (6), with meanings for determiners given both in quantifier notation and in set-theoretic notation. *Every* denotes the relation between two sets where the first is a subset of the second. *Some* denotes the relation between two sets whose intersection is not empty, and *four*, analogously, denotes the relation between two sets whose intersection is a set with four members. | | is the cardinality function assigning a cardinal value to a plurality, which we define in Section 2.2.1.

(6) a *Every:* $\lambda P\lambda Q.\forall x[P(x) \rightarrow Q(x)]$ OR $\lambda P\lambda Q.P \subseteq Q$
     b *Some:* $\lambda P\lambda Q.\exists x[P(x) \wedge Q(x)]$ OR $\lambda P\lambda Q.P \cap Q \neq \emptyset$
     c *Four:* $\lambda P\lambda Q.\exists x[P(x) \wedge |\ x\ | = 4 \wedge Q(x)]$ OR $\lambda P\lambda Q.|\ P \cap Q\ | \geq 4$

The DPs *every cat, some cat(s), four cats* denote respectively the set of sets of which CAT is a subset, the set of sets whose intersection with CAT is non-empty, and the set of sets whose intersection with CAT has four members.

(7) a *Every cat:* $\lambda Q.\forall x[CAT(x) \rightarrow Q(x)]$ OR $\lambda Q.CAT \subseteq Q$
     b *Some cat(s):* $\lambda Q.\exists x[CAT(x) \wedge Q(x)]$ OR $\lambda Q.CAT \cap Q \neq \emptyset$
     c *Four cats:* $\lambda Q.\exists x[CAT(x) \wedge |x| = 4 \wedge Q(x)]$ OR $\lambda Q.|\ CAT \cap Q\ | \geq 4$

The interpretations for sentences using these generalized quantifiers are given in (8):

(8) a *Every cat likes milk:* $\forall x[CAT(x) \rightarrow LIKE\ MILK(x)]$
        OR: $CAT \subseteq LIKES\ MILK$
     b *Some cat(s) like(s) milk:* $\exists x[CAT(x) \wedge LIKE\ MILK(x)]$
        OR: $CAT \cap LIKES\ MILK \neq \emptyset$
     c *Four cats like milk:* $\exists x[CAT(x) \wedge |\ x\ | = 4 \wedge LIKE\ MILK(x)]$
        OR: $|\ CAT \cap LIKES\ MILK\ | \geq 4$

(8a) asserts that all the cats are milk-likers, equivalently that the set of cats is a subset of the set of individuals who like milk. (6b) asserts that the some cats are milk-likers, equivalently that the intersection between the set of cats and the set of milk-likers is not empty. In (6c), the cardinal is treated as an enriched existential quantifier and the sentence asserts that four cats are milk-likers, equivalently that the intersection between the set of cats and the set of milk-likers contains at least four individuals.

  Despite the superficial similarity between cardinal numerals and expressions like *every*, there is good evidence that cardinals are not determiners, and I shall present this in Section 2.2.2. I shall first show that there is good reason to treat them as adjectives, based on their distribution (Section 2.2.2.1) and based on their interpretation (2.2.2.2). In Section 2.2.3, I shall show that they also occur as singular terms in argument position. In Section 2.3, I will give a semantic analysis of cardinal numerals which explains this data, showing that they are best treated as property-denoting expressions in the sense of Chierchia (1985), Chierchia & Turner (1988). I shall argue that, like properties, numericals alternate between a predicative interpretation in which they denote sets, and an argument interpretation in which they denote individual correlates of sets.

2.2.2 Cardinals as Predicates

2.2.2.1 *Cardinals are Adjectives*

There are several arguments in favour of treating cardinals such as those in (4b) and (8c) as predicate modifiers. Heim (1982) and Kamp (1981) have shown that there is good reason to analyse indefinites such as *a cat* as predicates, with *a* a syntactic determiner which does not denote a semantic determiner. This opens the way for treating cardinals in a similar (though not identical) way, showing that not all syntactic determiners are of the same semantic type.

Cardinal NPs are in several ways similar to indefinite NPs. They are indefinite, and so can appear in *there*-insertion sentences and as complements of possessives, as in (9).

(9)   a   There are two cats in the barn (but I have never seen them).
         b   Mary has two cats asleep on her lap.

Further, as the examples in (10) show, indefinites and nominals modified by cardinals occur as predicates where true DPs do not:

(10)   a   The speaker is a lecturer in the Linguistics Department.
        b   The inhabitants of the barn are four cats.
        c   # The guests are most students / some students. (on a non-partitive reading)[5]

In (10a), *a lecturer in the Linguistics Department* is the main predicate of the sentence. It denotes the set of individuals which have the property of being a lecturer in the Linguistics Department, and the sentence asserts that the speaker has this property. (10b) has the same syntactic and semantic structure. The primary predicate is *four cats*. It denotes the set of plural entities that have the property of being four cats, and the sentence asserts that the plurality of entities which are the inhabitants of the barn are in the set denoted by *four cats*. Quantifier phrases cannot appear in this position, as (10c) shows. This suggests that the quantifier phrase is an argument DP denoting a generalized

---

[5] '#' is the infelicity marker, indicating that the syntactic structure may in principle be generable, but that this sentence does not have a natural plausible interpretation.

quantifier, while the indefinite and cardinal phrases in (10a-b) are truly predicates (see also discussion in Rothstein 2001, and references cited there). But if these phrases are predicates and not generalized quantifiers, then presumably they are not headed by determiners, and so cardinals are not determiners. Further data support this.

First, we see that bare cardinals occur as predicates in predicate position. In (11), the cardinal *four* gives the cardinal property (i.e., the number) of the reasons denoted by the sentential subject.

(11) My reasons for saying this are four.

Second, cardinals do not necessarily occur in determiner position even when they are part of argument NPs, as in (12):

(12) a The four cats lay on the sofa.
      b Every two students got a questionnaire to fill in.

In (12a), the determiner position is filled by *the*, and in (12b) by *every*, and the cardinal fills a position of a normal attributive adjective. So, while (11) shows that cardinals can occur in predicative adjective position, (12) shows that they can also occur in attributive adjective position.

On the basis of these data, it is reasonable to suggest that cardinal numericals really are adjectives, and not determiners. This predicts that they ought to show other properties of adjectives. Landman (2003) argues that this is the case.[6] Crucially, strings of adjectives are permutable, and, in the right context, their order can be changed. For example, a cat can be described as *a black longhaired cat* or *a longhaired black cat*. The order of the adjectives may highlight or focus a particular adjective, but both are acceptable. Landman shows that when the determiner position is filled by a determiner like *the*, numericals may permute with other adjectives. The examples in (13) are based on Landman (2003), examples (4) and (5). (13b) is unacceptable as a variant of (13a), but (13c) and (13d) are both grammatical, since the cardinals are under the scope of the definite determiner.

(13) a We sent ten quiet lions to Artis (the Amsterdam zoo).
      b *We sent quiet ten lions to Artis.
      c We sent the ten fierce lions to Blijdorp (the Rotterdam zoo).
      d We sent the fierce ten lions to Blijdorp, and the quiet ten lions to Artis.

---

[6] Landman (2003) constructs a general theory of numericals as adjectives which he supports with several arguments, including an account of the semantics of downward entailing numerical expressions.

These permutations are possible (though less common) with *every* as well:

(14)   For every successful ten students, we hired a new teaching assistant.

    Landman suggests that the numerical is generated as the left-most adjective under a head NUM, and that when the determiner position is empty, NUM raises to determiner position.[7] When the numerical raises, as in (13a), then it is constrained to be the left-most element in the nominal, and permutations are impossible, However, if the determiner position is independently filled, the numerical does not raise and permutations are possible (13d/14). There is thus good evidence that cardinal numerals are adjectives, and we will adopt this position.

    We will assume a framework in which count nouns are of type $<e,t>$. Singular count nouns denote sets of atoms, and plural count nouns denote the closure of the singular denotation under sum, and thus denote complete atomic Boolean algebras. For details, see Landman (1991, 2011b), and for details of how to extend this to a type theory, see Landman (2000).

    Adjectives are intersective modifiers of N and are therefore also of type $<e,t>$. Cardinals are like other adjectives in this respect: they are of type $<e,t>$ and they have intersective semantics. *Four N* denotes the set of plural individuals that are both in the denotation of N and have the property *four*. The interpretation of numerals uses the cardinality function | | which applies to entities and gives the number of their atomic parts, as in (15a). *Four* has the interpretation in (15b). It denotes the function that maps entities onto the value TRUE if they have four atomic parts.

(15)   a $| x | = n \leftrightarrow |\{y: y \sqsubseteq_{ATOMIC} x\}| = n$
           'The cardinality of object x is n if the cardinality of the set of the atomic parts of x is n.'
      b $\lambda x. | x | = 4$
           'the set of objects whose cardinality is 4'

Four is of type $<e,t>$, like other predicative adjectives, and, like most predicative adjectives, it also has an attributive interpretation at type

---

[7] This proposal does not require all argument nominals to have an empty determiner. Bare plurals and mass nouns are arguments since they denote kinds (Carlson 1977; Chierchia 1998a,b; Landman & Rothstein 2010), but they are standardly analysed as NP arguments and not DP arguments with an empty determiner (Chierchia 1998a).

<<e,t>,<e,t>>. (16a) illustrates its use with the predicative interpreta-
tion (σ is the operator which maps a set X onto the unique maximal
sum of the members of X, if defined, giving the denotation of *the* X).
(16b) illustrates the attributive use. *Four cats* denotes the intersection
of FOUR and CATS. *Four* shifts to the modifier type at <<e,t>,<e,t>>,
and applies to the denotation of *cats*.

(16)   a   *The guests were four*:
           FOUR (THE GUESTS) $=$ $\lambda x. \mid x \mid = 4\, (\sigma(\text{GUESTS}))$
                               $=$ $\mid\sigma(\text{GUESTS})\mid = 4$
       b   *The animals were four cats*:
           FOUR (CATS) $=$ $\lambda P \lambda x.P(x) \wedge \mid x \mid = 4\, (\text{CATS})$
                               $=$ $\lambda x.\text{CATS}(x) \wedge \mid x \mid = 4$
           FOUR CATS (THE ANIMALS)
               $=$ $\lambda x.\, \text{CATS}(x) \wedge \mid x \mid = 4\, (\sigma(\text{ANIMALS}))$
               $=$ $\text{CATS}(\sigma(\text{ANIMALS})) \wedge \mid \sigma(\text{ANIMALS}) \mid = 4$

The above semantics gives an interpretation for numerical NPs as
predicates. Interpretation of numerical NPs in argument position
will either involve default existential quantification over the whole
sentence, as suggested in Kamp (1981) and Heim (1982), or raising
the predicate *four cats* to the type of generalized quantifiers. In the
latter case, the predicate $\lambda x.\, \text{CATS}(x) \wedge \mid x \mid = 4$ raises to the quantifier $\lambda P.\exists x\, [\text{CAT}(x) \wedge \mid x \mid = 4 \wedge P(x)]$, the interpretation proposed in
(7c). Both raising NP to a generalized quantifier and default existen-
tial quantification result in (17) as the interpretation for 'Four cats
were in the garden'.

(17) $\exists x[\text{CATS}(x) \wedge \mid x \mid = 4 \wedge \text{IN THE GARDEN}(x)]$

2.2.2.2   'Exactly' vs at 'least' readings of cardinals

In this section, we show that analysing numerals as adjectives will
provide insight into a puzzle which has occupied linguists for a long
time, namely the contrast between 'at least' and 'exactly' interpretations of numerals, already mentioned in connection with the example
in (5). It has long been known that numerical cardinals apparently can
be interpreted as meaning 'at least *n*' and 'exactly *n*' and that different
contexts favour each reading (Horn, 1972, 1989; Gadzar 1979;
Levinson 1983, 2000; Kadmon 1987). *Four N* naturally is interpreted
as meaning 'exactly four' in (18a,b), On the other hand, (18c) gives
a context in which the 'at least' reading is prominent:

(18)   a   I have four cats.
       b   A cat has four legs.
       c   A person with four cats gets a reduction at the animal clinic.

Horn (1972) argues that this reading is basic, and that the 'exactly' reading in (18a,b) follows from a scalar implicature. This works more or less as follows for (18a). Assumption A is that, following Grice's maxim of quantity, I, as the speaker, am giving you the most (relevant) information possible. Assumption B is that I know how many cats I have. Suppose I have five cats. In a neutral context in which I am asked how many cats I have, the answer '(at least) five' would be available (following assumption B) and more informative than '(at least) four' (following assumption A). So I ought then to answer 'five'. From the fact that I didn't, the listener can assume that 'four' was the most informative answer available, and consequently deduces the 'exactly' implicature. Horn (1972) extends this to a more general scalar principle that is not dependent on assumptions about the speaker's knowledge or beliefs: when an expression such as a cardinal is associated with a scale, choosing a weaker value on a scale implies that the stronger values do not hold. Scalar implicatures are defeasible. Because of what we know about vets' fees, (18c) can be taken to be a generalization about the minimal case in which a reduction is available, and the scalar implicature is cancelled. This allows us to deduce that (19a) follows from (18c). It also explains the fact that (19b) implies 'Mary has fewer than four cats'.

(19)   a John has six cats, so he qualifies.
        b Mary doesn't have four cats, so she doesn't qualify.

Other linguists, in particular Ariel (2006) and Cohen & Krifka (2010), have argued that the 'at least' reading is derived pragmatically, and that numerals, together with quantifiers like *most*, have an upper-bounded interpretation. This approach has gained some support from recent results in psycholinguistics (Huang, Spelke & Snedeker 2013) which suggest that small children acquire numericals with an 'exactly' reading.

Generalized quantifier theory, which treats cardinals as determiners, is forced to make a decision as to whether the *at least n* or *exactly n* interpretation is basic, and to explain how the other interpretation is derived. Landman (2003) shows that treating cardinals as adjectives within a Boolean theory of noun denotations allows us to solve the problem in an elegant way.

Landman (2003) adds two crucial observations to the debate. Following observations which he attributes to Barbara Partee (pc) and Kadmon (1987), also Kamp & Reyle (1993), he notes that, while an 'at least' interpretation is available for a numerical NP in argument position, as was the case in (18a), it is not available when the same NP is in predicate position. Thus, the 'exactly' implication is felicitously cancelled in (20a), but not in (20b) or (20c). In these cases, changing the value of the numeral can only be interpreted as a correction (from exactly four to exactly five), as indicated in (20d).

(20)   a   Certainly I have four cats, in fact I have ten.
       b   #The inhabitants of the barn are four cats, and in fact there are ten of them.
       c   #My reasons are four and in fact they are five.
       d   My reasons are four, or rather, they are five.

Secondly, Landman points out that cardinals also have an 'exactly n' reading when embedded under *the*, or any other determiner. (21a) entails that at least, but no more than, three students passed the exam. (21b) assigns a single research assignment to exactly three students.

(21)   a   The three students who passed the exam will go in for the competition.
       b   Every three students got a different question to research.

Landman, following Kadmon (1987), argues that numericals are not ambiguous between an 'exactly' and an 'at least' interpretation. The 'exactly' meaning is basic, with numericals interpreted as in Section 2.2.2.1, i.e. n denotes $\lambda x.\ |\ x\ |\ = n$. He shows that the 'at least' interpretation does not require a change in the meaning of the numerical, but follows as a semantic consequence of the existential quantification required to interpret the predicate NP in argument position. *Four cats* has the basic 'exactly' interpretation in (22a). Existential quantification raises this predicate to the generalized quantifier at type $<<e,t> t>$ in (22b), incorporating the meaning of the predicate with its 'exactly' reading:

(22)   a $[\![\text{four cats}_{<e,t>}]\!] = \lambda x.\text{CATS}(x) \wedge |\ x\ | = 4$
       b $[\![\text{four cats}_{<< e,t > t >}]\!] = \lambda P.\exists x[\text{CATS}(x) \wedge |\ x\ | = 4 \wedge P(x)]$

Four cats live in the barn has the interpretation in (23):

(23)   FOUR CATS(LIVE IN THE BARN) =
       $\lambda P\exists x.[\text{CATS }(x) \wedge |\ x\ | = 4 \wedge P(x)]\ (\lambda y.\text{LIVE IN THE BARN}(y)) =$
       $\exists x[\text{CATS}(x) \wedge |\ x\ | = 4 \wedge \text{LIVE IN THE BARN}(x)]$

This asserts that there is a plurality of exactly four cats who live in the barn. Landman shows that the 'at least' commitment of (23) is available, not because the semantic contribution of *four* has changed (it hasn't), but because the truth of the existential assertion that there is a plurality of exactly four cats living in the barn is compatible with the situation in which another and bigger plurality of cats lives in the barn too. In other words, instead of the semantic meaning of the cardinal being 'at least n' and the 'exactly' reading being the result of a scalar implicature, the meaning of the cardinal is 'exactly n', i.e. $|x| = 4$. The sentence as a whole has an 'at least' entailment, since, while it asserts that a plurality of exactly four cats lives in the barn, it leaves open the possibility that a larger plurality of cats may have the same property. Still, it follows from the Gricean principle of maximality that the speaker is presumed to make the most informative statement relevant. We therefore assume that the speaker has a good basis for making the statement that a group of exactly four cats live in the barn, and unless there is good contextual reason to do so, we do not raise the question of whether this group is a proper part of a group with a bigger cardinality. This means that, in a context in which the speaker is assumed to be referring to a unique maximal set, the 'exactly' implication will be almost impossible to override. If *four cats* is the antecedent for a pronominal anaphor, the 'exactly' reading will be very strong, as Kadmon (1987, 1990) shows:

(24)   Four cats were drinking milk in the kitchen. They were very beautiful.

Kadmon argues that this is because of the uniqueness requirement of the anaphor.

Landman shows that when the numerical is embedded under a definite determiner as in *the four cats* in (12a), the definite determiner imposes a unique interpretation and the 'exactly' reading cannot be overruled. *The four cats* denotes the $\sigma(\lambda x.CAT(x) \wedge |x| = 4)$, the unique sum of cats whose cardinality equals 4, and thus is defined only in a situation in which there are exactly four cats.

The claim that the 'at least' commitment follows from the existential quantification is supported by the fact that the numerical noun phrase in (25) also allows an 'at least' entailment.

(25)   There are four cats living in the barn (and maybe even more).

The NP in *there-* constructions has been argued to be a predicate position (Higginbotham 1987; Landman 2004), with *there* introducing or marking an existential quantifier. Numerical NPs in these constructions are predicates, and should in principle have 'exactly' readings like all other numerical NPs. However, if we assume that numerical NP predicates are bound by the existential quantifier associated with *there*, and that the sentence has the same truth conditions as (23), then the 'at least' reading is predicted.

On the basis of all this evidence, I will now assume that cardinal numericals are born at the predicate type <e,t>, and that a cardinal expression n has the interpretation $\lambda x. \mid x \mid = n$. Cardinal numericals have an 'exactly' reading, and the 'at least' implication follows in when the numerical phrase is used in argument position as a consequence of existential quantification which binds the predicate variable.

We can now extend our analysis to bare cardinals in argument position.

2.2.3 Cardinals as arguments

Cardinals do not only occur as prenominal modifiers. They also occur as bare numerical expressions in different kinds of contexts. These include sequences of numbers, as in (26a), mathematical statements of (in)equality as in (26b) and statements about properties of numbers as in (26c–e).

(26) a one, two, three ... eighteen
      b Two times two is four. / Two plus two is four.
      c Two, four, six and eight are the first four even numbers.
      d Two is the only even prime number.
      e Eighteen is the ninth even number in the sequence of natural numbers.

(26) shows that bare numericals can fill argument positions and are subjects of predicates. This means they must have properties, the properties expressed by the predicates. *Two* has the property of being even, of being the only even prime number, of being the smallest prime number, and so on. This makes it natural to think of bare cardinals in contexts such as (26) as denoting abstract objects, numbers, which have properties, or, equivalently, generalized quantifiers in the domain of numbers. Numericals then are names for numbers analogous to proper names which denote individuals, or the sets of properties which hold of the individual.

Some recent papers, including Hofweber (2005) and Ionin & Matushansky (2006), have argued that, despite the data in (26), numerals do not ever denote abstract objects. Hofweber, following Barwise & Cooper (1981), argues that cardinals are always determiners, while Ionin & Matushansky propose that they are always predicate modifiers. We have already argued that prenominal numericals are derived from predicates; we provide further evidence for this in Section 2.6. Here we are concerned with the more general question or the relation between prenominal cardinals and the bare cardinals in (26). Should the two uses be assigned to different syntactic categories or not?

Hofweber and Ionin & Matushansky both argue that bare numericals and prenominal numericals belong to the same syntactic category. Both claim that the apparently bare numericals in (26) are prenominal numericals which precede a null noun. They analyse (27a) as (27b):

(27)   a Two and two make four.
        b Two things and two things make four things.

While paraphrasing (27a) as (27b) is just plausible, other cases suggest that this analysis cannot be correct.

First, (28) shows that *count* can be used in two ways: *count how many x there are* as in (28a) or *name a sequence of natural numbers* as in (28b). In each case, *count* subcategorizes for a different complement.

(28)   a I counted thirteen (*things, people, books*)
        b I counted to thirteen (*#things, #people, #books*)

Count how many in (28a) takes a direct object, either a bare numerical or a numerical+N string. It is quite plausible that the bare numerical in (28a) is followed by an elliptical N, since *I counted thirteen* naturally invites the question 'Thirteen what?', and expects an answer. In fact, 'counting how many' is always counting how many of a certain kind of object, counting how many N, a point we come back to in Chapter 4, where we connect it with the semantics of count nouns. If *thirteen* in (28a) modifies an elliptical N, it reflects this intuition nicely. In contrast, *count* in the sense of *name a sequence* of numbers must be followed by the preposition *to* and the cardinal following *count to* is obligatorily bare. The question 'Thirteen what?' is not appropriate in (28b). Modal contexts like (29) show this even more clearly.

(29)   a I can count thirteen. – Thirteen what?
        b I can count to thirteen – #Thirteen what?

A similar contrast shows up in other languages. In French, it is particularly salient.

(30)   a J'#(en)   ai   compté   treize.
           I of them   have   counted   thirteen
           'I counted thirteen (of them).'
        b J' (?#en)   ai   compté   jusqu'à   treize.
           I of them   have   counted   until   thirteen
           'I counted up to thirteen.'

In (30a), *compter* is understood as 'count how many' and the clitic *en* 'of them' is obligatory. *Compter* selects a direct object. *Treize* plausibly modifies a null N, which is anaphorically dependent on the proform en. In (30b), *compter jusqu'à* means *count a sequence up to*, and *en* is strongly dispreferred, with the result that *treize* is a bare numerical. If *en* is inserted, the sentence is highly marginal and its meaning reverts to 'count how many'. (28)–(30) indicate that *count/compter* have two different meanings, associated with structurally different numerical complements.

Second, the paraphrase technique illustrated in (27) is impossible when properties are ascribed directly to numbers.

(31) a *Two is even / is a prime number.*
      b #*Two things are even / are a prime number.*

Numbers and plural objects have different properties. (31a) is true, but (31b) infelicitous, on the assumption that predicating numerical properties of objects involves presupposition failure or type mismatch. (If not infelicitous, it is false.) (32) makes the same point. Numbers stand in the *bigger than / smaller than* relation as in (32a), while plural objects with cardinalities stand in the *more than / fewer than* relation (32b,). Note that (32b) seems clearly infelicitous here, and not false.

(32) a Two *is smaller than* three.
      b #Two things *are smaller than* three things.
      c Two things *are fewer than* three things.

Third, agreement features support the claim that *two things* and *two* denote different objects. (33) shows that cardinal modifiers take plural agreement with an explicit or elliptical N.

(33) a Four (things) are/#is more than three (things).
      b There are ten balls in the box. Six are/#is red and four are/#is black.

If the choice of predicate forces a bare cardinal to be interpreted as the name for a number, singular agreement is required, as in (34). This strongly suggests that *four* in (33a) modifies a plural noun, while in (34), *four* is a name of a number and singular:

(34) Four *is/#are* bigger than three.[8]

Cardinal numerals can themselves be counted, in which case verbal agreement is plural. The examples in (35) illustrate a standard way for children to learn their 'tables' in the UK. Numbers here behave like proper names, with (35) analogous to (36a). Note that adjectives do not

---

[8] Note that *more than /less than* can occur with bare cardinals and singular agreement as in (i):

(i) Four is more than three and less than five.

usually shift to plural nominals in this way. They can only be nominalized as definite singulars, in which case they have a kind interpretation (36b).

(35) a Two twos are four, three twos are six.
       b 'What are twelve sevens? Eighty-four' (Roald Dahl, Matilda, New York: Puffin Books, p. 57)

(36) a There are two Johns in the class. The John I know sits on the right.
       b The meek / #Many meeks / #Ten meeks will inherit the earth.

Together, these data show that, alongside examples like (33) where the cardinal is a predicate modifying an elliptical N, there are cases where a bare cardinal numerical must be a singular term. In the examples which we have given so far, cardinals are used as singular terms in mathematical statements. However, in Chapter 3 we will show that cardinal numerals are widely used as singular terms in measure constructions, and that this use is not restricted to mathematical metalanguage.

In the next section, we offer a semantics for numericals in the framework of property theory, based on Rothstein (2013a), which will allow us to account for this whole range of data.

2.3   A FORMAL ANALYSIS OF NUMBER AND NUMERICALS

2.3.1   Numbers as Properties

Chierchia (1984, 1985), following Frege (1884), developed property theory to account for the 'double nature' of property expressions. Properties can be predicated of arguments, in which case they are grammatically adjectives. In (37a), Mary has the property WISE, in (37b) her eyes have the property BLUE and so on.

(37) a Mary is **wise.**
       b Mary has beautiful **blue** eyes.
       c John is **crazy.**
       d Not eating all day is **crazy.**
       e Craziness is **crazy.**

But (38) shows that properties can also be subjects of predication, and that properties can be attributed to them. For example, the property of being valuable is attributed to wisdom in (38a). In this case, properties are abstract objects, expressed by nouns in argument position.

(38)   a **Wisdom** is valuable / is a valuable property.
      b **Blue** is the colour of light on the visible spectrum between violet and green.
      c **Craziness** is frightening.

The adjectival and nominal forms of the property expression may differ morphologically (*wise/wisdom*) but need not do so (*blue/blue*). Properties as predicates can be predicated both of first-order entities and of abstract property entities (*craziness* is predicated of John and of craziness and not eating all day). Some properties may select only for a particular type of argument – for example, *valuable* can be predicated of both wisdom (38a) and a diamond ring, but *is a valuable property* can be predicated only of *wisdom*. Cardinal numbers, as we have seen above, show exactly the same dual behaviour, and we will treat them as a special type of property, namely a cardinal property.

In Chierchia's (1985) theory, properties are associated with two linguistic expressions. They have a familiar, applicative interpretation at the predicative type <e,t>, where they denote functions from individuals into truth values (or, equivalently, sets). This is the adjectival use, illustrated in (39):

(39)   a *wise*: $\lambda x.\text{WISE}(x)$
      b *crazy*: $\lambda x.\text{CRAZY}(x)$

In addition, they are associated with an individual correlate, at the type of properties, π. Chierchia assumes that the type of individuals is sorted into three groups: e-type individuals or 'ordinary entities', propositions at type t, and individual properties at type π. Two operations relate properties at type <e,t> and properties at type π. $^\cap$ applies to an applicative interpretation at type <e,t>, and derives a property correlate at type π, while $^\cup$ applies to a property at type π and derives the applicative correlate at type <e,t>. Given the applicative $\lambda x.\text{WISE}(x)$, $^\cap\lambda x.\text{WISE}(x)$ is its individual property correlate, the denotation of *wisdom*. Crucially $^{\cup\cap}\lambda x.\text{WISE}(x) = \lambda x.\text{WISE}(x)$. This gives (40a) as the interpretation of (37a) and (40b) as the interpretation of (38a).

(40)   a $\lambda x.\text{WISE}(x) (\text{MARY}) = \text{WISE}(\text{MARY})$
      b $\lambda x.\text{VALUABLE}(x) (^\cap\lambda x.\text{WISE}(x)) = \text{VALUABLE}(^\cap\lambda x.\text{WISE}(x))$

I propose using the same approach to account for the duality of cardinal expressions, which can, as we have seen, also be both predicates and bare arguments.

In the same way that the predicate interpretation of *wise* is the set of entities which are wise, we will assume that the predicate interpretation of a cardinal number *n* at type <e,t> is the set of (plural) entities which have *n* atomic parts. *Four* as a predicate has the denotation that we specified in (15b), repeated here as (41):

(41) $four_{<e,t>}$: $\lambda x. \mid x \mid = 4$, equivalently $\lambda x. \mid\{y: y\sqsubseteq_{\text{ATOMIC}} x\}\mid = 4$

Thus *four* at its predicative type denotes the set of plural entities that have four atomic parts.

The singular term *four* used as an argument is an expression of type n and denotes the individual property correlate of the set in (41). This is given in (42):

(42) $^{\cap}\lambda x. \mid x \mid = 4$

In the same way that *wisdom*, or $^{\cap}\lambda x.\text{WISE}(x)$, is whatever the property is that all people who are wise share, the property correlate in (42) is the property that all and only pluralities with exactly four atomic parts share.

Numbers, then, are the individual property correlates of properties like those in (41).

We assume that the type of numbers, n, is a subtype of Chierchia's type π, and we assume that the cardinality function is a function from plural individuals into type n. With this, we assume that numbers satisfy the equation in (43):

(43) $n = {}^{\cap}\lambda x. \mid x \mid = n$

So, numbers are the abstract individual property correlates of cardinality predicates, and the denotation of cardinality predicates shifted to type n. They are instances of a particular kind of property, cardinal properties. Second-order properties at type <n,t>, such as *is a prime number*, apply only to expressions at type n, while predicates of type <π, t>, such as *is a valuable property*, apply felicitously to properties in general.

The theory we have outlined here is essentially a Fregean theory of numbers in two senses. First, property theory as developed in Chierchia (1984, 1985), Chierchia & Turner (1988) expresses formally Frege's (1892) insight that properties have what he called 'two modes of presentation', an unsaturated mode in which they apply to an argument, and a saturated mode in which they can themselves be the subject of a predication. Our analysis takes the data in Sections 2.2.2 and 2.2.3 as a direct expression of this duality. At type <e,t>, numericals are unsaturated and express properties which can be predicated of pluralities, while at type n they are saturated and can be subjects of predications.

Second, this theory captures Frege's insights as to what numbers are. Frege (1884) treated numbers in set theory as equivalence classes of sets which all had the same cardinality. For Frege, the number denoted by *four*, for example, is the set of all sets with four members as in (44):

(44) $\{X: |X| = 4\}$

This definition was, of course, open to set theoretic paradoxes. In the typed lambda-calculus, the abstraction in (44) would be restricted to variables of type $\langle e,t\rangle$:

(45) $\lambda X_{\langle e,t\rangle}. |X| = 4$

(or, more generally, by a definition schema $\lambda X_{\langle a,t\rangle}. |X| = 4$). In the mereological framework following Link (1984), type e is turned into a domain of singularities (atoms) and pluralities (sums of atoms). Pluralities in the domain of type e are sums which correspond to properties of atoms. Thus, we restrict the Fregean 'definition' in (45) once more:

(46) $\lambda X_{\langle e,t\rangle}. X \subseteq \text{ATOM}_e \wedge |X| = 4$

(or a presuppositional version of this, which restricts the application to sets of atoms). We now define function **F** from $\langle\langle e,t\rangle, t\rangle$ into sets of individuals at type $\langle e,t\rangle$:

(47) $\mathbf{F(Q)} = \lambda x.\exists X[X \in \mathbf{Q} \wedge x=\sqcup X]$

And we derive:

$\mathbf{F}(\lambda X_{\langle e,t\rangle}. X \subseteq \text{ATOM}_e \wedge |X| = 4) =$
$\lambda x. \exists X_{\langle e,t\rangle}[X \subseteq \text{ATOM}_e \wedge |X| = 4 \wedge x=\sqcup X] =$
$\lambda x. |\{y: y\sqsubseteq_{\text{ATOMIC}} x\}| = 4$

This gives us the set of plural individuals, each of which is a sum of atoms with a cardinality of 4. Lowering this via the $\cap$ operation gives us the property-correlate interpretation at type π, and in fact at type n:

(48) $\cap\lambda x. |\{y: y\sqsubseteq_{\text{ATOMIC}} x\}| = 4$

We have added a new type of individual to our theory, numbers at type n, expressing the intuition that cardinals express a special kind of property, and that individual property correlates of cardinals are a special type of individual. We have already seen that this is supported by both syntactic and semantic arguments. As an attributive predicate, a cardinal numerical has a privileged syntactic position at the left periphery of the NP, preceding all other adjectives. As subjects of predications, numericals are arguments of special numerical properties (of type <n,t>), and relations (at type <n<n,t>> and <n,<e,t>>). We have already seen examples of these in Section 2.2.3, and we will discuss more of them in the rest of this chapter and the next one.

2.3.2 Operations on Numbers

The examples in (26b–d) show that numbers as individuals have properties just like other kinds of individuals. *Is the only even prime number, is smaller than three* are expressions of type <n,t>, denoting properties of the individual denoted by *two*. *Is smaller than* is <n,<n,t>>, denoting a relation between numbers, and is structurally analogous to a transitive verb, at type <e,<e,t>>.[9] Like a transitive verb, *is smaller than* takes two arguments and maps them in two stages onto a truth value:

(49)   a *is smaller than*$_{<n,<n,t>>}$: $\lambda m\lambda n.\ n < m$
       b *is smaller than three*$_{<n,t>}$: $\lambda m\lambda n.\ n < m\ (3) = \lambda n.\ n < 3$
       c *Two is smaller than three*$_t$: $\lambda n.\ n < 3\ (2) =\quad 2 < 3$

Equals, is the square of and so on, work the same way.[10]

Two-place operations on numbers of type <n <n, n>> map pairs of numbers onto a third number. *Plus, times* and *minus* are the most obvious examples:

(50)   a Two plus three equals five.
       b Two times three equals six.

In (50a), *plus* applies to a number *three* to give the expression *plus three*. This applies to *two* to give the subject of (50a). *Times* works similarly. *Plus* and *times* are thus expressions of type <n,<n, n>>, mapping two numbers arguments onto a number, as in (51a,b). *Equals* at type <n,<n, t>> maps two numbers onto a truth value as in (51c). A derivation for (51a) is given in (52).

(51)   a *plus*: $\lambda m\lambda n.n+m$
       b *times*: $\lambda m\lambda n.n\times m$
       c *equals*: $\lambda m\lambda n.n=m$

---

[9] *Is smaller than* can compare two numbers at type n, or two individuals as in 'This kitten is smaller than that kitten', so its type is actually <a<a,t>>. What this crucially captures is that the two objects compared must be of the same type. 'This kitten is smaller than 3' and '3 is smaller than this kitten' are infelicitous.

[10] For simplicity, we restrict the domain and range of these functions to the natural numbers. To allow the full range of mathematical statements, these will have to be extended to the real numbers, imaginary numbers and so on.

(52)   a *plus:* $\lambda m \lambda n.n+m$

        b *plus three:* $\lambda m \lambda n.n+m$ (3)   = $\lambda n.\ n+3$

        c *two plus three:* $\lambda n.n+3$ (2)   = $2+3$

        d *two plus three equals five:* $\lambda m \lambda n.n=m$ (5)   = $\lambda n.\ n=5$

                                           $\lambda n.n=5$ (2+3)   = $2+3=5$

(51) gives the interpretation of the *plus* and *times* functions in terms of + and ×, but do not, of course, say what the addition and multiplication operations represented by + and × are. This question is far beyond the scope of this book, and I will not discuss it. Hofweber (2005) raises a different point. He does not discuss what multiplication and addition are, but does suggest that statements like (50) are generalizations over statements such as (53).

(53)   Two things and three things are five things.

While we have shown that (50a) cannot be derived syntactically from (53), it is important to show the relationship between the mathematical statement and the statement about objects. Treating numericals as property expressions allows this to be stated simply, without requiring a syntactic relation. We want to show that the sum of two non-overlapping pluralities with cardinalities n and m will always have the cardinality n+m. We define the overlap relation in (54), such that two entities overlap if they have some non-null part in common.

(54) $O(x,y)$ iff $\exists z[\neg z = 0 \wedge z \sqsubseteq x \wedge z \sqsubseteq y]]$

The required property follows from the structure of the Boolean domain if $\mid x \mid = n \wedge \mid y \mid = m$ then $\mid \{a: a \sqsubseteq_{\text{ATOMIC}} x\} \mid = n$ and $\mid \{a: a \sqsubseteq_{\text{ATOMIC}} y\} \mid = m$. The Boolean structure guarantees that $\{a: a \sqsubseteq_{\text{ATOMIC}} x \sqcup y\} = \{a: a \sqsubseteq_{\text{ATOMIC}} x\} \cup \{a: a \sqsubseteq_{\text{ATOMIC}} y\}$. If $\neg O(x, y)$ then $\mid \{a: a \sqsubseteq_{\text{ATOMIC}} x \sqcup y\} \mid = \mid \{a: a \sqsubseteq_{\text{ATOMIC}} x\} \mid + \mid \{a: a \sqsubseteq_{\text{ATOMIC}} y\} \mid = n+m$:

(55) $\forall x \forall y: \mid x \mid = n \wedge \mid y \mid = m: \neg O(x, y) \rightarrow \mid x \sqcup y \mid = n+m$

Multiplication is defined in terms of iterations of additions, so the relation between multiplication of abstract numbers and the corresponding operation on plural entities can also be made explicit. Intuitively, the value of *three times two* will correlate with the cardinality of the sum of three non-overlapping pluralities in the denotation of the predicate *two*. So, without defining mathematical operations, we can show that the appropriate correlations hold between operations on numbers such as addition, and operations on objects such as the summing of pluralities. (This holds as long as the operations are operations on natural numbers. Since we have defined cardinality in terms of the atomic parts, the situation with operations on rational and real numbers will be different, but we will not discuss this here.)

While the truth of the mathematical statement in (50a) and the statement about objects in (53), can be derived from each other, we note their grammatical differences. First, English distinguishes the operation of adding numbers, which is expressed by *plus* in (50a), from the operation of summing pluralities, which is expressed by *and* in (53). The subject of the mathematical statement is a singular term, and verb agreement is always in the singular.

(56) a Two plus three equals/is/#equal/#are five.
      b Two times three equals/is/#equal/#are six

In (53) agreement must be plural. When *and* is used with bare numericals, either singular or plural agreement can be used in English, but other languages make stricter demands:

(57) a Two and two is/are four.
      b 'Two and two make five.' (Orwell, 1984: Part III, ch. 4)
      c 'Two and two are four, four and four are eight ...' (Danny Kay, Inchworm)
      d Twee   en   twee   is | #zijn   vier. (Dutch)
         two   and   two   be.SG | #be.PL   four
      e Deux   et   deux   font   quatre. (French)
         two   and   two   make.PL   four
         Both: 'Two and two are four'

Grammatically, *two plus three* and *two times three* are complex expressions denoting a single number, 5 and 6 respectively, and thus take singular agreement. *Two and two* can take either singular agreement or plural agreement. When agreement is singular *and* seems to be interpreted exactly like *plus*. When agreement is plural, *and* seems to denote a summing operation which maps two abstract objects onto a plural sum. This is possibly related to the examples in (35), e.g. *two twos are four*, in which numerical expressions are treated as count nouns and pluralized, and the verb is always plural. Note that agreement properties differ from language to language. In Dutch, agreement must be singular as in (57d), while in French, the verb is plural as in (57e).

In this section, we have looked at simple numericals denoting numbers, and at the complex expressions which can be formed using the operators *plus/and* and *times*. There are many more such operators, including *minus, square root of, square of* and so on. These operations are syntactically similar to the ones we have discussed, although their interpretation takes us beyond the range of the natural numbers and we will not discuss them here. In the next section, we will look at complex numerical expressions which raise grammatical, rather than mathematical, issues.

2.4 COMPLEX NUMERICALS

2.4.1 The Numbers from Thirteen to Ninety-nine

In addition to simple numerical expressions, there are an infinite number of syntactically complex cardinal numerals which can be used as simple adjectives.[11] These are formed by two processes, addition and multiplication, either singly or together. Additive constructions are formed using strings of numericals as in (58):

(58) a twenty-two
      b ninety-eight
      c fourteen

The denotation of (58a), the number 22, is derived compositionally from the denotation of *twenty* and the denotation of *two* using a null *plus* operator from (51a), repeated here as (59a).

(59) a [+]: $\lambda m \lambda n.n+m$
      b *twenty-two*: $\lambda m \lambda n.m+n$ (20)
                     $\lambda n.20+n$ (2)
                     $20+2$

While the operation in (59a) could be either a lexical or a syntactic operation, I shall assume it is lexical for several reasons. There are strong lexical constraints on how the numericals up to *ninety-nine* can be composed. The operations combining numericals with the two allomorphs of *ten*, namely *-teen* and *-ty*, must be lexical, since these allomorphs are bound morphemes. These derive the numericals in the sequence *thirteen* to *nineteen*, and the multiplication operation used to construct the decades in the sequence *twenty, thirty . . . ninety*. Numericals denoting decades such as *twenty* and *thirty* can be composed via addition with the numericals *one* to *nine* (in the strict order decade + unit), but not with any other numbers; #*twenty-thirty*, #*thirty-twenty*, #*twenty-fourteen* are all impossible. The addition operation generating numericals up to *ninety-nine* is not recursive. Together, this

---

[11] The twenty-three cats, or even *the three and twenty cats*, are perfectly felicitous, with the cardinal being used as a prenominal adjective. Expressions such as *the twenty plus three cats* or *the thirty minus seven cats* are not.

indicates that these numericals are probably all derived in the lexicon (in English). Furthermore, in complex numericals above one hundred, the last syntactically conjoined numerical is preceded by *and* (60a,b). In (60c), *and* is placed before *twenty-two*, showing that it is considered the last numerical, and is probably thus a single lexical item. This contrasts with (60d), where the archaic form *two and twenty* is not considered a single lexical item, and *and* follows *two* and precedes *twenty*.

(60)   a two hundred and twenty
         b two hundred and two
         c two hundred and twenty-two.
         d two hundred, two and twenty

2.4.2 Multiplicative Constructions

2.4.2.1 *Lexical Powers and Multiplication*

Above *ninety-nine*, English (like many other languages) uses a recursive system to make possible an infinite sequence of numerals. As we saw, this is done by selecting certain numbers as powers which are combined with multipliers, and which we called 'lexical powers'. This is a mechanism which seems to be essential in any language which allows infinite sequential counting, though the morphosyntactic characteristics of lexical powers vary crosslinguistically.

English, which is a base ten language, counts by allowing multiplication of *hundred* (= 10^2), *thousand* (= 10^3), *million* (= 10^6) and *billion* (= 10^9).[12] English also has *myriad* (= 10^4), though this has fallen into disuse, but there is no lexical expression for 10^5, 10^7 or 10^8. *Dozen* (= 12^1), and *gross* (= 12^2 or 144), as well as *score* (=20^1) are lexical powers, though they do not denote powers of ten. The lexical powers are characterized by specific morphosyntactic characteristics which distinguish them from other cardinal numericals. Unlike other cardinals, lexical powers can never appear bare, but are always preceded by a numeral (the 'determiner numeral', a definite determiner or an indefinite determiner, as shown in the counting sequences in (61), as well as in the sentences in (62).

(61)   a ninety, ninety-one, ninety-two .... ninety-eight, ninety-nine, #hundred
         b ... ninety-eight, ninety-nine, one/a hundred
         c a hundred, one hundred, two hundred

---

[12] Creatively, the language allows *trillion*, *zillion*, etc., although there is considerable confusion as to what powers they refer to.

(62) a Two/one/a hundred people stood in line.
      b #Hundred people stood in line.
      c The (one/two) hundred lucky people who got tickets ...

Note that there is a contrast between *two hundred* which names a number, and *two hundreds* in which *hundred* is a plural count noun and can be used in arithmetical statements analogous to *two twos are four* (see 35a). The contrast shows up in (63):

(63) a Nine hundreds are nine hundred, ten hundreds are a thousand.
      b Nine hundred is nine hundred.

While both the examples in (63) are tautological, (63a), analogous to (35a) with plural agreement on the verb, is informative in the same way that *The Morning Star is the Evening Star* is informative, while (63b), where the verb has singular agreement, is uninformative, analogous to *The Morning Star is the Morning Star*.

Semantically, the determiner numeral denotes the multiplier and the lexical power denotes the multiplicand, as in (64a,b), where the numericals denote 2×100 and $2 \times 1{,}000$ respectively. Only lexical powers can be preceded by multipliers in this way, as (64c,d) show:

(64) a two hundred cats
      b two thousand cats
      c #two twenty cats
      d #three ninety cats
      e two score cats

Two twenty cannot be interpreted analogously to *two hundred* with *two* as the multiplier and *twenty* as the multiplicand. The contrast between (64c) and (64e) shows that this is a grammatical restriction and not a semantic restriction, since *score* and *twenty* both denote 20. Clearly, *twenty* and *score* have different combinatorial properties. In (65) *two hundred* is the multiplier of the lexical power *thousand*, showing that the system is recursive.

(65) [[two hundred] thousand] cats

Two combines with *hundred* to make a numerical expression denoting 200, which itself is the multiplier of *thousand* resulting in the numerical denoting 200,000.

Lexical powers have another characteristic: they are the only numerical expressions which can also be used as approximative classifiers, as in (66):

(66) a hundreds of cats
      b thousands of cats

c hundreds of thousands of cats
d scores of cats, dozens of cats
e #twenties of cats, #twelves of cats, #sixties of cats, #nineties of cats

Again, the contrast between (66d) and (66e) shows that this is a grammatical and not a conceptual issue.

These data suggest that the semantic type and interpretation of lexical powers must be different from those of other numericals. While a non-argument numerical like *four* is a predicate at type $\langle e,t \rangle$ and shifts to the argument type n, a lexical power like *hundred* must be of type $\langle n,\langle e,t \rangle \rangle$, in other words an expression which combines with a numerical expression at type n to give a predicate. The meaning for *hundred*, which is a typical meaning for a lexical power, is given in (67a). *Hundred* combines with a number *n* to give a property of individuals, the property that a plural individual has if it has *n* hundred atomic parts. (67b) gives the result of applying (67a) to the number 2. The meaning for *two hundred* at type n is given in (67c). (67d) shows how this works recursively: *thousand* applies to the number *two hundred* to give *two hundred thousand*.

(67) a *hundred*$_{\langle n,\langle e,t \rangle \rangle}$: $\lambda n \lambda x. \mid x \mid = 100 \times n$
     b *two hundred*$_{\langle e,t \rangle}$: $\lambda x. \mid x \mid = 100 \times 2$
     c *two hundred*$_n$: $^{\cap}\lambda x. \mid x \mid = 100 \times 2$
     d *two hundred thousand*: $\lambda n \lambda x. \mid x \mid = 1{,}000 \times n \, (^{\cap}\lambda x. \mid x \mid = 100 \times 2) =$
        $\lambda x. \mid x \mid = 1{,}000 \times {}^{\cap}\lambda x. \mid x \mid = 100 \times 2 \quad =$
        $\lambda x. \mid x \mid = 1{,}000 \times 200$

The only configuration in which *hundred* does not appear with a number is when it appears with a determiner, as in *a hundred* or *the hundred*. I assume that *the hundred* N is an elliptical form of *the one hundred* N, and thus directly analogous to *the two hundred* N. The indefinite may work the same way, but it is more probable that *a* is interpreted semantically as *one*, since *a one hundred* is usually considered infelicitous.

Numbers constructed out of lexical powers combine with numericals additively. Sometimes, the additive operator is explicit as in (68a,b), and sometimes it is optional as in (68c). In English, *and* is obligatory if the number added is less than 100:

(68)   a two hundred and twenty-two
       b nine hundred and ninety-nine
       c two thousand (and) three hundred
       d two thousand #(and) ninety-nine

We assume a lexical item *and* at type <n <n, n>> as in (69a), with the semantics of the lexical *plus* operator given in (51a) above. A numerical constructed using it is given in (69b).

(69)   a   *and:* $\lambda m \lambda n.n+m$
       b   *two hundred and three:* $200 + 3 = 203$; $^{\cup}203 = \lambda x. \mid x \mid = 203$

Not all additive operations are expressed lexically. In *two thousand three hundred and ninety-three*, there are three conjuncts joined by the operation in (69a), since the expression denotes the result of adding 2,000, 300 and 93. However, only the last two conjuncts are joined by an explicit *and*. The same is true of all lists of conjunctions in English – for example, in the list *John, Mary and Bill, and* is lexically realized only once.

2.5   SOME NON-CARDINAL NUMERICALS

2.5.1   Approximatives

Up till now, we have looked only at cardinal numericals. In this section, we look briefly at two other types of numerical expressions. We will start with approximatives, derived from the lexical powers just discussed. In Section 2.5.2, we will look briefly at the semantics of ordinals.

Lexical powers (and only lexical powers) also occur as approximatives, as we saw in (66). Approximatives have the syntax of classifiers (Rothstein 2012). They take an *of* -complement, and the complement of the preposition must be a bare plural. Plural marking on the classifier is obligatory (as in 70b), and a determiner numerical is impossible. The determiners *the* and *some* are felicitous, as is the adjectival *many*.

(70)   a   Thousands of cats were in the garden.
       b   #(a/two) thousand of cats ...
       c   #two thousands of cats ...
       d   The (many) thousands of cats in the garden ...
       e   Some thousands of cats gathered in the garden.

(70a) is true if there were more than 2,000 cats in the garden, and beyond that implies that the appropriate lexical power to use in counting the cats is *thousand*. Since only lexical powers can be approximative classifiers, the operation deriving the approximative from the numerical must exploit the semantic properties of the lexical power, namely that it is of type <n,<e,t>>. (We will argue that this is the type of measures in Chapter 9.) As approximatives are syntactically classifiers which apply to a bare NP and yield an NP, they must be of type <<e,t>,<e,t>>. So the operator deriving approximatives must shift an expression of type <n,<e,t>> to type <<e,t>,<e,t>>. The operation in (71) does this and gives the right semantics:

(71)   a   APPROX($N_{<n,<e,t>>}$):
           morphology: N → Ns
           semantics: APPROX$_{<n,<e,t>>}$ → $_{<e,t>}$:
           $\lambda a \lambda P \lambda x.P(x) \wedge \exists n[n \geq 2 \wedge | \ x \ | \geq {}^{\cap}a(n)$ a of type <n,<e,t>>
       b   *thousand* : $\lambda m \lambda y.|y| = m \times 1,000$
       c   APPROX(*thousand*):
           APPROX($\lambda m \lambda y.|y| = m \times 1,000$) =
           $\lambda a \lambda P \lambda x.P(x) \wedge \exists n[n \geq 2 \wedge | \ x \ | \geq {}^{\cap}(a(n))] \ (\lambda m \lambda y.|y| = n \times 1,000) =$
           $\lambda P \lambda x.P(x) \wedge \exists n[n \geq 2 \wedge | \ x \ | \geq {}^{\cap}(\ \lambda m \lambda y.|y| = m \times 1,000 \ (n))]=$
           $\lambda P \lambda x.P(x) \wedge \exists n[n \geq 2 \wedge | \ x \ | \geq {}^{\cap} \ \lambda y.|y| = n \times 1,000]$
           $\lambda P \lambda x.P(x) \wedge \exists n[n \geq 2 \wedge | \ x \ | \geq n \times 1,000]$

The APPROX operation marks the lexical power as plural. Semantically it does three things: it existentially quantifies over the n argument, it 'changes the = to ≥' and it adds the clause 'n ≥ 2'. Of course, for compositionality reasons, 'changing the = to ≥' is a complex operation.

Thousands of cats denotes (72), namely the set of pluralities of cats which have a cardinality greater than $1,000 \times n$, where n is greater than or equal to 2 – in other words, the set of pluralities of cats which have a cardinality greater than 2,000.

(72) $\lambda x.\exists n[n \geq 2 \wedge | \ x \ | \geq n \times 1,000 \wedge CATS(x)]$

Approximatives can stack, as in *hundreds of thousands of cats*. Here the numericals compose to make a complex classifier, and the expression denotes the set of pluralities of cats whose cardinality is more than $2 \times 10 \times 1,000$. The derivation is given in (73). The denotations of *hundred* and *thousand* are composed via function composition as in (73a). We first applying the meaning of *hundred* to a variable *n*, and shift it via the $^{\cap}$ function to type n. We apply the interpretation of *thousand* to the result and abstract over variable *n*. We write $^{\cap}\lambda x. | \ x \ | = n \times 100$ as $n \times 100$, by the equivalence principle. We apply APPROX to the result in exactly the same way as above and apply the result to CATS:

(73)   a   *thousand* ∘ *hundred* =
           $\lambda m \lambda x. | \ x \ | = m \times 1,000 \circ \lambda n \lambda x. | \ x \ | = n \times 100 =$
           $\lambda n.(\lambda m \lambda x. | \ x \ | = m \times 1,000 \ (^{\cap}\lambda x. | \ x \ | = n \times 100)) =$
           $\lambda n.(\lambda m \lambda x. | \ x \ | = m \times 1,000 \ (n \times 100)) =$

$$\lambda n.(\lambda x. \mid x \mid = n \times 100 \times 1,000) =$$
$$\lambda n \lambda x. \mid x \mid = n \times 100 \times 1,000$$
b APPROX(*thousand ∘ hundred*) =
$$\lambda P \lambda x.P(x) \wedge \exists n[n \geq 2 \wedge \mid x \mid \geq n \times 100 \times 1,000]$$
c *hundreds of thousands of cats*:
$$\lambda P \lambda x.P(x) \wedge \exists n \ [n \geq 2 \wedge \mid x \mid \geq n \times 100 \times 1,000] \ (CATS) =$$
$$\lambda x. \exists n \ [CATS(x) \wedge n \geq 2 \wedge \mid x \mid \geq n \times 100 \times 1,000]$$

As we see in (73c), this gives us the meaning we want: *hundreds of thousands of cats* denotes pluralities of cats whose cardinality is greater than $n \times 100 \times 1,000$, where n is at least 2 – that is, cats in quantities of more than 200,000.

The APPROX operation makes use of the structure of lexical powers at type $<n,<e,t>>$, since it existentially binds the n argument. This explains the contrast between *scores/dozens of cats* and #*twenties/twelves of cats* since only *scores/dozens* is of the type that APPROX can apply to. We also explain why approximatives cannot occur with numerical determiners, i.e. why #*two thousands of cats* is ungrammatical. Since n is bound by an existential quantifier, *thousand* can no longer apply to a numerical argument.

Note that there is one exceptional numerical, *ten*, which can be used as an approximative, but which does not have the usual grammatical properties of a lexical power.

(74)   a Ten people / tens of people stood in line.
        b Tens of thousands of people were in the square.

As we saw, the allomorph -*ty* is used as a lexical power in *twenty*, *thirty* and so on, but these numericals are constructed via lexical operations and not via recursive, syntactic operations. This suggests that the numerical *ten* has a number of different allomorphs which are lexically derived. These include the simple numerical *ten* at type n, the lexical power -*ty*, the additive base -*teen* and the approximative classifier *tens*.

2.5.2   Ordinals

Ordinals are numerical expressions such as *first/second/third*. They give information about the ranking of an individual within a partially ordered set, where the ordering is contextually defined. Ordinals can be adjectival or adverbial.

(75)   a The book is on the third shelf from the top.
        b Mary won first/second prize.
        c Mary was the first/second speaker.
        d Mary spoke first.

In (75a), shelves are ranked in order of height; in (75b), prizes are ordered in terms of degrees of achievement; while in (75c,d), speakers, or events of speaking, are ordered in terms of temporal precedence. If R(x,y) is the relation 'x spoke before y' then (75c) is true if there is no x such that R(x,M).

Unlike cardinals, ordinals are inherently modificational. *Mary was (the) first* requires a comparison set naturally supplied by an elliptical N.

We can define the meaning of the ordinal numerical in terms of the related cardinal numerical. If Mary is the first or 1st speaker, then Mary is a speaker, and the cardinality of the set of individuals who spoke before her is 1–1, i.e. zero. If Mary is the second or 2nd speaker, then the cardinality of the set of preceding speakers is 2 – 1, and if she is the nth speaker, then the number cardinality of the set of speakers preceding her is n – 1 and so on.

An ordinal n^{th} (realized as st and nd in the case of 1 and 2) is thus derived from a cardinal via an operation th of type <n,<<e,t>, <<e<e,t>>,<e,t>>>>. Th combines with a cardinal n, a predicate P and a relation R, which is a contextually determined partial order on P. *Second* denotes $^{th}(2,P,R_P)$, *fourth* denotes $^{th}(4,P,R_P)$ and so on. P is predicate, and R_P is a partial order on the set denoted by P. n^{th} P denotes the property that an individual x has if x is P, P is partially ordered by R_P, and the cardinality of the set $\{y: R_P(y,x)\} = n$ – 1, as in (76a). This gives (76b) as the interpretation of *first* and (76c) as the interpretation of (75c), with R(y,x) interpreted as the partial order 'y spoke before x':

(76) a $[n^{th}] = \lambda n \lambda P \lambda R \lambda x.P(x) \wedge |\ \{y: R(y,x)\}\ | = n–1$
      b $[FIRST] = \lambda P \lambda R \lambda x.P(x) \wedge |\ \{y: R(y,x)\}\ | = 1–1$
      c *Mary is the first speaker:*
             SPEAKER(MARY) $\wedge |\ \{y: y$ SPOKE BEFORE MARY$\}\ | = 0$

The property $\lambda x.P(x) \wedge |\ \{y: R(y,x\}\ | = n–1$ is very often a singleton set, and used to define a familiar object, which is why ordinals frequently occur with the determiner *the*. However, this need not be the case, as in (77):

(77) a Today we have two first prize-winners.
      b Mary won three second prizes in last year's running season.

Obviously, this is a very preliminary account of ordinals, leaving many questions unanswered, but it does in principle show how ordinal numericals can be given an interpretation in terms of the cardinals to which they are related.

2.6   OTHER APPROACHES TO CARDINAL NUMERICALS

In this chapter, I have proposed treating numericals as a special kind of property expression, in the framework of Chierchia & Turner (1988). I have argued that cardinal numericals are ambiguous between predicates and arguments: at type <e,t>, a cardinal denotes a property of pluralities, the property that an entity has if the set of its atomic parts has n members. As an argument at type n, a cardinal denotes the individual correlate of that property, an individual which itself has properties. Properties of cardinals are expressions of type <n,t> – for example, *is equal to 6, is a prime number* and so on.

Cardinals at type <e,t>, like most other modifiers, shift easily to the predicate modifier type <<e,t,>,<e,t>>, and modify nouns, as in *four cats*. Other numericals, in particular approximatives such as *hundreds (of)* and ordinals such as *second, third*, are derived from the basic cardinal property meanings, via operations such as those proposed in Section 2.5.

This is not the only possible approach to the semantics of numericals. Two recent influential proposals are Hofweber (2005) and Ionin & Matushansky (2006). As discussed in Section 2.2, Hofweber has argued that cardinal numericals are determiners, following Barwise & Cooper (1981) and Keenan & Stavi (1986). We showed there that Hofweber's account does not give a plausible explanation of either the bare predicate or the bare argument use of cardinals, nor does it explain the distribution and interpretation of cardinals under the scope of determiners such as *the*.

A different approach is proposed in Ionin & Matushansky (2006), who argue that all numerical expressions are predicate modifiers at type <<e,t><e,t>>. Some of the criticisms of Hofweber apply also to their account, since they basically adopt his view that bare numerals such as *four* are equivalent to *four things*. However, they make two additional claims, which if correct would have far-reaching consequences, and these need to be discussed independently.

First, they claim that numericals are heads, taking nominal complements. This is based on the fact that in some languages, for example Russian, cardinals assign case to the noun that follows them, strongly suggesting that cardinals are heads which take complements. Second, they claim that all cardinal numericals must be of the same type – for example, *four* must have the same interpretation in (78a) and (78b):

(78)   a *four* cats
       b *four* hundred cats

They claim that, in (78a), *four* is a predicate modifier modifying *cats*. (78b) has the structure in (79), involving recursive modification: *hundred* modifies *cats* and *four* modifies *hundred cats*.

(79)   [four[hundred[cats]]]

They argue that the semantics for numericals is based on partitions: *four cats* denotes a set of cats partitioned into four non-overlapping cells each containing a singleton cat, while *four hundred cats* denotes a set of pluralities of cats which can be partitioned into four non-overlapping cells, each cell containing one-hundred (singleton) cats. The recursive nature of the interpretation is linked to the fact that numericals are analysed as heads. Complex additive numbers are derived from explicit conjunctions as in (80).

(80)   [two [hundred ~~students~~]] and [thirty students]

There are a number of points to criticise in this analysis (see Rothstein 2013a). I will here focus only on one crucial issue, the assumption that it is desirable to treat lexical powers and other cardinals as being of the same semantic type, and that examples like (79) should be derived via a simple recursion procedure. We have seen plenty of evidence that this assumption is unjustified. Lexical powers like *hundred* must co-occur with a numeral determiner, while other cardinals cannot occur as complements of other numericals. Ionin & Matushansky fail to account for the ungrammaticality of either (81a), where the lexical power is missing a numerical determiner, or (81b), where a cardinal which is not a lexical power occurs with a numerical determiner:

(81)   a #Hundred cats miaowed.
       b #Four thirty cats miaowed.

Furthermore, in some languages, lexical powers have morphosyntactic properties which distinguish them from other cardinals. In Hebrew, the cardinals such as *šloša* 'three' and *arba'a* 'four' agree in gender with the noun they modify, while lexical powers such as *mea* 'hundred' and *elef* 'thousand' have fixed grammatical gender, and have singular and plural forms. In (82a), *elef* is singular. In (82b), it is marked masculine plural, despite the fact that it is modifying a feminine plural noun.

(82) a elef   ban-ot
         thousand.SG   girl-F.PL
         'a thousand girls'
      b šlošet   alaf-im   ban-ot
         three.CS   thousand-M.PL   girl-F.PL
         'three thousand girls'

A semantic account of cardinals needs to explain the fact that the possibility of generating recursively an infinite number of cardinal numerals is a consequence of the special grammatical properties of a limited number of lexical powers, the only numerals to occur with numerical determiners. In the analysis I gave above, the difference in semantic type between cardinals at $<e,t>$ and lexical powers at $<n,<e,t>>$ captures this. Furthermore, the semantic type of lexical powers at $<n,<e,t>>$ is exploited to explain that, crosslinguistically, lexical powers and only lexical powers give rise to the approximative interpretations of *hundreds* and *dozens*, which occur when the numerical determiner is existentially bound.

Ionin & Matushansky also raise the issue of the syntactic relation between cardinal numerals and the noun they modify. They claim that numerals must be heads because, in a number of languages, for example Russian, they assign case to their complements. Danon (2012) discusses this in detail, arguing against the assumption that all numerals occur in the same syntactic configuration and against the claim that all numerals assign case to their complements. He points out that variation occurs crosslinguistically, and even within single languages. For example, in Hebrew, many numerals have two forms, one of which he argues is a modifier appearing in specifier position, while the other is a bound form in what is known as the construct state, taking a complement to which it appears to assign genitive case. (We will discuss the syntax and semantics of constructs in Chapter 3.) This is illustrated with *šloša* 'three', which is free in (83a) and bound in (83b).

(83) a šloša dub-im
         three bear-PL
         'three bears'
      b šlošet   ha-dub-im
         three.CS DEF-bear-PL
         'the three bears'

The choice between these two forms in (83) is dependent on whether the complement is definite. The bound form is obligatory with a definite complement, but impossible with an indefinite complement, but there is no detectable difference in the interpretation of the numerical.[13] Furthermore, as (82b) above shows, 'three' will have the bound morphology when it occurs as the determiner of a lexical power like *alafim*. This means that morphosyntactic status of the noun is independent of its semantic interpretation.

The Hebrew data contribute one more point to the comparison between lexical powers and other cardinals, and to the discussion of numericals as case assigners. As pointed out in Rothstein (2012) and Danon (2012) the plural of 'thousand' can occur in both a free form as in (82b) and a bound form as in (84):

(84)   alfey   xatul-im
        thousand.CS.PL   cat-PL
        'thousands of cats'

However, as the gloss shows, the bound form can only be interpreted as an approximative classifier, and does not occur felicitously with a determiner numeral. Although (85) does occur, informants consider it very degraded.

(85)   #šlošet   alf-ey   xatul-im
        three.CS   thousand-CS.PL   cat-PL

This shows that, contrary to what Ionin & Matushansky predict, the bound numericals which are assumed to assign case do not (normally) occur recursively in the way structures like (79) predict.

2.7 CONCLUSIONS

I have argued in this chapter that cardinal numericals are best treated semantically within the framework of property theory (Chierchia 1985, Chierchia & Turner 1988), and that they have an argument denotation at type n, as well as a predicative interpretation at <e,t>. As predicates, they can modify nouns attributively, and though they may in some situations assign case to the N following them, this does not indicate that the cardinal is the syntactic head of the phrase. Crucially, lexical powers are of a different type from 'ordinary' cardinals, and they combine with numericals at type n to form complex cardinals. We have thus identified two kinds of environments in which numericals occur at type n, mathematical statements about

---

[13] There are some exceptions to this generalization. As Danon shows, the bound form of *šnayim* 'two' is always used when the numerical is adjacent to the verb. Lexical powers also occur with indefinite complements in the construct state, as shown below. For other exceptions, see Moshavi & Rothstein (in press).

numbers, and numerical determiners of lexical powers. In the next chapter, we will explore another context in which cardinals occur at type n, namely measure phrases.

2.8   QUESTIONS FOR FURTHER DISCUSSION AND INVESTIGATION

1 For any language that you have access to, explore in detail how the system of cardinal numericals works, paying particular attention to the morphosyntax of lexical powers. Do all cardinals have the same grammatical properties? (For example, in Hebrew, the word for *one* is a normal adjective which follows the noun as in (86a), while other numericals, unlike adjectives, precede the noun as in (86b):

(86) a xatul   exad
         cat.M.SG   one.M
         'one cat'
      b šloša   xatul-im
         three.M   cat-M.PL
         'three cats'

What other numerical expressions are derived from or related to cardinals? What exactly is their meaning usage? For example, Mel'čuk (1985) observed in Russian a contrast between cardinal numericals and so-called collective numericals, illustrated in (87), where the collective numerical implies that the four students came as a group.

(87)   včera   ko   mne   prixodili cetyre^{CARDINAL} studenta
       yesterday to   me   came   four^{CARDINAL} student
       /cetvero   studentov
       /four^{COLLECTIVE} student
       'Yesterday four students came to see me.'

Similar contrasts have been observed in other Slavic languages. Recent work on Czech (Dočekal & Ziková 2013), Polish (Wągiel 2015) and Russian (Khrizman 2015, 2017) investigates the precise nature of the contrast involved, which is not necessarily the same crosslinguistically.

2 Approximatives such as *hundreds* and *thousands* turn up crosslinguistically. They seem consistently to be related to lexical powers, supporting the idea that the interpretation of approximatives is inherently dependent on the <n,<e,t>> type of the lexical powers. There are many unexplored issues to be investigated. An obvious question is what crosslinguistic similarities and variations are there

in the morphosyntax of approximatives? In English, approximatives are associated with constructions such as (88):

(88)   People came in (their) hundreds.

What kind of interpretation can the approximative be given in (88)?
Can it be derived from the semantics proposed in (71)? Is (88)
a peculiarity of English or is it a use of approximatives that is
available crosslinguistically?

3 The use of *hundreds* in (89) is not an approximative use:

(89)   The number of people there was somewhere in the hundreds.

(89) is true if the number of people is above 100 (while *hundreds of
people* normally denotes a set of people whose cardinality is well
above 200). In fact, *in the hundreds* seems to denote a property of
numbers. How is this construction used? Does it occur crosslinguistically? Is it always the same form as the approximative?

4 What is the grammar of fractions? Decimals?

5 What patterns of singular/plural agreement with numericals are
there? See, for example, Acquaviva (2006).

3 Counting and Measuring

'The prisoner explained that in her statement she used the phrase "a cup of coffee" merely as denoting "a certain quantity of coffee". You yourselves will be able to judge whether that is a usual and natural form of expression.'

D. L. Sayers, *Strong Poison*

3.1 INTRODUCTION – THE DISTINCTION BETWEEN COUNTING AND MEASURING

This chapter introduces the difference between two of the primary functions associated with numerical expressions – counting and measuring. Intuitively, counting involves saying 'how many' individuated relevant entities or objects there are in a particular context, while measuring involves saying how much of a particular substance there is. These are not the only functions associated with numericals, as discussed in Chapter 1. However, counting and measuring uses of numericals are central linguistic expressions of numerosity, and, as we will see, they have different grammatical properties. Furthermore, as I shall argue in Chapters 4 and 5, the count/measure contrast is fundamental to understanding another central opposition in grammar, the contrast between count and mass nouns.

The structure of this chapter is as follows. In this introductory section, I shall argue for a distinction between counting and measuring. In Section 3.2, I will introduce the general theoretical issues, arguing that counting and measuring are associated with two different syntactic structures, and that *two* in *two cats* is a cardinal predicate denoting the property $\lambda x. \mid x \mid = 2$, while in *two kilos* it is a bare singular denoting the number at an individual property type n, i.e. $^{\cap}\lambda x. \mid x \mid = 2$. Central to the discussion will be examples like *two glasses of wine*, which we will see are ambiguous between counting and measure readings, and which are also structurally ambiguous. In Section 3.3, I will present evidence that the syntactic contrast between counting and measuring occurs in Modern Hebrew, based largely on Rothstein (2009, 2012). Section 3.4 presents briefly further crosslinguistic evidence supporting the claim that counting and measuring are associated with different syntactic structures. (More evidence will be offered in Chapter 6, where I present in-depth case studies of Mandarin, Hungarian and Brazilian Portuguese.) Later, in Chapters 8 and 9, I discuss whether a two-way ambiguity between counting and measuring captures all the possible readings of *two glasses of wine*, or whether more readings are available, as suggested in Partee & Borschev (2012), who distinguish between at least three different measuring constructions, and by Khrizman *et al.* (2015), who argue that several different count interpretations can be distinguished. However, for the moment, we will be concerned only with the count/measure distinction.

I assume in this chapter a basic distinction between count nouns and mass nouns, a distinction which we will examine in detail in Chapters 4 and 5. It is a bit unusual to discuss counting and measuring before analysing the mass/count distinction; however, I hope my reasons for doing so will become clear in the course of the next three chapters.

Typical counting constructions are constructions such as (1), where numeral modifiers modify count nouns. In English (but not in all languages), N is plural when the numerical is *two* or higher:

(1)   three flowers, four books, two hundred and twenty cats

Mass nouns are nouns which cannot be directly modified by numericals, as in (2):

(2)   #one furniture, #two flour(s), #three mud(s)

Classifiers like *box of N, cup of N* are used to count mass nouns, as in #*three flours* vs *three cups of flour* or *three packs of flour*. Denotations of plural nouns can also be counted as in *three boxes of books*, where the classifier is used to 'repackage' pluralities into higher-order entities which can then be counted.

Lexical measure phrases such as *kilo* and *litre* combine with cardinals and both mass and plural count nouns, as in *four litres of water, three kilos of books*. Selkirk (1977) called these measure phrases 'pseudopartitives'. They are distinguished from true partitives such as *three kilos of the beans*, which take definite DP complements, and involve a part-of operation on the DP complement. Pseudopartitives have bare NP complements. The partitive *three kilos of the beans* denotes a part (equal to three kilos) of the definite sum denoted by *the beans*.

The pseudopartitive *three kilos of beans* denotes beans measuring a certain amount, and seems to involve normal intersective modification on the NP complement denotation. As has been shown (Koptjevskaja-Tamm, 2001, 2009; Schwarzschild 2006), differences between pseudopartitives and true partitives show up differently in different languages.

Numericals like *three* occur in both counting contexts like *three books* and measuring pseudopartitives like *three kilos of books*, and an obvious question is whether they have the same use in both contexts, and more generally whether the quantity judgements expressed in counting and measuring contexts are the same kind of quantity judgements. There seem to be three possible answers. First, measuring could be a form of counting, in which units (determined by the so-called 'mensural classifier') are counted instead of objects. This is what is suggested in Gil (2013), who writes that 'Mensural classifiers provide nouns of low countability with a unit of measure by means of which they may then be counted.' Gil builds on an intuition in Lyons (1977), who suggests that 'a mensural classifier is one which individuates in terms of quantity' (p. 463). A second possibility is that counting could be a form of measuring. This is essentially the position of Krifka (1989, 1995), who suggests that *two cows* measures a quantity of cows in terms of natural units, analogously to the way in which *two kilos of meat* measures a quantity of meat in terms of kilo-units. A third possibility is that measuring and counting could be two independent operations. I am going to argue (based on Rothstein 2009, 2011) that this third possibility is the correct one, based largely on an analysis of classifier constructions such as *two glasses of water*.

It has long been observed (Doetjes 1997; Chierchia 1998a; Landman 2004; and others) that these classifier phrases are ambiguous between what we will call an 'individuating' or 'counting' reading, illustrated in (3a), and a 'measure' reading, illustrated in (3b):

(3)   a Mary, bring two glasses of water for our guests!
       b Add two glasses of water to the soup!

If the instructions in (3a) are fulfilled, then we expect Mary to bring two concrete glasses, filled with water. *Two* then counts the glasses containing water: the plural object that Mary brings has two atomic parts, each one a glass of water. In (3b), the instructions are to add an amount of water to the soup which is equivalent to the contents of two standard-size glasses. If the right quantity of water (say 2 x 100ml), is added to the soup from a plastic jug, then the instructions in (3b) have been fulfilled adequately. In fact, Mary can do what she is asked to by adding water straight from a bottle or from the tap, as long as she adds the right overall quantity. In contrast, if Mary comes into the room carrying only a jug or a bottle containing 200ml of water, there is a sense in which she has not fulfilled the instructions in (3a).

In English, as (3) shows, both these readings are expressed by the same expression *two glasses of water*. The individuating reading involves two concrete glasses and two individuated quantities of water, one in each of the glasses. *Glasses* is a relational nominal derived from the one-place sortal predicate *glass*, which denotes a set of glasses. It combines with *water* and is modified by *two*. We count the glasses of water, and thus indirectly give a quantity evaluation of the water contained in the glasses.

In the measure reading, no actual glasses need be involved, nor need there be two individuated bodies of water. *Glasses* expresses a unit of measure. If the glasses are contextually understood to be pint glasses, then (3b) is truth-conditionally equivalent to 'Add two pints of water to the soup!' In contrast to (3a), fulfilling the instruction in (3b) can involve only one body of water whose overall measure is equivalent to two pints or two glasses. (4a) shows examples of measure contexts which use the lexical measure head *kilo*, which is not derived from a sortal noun. While (4a) looks identical to (3b), it is (normally) not ambiguous, but only has a measure interpretation. For the reading that Mary bought six individual bodies of flour each weighing one kilo, we need a sentence like (4b):

(4)   a   Mary bought six kilos of flour/beans (in one sack).
        b   Mary bought six kilo-packs of flour.

Doetjes (1997) notes that, in Dutch, lexical measure expressions such as *liter, kilo* can be distinguished explicitly from nominal classifiers since, unlike nominal classifiers, they do not necessarily agree in number with a numeral modifier:

(5)   a   Jan   heeft   twee   kilo(-s)   pruimen   gekocht.
            Jan   has   two   kilo(-PL)   plums   bought
            'Jan has bought two kilos of plums.'
        b   Jan   heeft   twee   #zak /   zakk-en   pruimen   gekocht.
            Jan   has   two   #sack.SG /   sack-PL   plums   bought
            'Jan has bought two sacks of plums.'

In (5a), plural agreement on *kilo* is optional, while in (5b) it is obligatory, whether or not *zakken* has an individuating or a measure reading. In fact, these data can be used to make an even stronger point. In (5b), *twee zakken* is ambiguous between a counting or individuation reading and a measure interpretation. However, in

(5a), when *kilo* is marked plural, the preferred reading is individuating: Jan has bought two individuated bodies of plums each weighing
a kilo. When *kilo* is bare, there is no such implication. This holds for
all measure expressions. (6a) makes no commitment about the
number of items delivered, and is true if the grocer delivered
a single barrel of soft drinks whose volume was twenty litres. (6b)
is naturally interpreted as asserting that twenty one-litre-bottles
were delivered:

(6)   a Ik heb twintig liter frisdrank bezorgd voor het feestje.
          I have 20   litre soft-drink delivered for the party
          'I have delivered 20 litres of soft-drinks for the party.'
    b Ik heb twintig liter-s frisdrank bezorgd voor het feestje.
          I have 20   litre-PL soft-drink delivered for the party
          Preferred reading: 'I have delivered 20 litre-bottles of drink for
          the party.'

So, lexical measure heads in Dutch contrast with nouns used as
measure heads, since only the latter are marked plural. However, if
inherent measure phrases are used as individuating classifiers, the
shift to nominal classifier use shows up grammatically in the plural
marker. This is good evidence that measure heads and nominal
classifiers belong to different syntactic categories. Fred Landman
(p.c.) supports this with the observation that *twintig halve liters bier*
(with *litres* marked plural) is a natural way of referring to 20 half-
litre bottles of beer. However, *twintig halve liter bier*, with a bare
measure head, is infelicitous. Since *halve liter* is not a natural
measure unit, using it as if it is a lexical measure expression is
inappropriate.

German distinguishes between lexical measure heads and lexical
nouns in a similar way, as shown also in Grestenberger (2015),
with an interesting difference. In some dialects of German, nouns
like *Glas* 'glass' are ambiguous between a noun interpretation and
a homonym denoting standardized measure units. Used in
this second way, the plural marker can be dropped. (7a), where
the noun is marked plural, is ambiguous between a count and
a measure reading, just like (5b). However, in (7b) (Mosel-Fränkisch
dialect: Franz d'Avis p.c.), the plural marker has been dropped,
and, crucially, the reading is unambiguously measure.
The infelicity of (7c) shows that the plural can be dropped only
from nouns which have a canonical or standardized measure interpretation. Grestenberger (2015) shows that similar contrasts occur
in Viennese German.

(7)   a zwei Gläser   Wasser   (ambiguous)
        two   glass.PL   water
      b zwei Glas   Wasser   (measure reading)
        two   glass.SG   water
      c zwei Kiste/#Kisten Bücher
        two   box.#PL   books

In English, the measure and individuating interpretations of classifiers can be distinguished, as shown in the following examples. In all cases, *bring two glasses of wine* or *the two glasses of wine on this tray* are taken to be contexts which favour a counting interpretation, in which the nominal phrase denotes individual glasses filled with wine. *(The) two glasses of wine in the soup* favours a measure reading where the nominal denotes wine to a quantity.

(i) Measure suffixes
When the measure suffix -*ful* is suffixed to container-nouns, the result is unambiguously a measure interpretation. (8) shows that -*ful* cannot be used in contexts favouring an individuating reading.

(8)   a Add two glasses(ful) of wine to the soup.
      b Bring two glasses(#ful) of wine for our guests.
      c We needed three bucket(ful)s of cement to build that wall.
      d Three bucket(#ful)s of mud were standing in a row against the wall.

(ii) Pronominalization
Plural individuating classifiers provide natural antecedents for individuating pronouns:

(9)   There are two glasses of wine on this tray.
      a They are blue.
      b They (each) contain 100 millilitres.
      c They (each) cost 2 euros.

(10) There are two glasses of wine in this soup.
      a #They are blue.
      b #They (each) contain 100 millilitres.
      c #They (each) cost 2 euros.
      d It adds flavour / ??They add flavour.

(iii) Grammatical agreement
Plural individual classifiers require plural agreement, measure phrases may allow singular agreement, especially in existential and copular constructions. (Note that the distribution of reduced 's is marginally OK in (11b)):

(11) a There are two glasses of wine on this tray.
      b #There is / ?There's two glasses of wine on this tray.

(12) a There are two glasses of wine in this soup.
      b There's two glasses of wine in this soup.

(13) a Two pieces of cake are/is enough for you to eat.
      b Two spoonfuls of sugar were/was added to the sauce.

(iv) Distributive operators
Distributive operators, such as *each*, operate on the individuals in the
denotation of individuating classifier expressions and are unacceptable with measure phrases:

(14) a Two packs of flour cost 2 euros each.
      b #Two kilos of flour cost 2 euros each.
      c The two glasses of wine (#in this soup) cost 2 euros each.

(v) Relative clause formation (Carlson 1977; Heim 1987; Grosu & Landman
1998) Relative clauses denoting sets of individuals can be headed by
that or *which*, while relative clauses denoting quantities are headed
only by *that*. If a classifier like *bottle* is ambiguous between an individuating and a measure reading, either complementizer is acceptable
(as in 15a), though choice of *which* forces an individuating reading.
With a measure head like *litre*, only a *that*-clause is acceptable, as
shown in (15b). Since bottles of wine can only be drunk once, (15c)
can have only the measure reading, and, as a consequence, a *which*-
relative is infelicitous:

(15) a I would like to be able to buy the bottles of wine that/which they
         bought for the party. (ambiguous)
      b I would like to be able to buy the litres of wine that/#which they
         bought for the party.
      c It would take us a year to drink the bottles of wine that/#which
         they drank that evening.

The evidence shows that the individuating/measure contrast in the
interpretation of classifiers is a genuine semantic ambiguity, even
though it is not, in English, grammatically encoded on the classifier
itself.

3.2 SYNTACTIC STRUCTURE

The next question is how this semantic ambiguity is encoded in
structure. Gawron (2002) suggests that measure pseudopartitives
have different syntactic structures from other classifier constructions.

Rothstein (2009) argues that there is syntactic evidence from English and Modern Hebrew that two different structures are associated with the two different interpretations. Recent work shows that this holds in other languages too: Partee & Borschev (2012) make the case for Russian, Li (2011, 2013) and Li & Rothstein (2012) have argued the same for Mandarin, and Schvarcz (2014) makes the case for Hungarian.

Landman (2004) gives an analysis in which, on the individuating reading, *three glasses of wine* denotes three actual glasses containing wine. Rothstein (2009) proposes (16) as the syntactic structure for individuating readings of classifiers. *Of*-insertion is a late phenomenon, projecting no PP node (see Chomsky 1981):

(16)
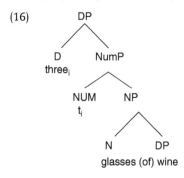

Glass(es) starts off as a sortal nominal of the predicate type at <e,t>, denoting the set of glasses. (*Glass* denotes the set of individual glasses, *glasses* denotes the set of pluralities of glasses.)

(17) $\lambda x.\text{GLASS}(x)$
        the set of singular glasses

(17) provides the sortal interpretation of *glass* in *I bought three glasses and a jug*, the interpretation on which *glass* denotes a one-place predicate. In (18), *glass* has shifted from its sortal use to a relational noun which takes an NP complement, and is interpreted as a relation at type <<e,t>,<e,t>>. Interpretation is via NP incorporation (van Geenhoven 1998). As a relational noun, *glass* denotes the relation between entities which are *glasses* and what they contain, as in (18).

(18) $\lambda P \lambda x.\text{GLASS}(x) \wedge \exists y[P(y) \wedge \text{CONTAIN}(x,y)]$

Connecting this with *wine* gives (19) as the interpretation of *glass of wine*:

(19) $\lambda x.\text{GLASS}(x) \wedge \exists y[\text{WINE}(y) \wedge \text{CONTAIN}(x,y)]$

The resulting NP is a nominal predicate at type $<e,t>$. It is at this level that semantic pluralization takes place. Pluralization operation * is a predicate operation such that *P is the closure of P under sum, or equivalently:

(20) $*P = \lambda x.\forall a[a \sqsubseteq_{ATOMIC} x \rightarrow P(a)]$

Hence *glasses of wine* is interpreted as:[1]

(21) $\lambda x.\forall a[a \sqsubseteq_{ATOMIC} x \rightarrow GLASS(a) \wedge \exists y[WINE(y) \wedge CONTAIN(a,y)]]$

Three is an $<e,t>$ predicate, as in (22a), which shifts to the modifier type $<<e,t>,<e,t>>$, as in (22b), and applies to (21) to give (22c) as the meaning for *three glasses of wine*.

(22) a *three:* $\lambda x. \mid x \mid =3$
     b *three:* $\lambda P \lambda x.P(x) \wedge \mid x \mid =3$
     c *three glasses of wine:*
            $\lambda x.\forall a[a \sqsubseteq_{ATOMIC} x \rightarrow GLASS(a) \wedge \exists y[WINE(y) \wedge CONTAIN(a,y)]]$
            $\wedge \mid x \mid =3$

This is the function characterizing the set of pluralities of glasses which contain wine and which consist of three atomic glasses. It is a *counting* reading, since *three* counts the atomic parts of the plural individuals which are pluralities of glasses of wine. The counting reading presupposes *individuation* of the atomic glasses of wine.

In contrast to (16), Rothstein (2009) posits (23) as the syntactic structure for the measure reading. As in (16), *of*-insertion is a late phenomenon satisfying surface constraints and projecting no PP node.

(23)

In this structure, *glass* is a measure head and denotes a unit of measurement analogous to *litre* or *kilo*. Krifka (1989) and Landman (2004)

---

[1] There is an alternative analysis where the interpretation of *glasses* starts out as plural *GLASS. The shift to the relational interpretation must then be distributive as in (i). I will use the simpler formulation here.

(i) $\lambda P \lambda x. *GLASS(x) \wedge \forall a[a \sqsubseteq_{ATOMIC} x \rightarrow \exists y[P(y) \wedge CONTAIN(a,y)]] \wedge \mid x \mid =3.$

propose that measure heads like *kilo* combine with numericals to give measure operators on nouns. In *three kilos, kilo* denotes an operator of type <n< e,t>> as in (24a), which applies to a numerical to give (24b), equivalently (24c):

(24) a $\lambda n \lambda x.KILO(x) = n$
      b $\lambda x.KILO(x) = 3$
      c $\lambda x.MEASURE_{WEIGHT, \, KILO}(x) = 3$

The numerical has its argument usage at type n, discussed in Chapter 2. *Glasses* is a measure head at type <n,<e,t>>, as in (25a) and combines with *three* to give the measure predicate *three glasses* in (25b). (25b) denotes bodies of wine whose volume is equal to that contained in three glasses.

(25) a $\lambda n \lambda x.MEASURE_{VOLUME, \, GLASS}(x) = n$
      b $\lambda x.MEASURE_{VOLUME, \, GLASS}(x) = 3$

Wine in (23) is an N predicate denoting the set of entities that are wine (as in 26a), and is modified by the measure predicate *three glasses*. In (26b), this has shifted to the attributive modifier type <<e,t>,<e,t>>, just as *three* did in (22b), and modifies *wine*. The result is (26c):

(26) a wine$_{<e,t>}$: $\lambda x.WINE(x)$
      b three glasses$_{<<e,t>,<e,t>>}$: $\lambda P \lambda x.P(x) \wedge MEASURE_{VOLUME, \, GLASS}(x) = 3$
      c three glasses of wine$_{<e,t>}$: $\lambda x.WINE(x) \wedge MEASURE_{VOLUME, \, GLASS}(x) = 3$

(26c) denotes the set of entities that are wine which measure three glassfuls. It is a *measure reading*, since it gives the overall measure of a body of wine without reference to the internal structure of the measures of its parts (unlike in the case of counting, where the count of a plurality is always calculated in terms of its atomic parts). *Glass* gives the measure unit just as *kilo* does.

Three glasses of wine, as interpreted in both (22c) and in (26c), is a predicate. (22c) gives the set of pluralities of glasses with three atomic parts, and (26c) the set of bodies of wine which each measures three glasses. As arguments, these either shift to the type of generalized quantifiers via existential closure (see, e.g., Landman 2003) or are bound by default existential closure (Heim 1982; Kamp 1981) over the sentence.

So far, the justification for the two different structures in (16) and (23) is that they allow appropriate semantic interpretations. However, there are some syntactic arguments to support these structures. First, phrases consisting of numericals and units are used as bare predicates in sentences such as *That weighs ten kilos*, where the V takes a predicate complement. Second, as was noted in Gawron (2002), measure phrases such as *two litres / two gallons* can be preceded by another adjective under the scope of an indefinite determiner, as in (27). The examples are taken from advertisements for a cleaning fluid and a dehumidifier respectively:

(27) a This little 16 oz bottle creates **an unbelievable 48 gallons** of super-safe, really powerful, all purpose cleaner.
       b Capable of removing up to **an amazing 10 litres** of water from its surroundings every day . . ..

These adjectives modify the measure phrase. In (27a), it is the quantity of super-safe really powerful, all purpose cleaner which is unbelievable, and in (27b), it is the quantity of removable water which is amazing. The indefinite determiner, *a/an*, indicates that reference is to single quantities.

Rothstein (2009) shows that adjectival modification can be used to distinguish between the measure and counting readings of *three glasses*. When *three glasses* is a measure predicate, it is felicitous under the scope of an adjective evaluating the quantity measured. This is shown in (28). *Spill* and *drink* facilitate a context in which the measure reading of *three glasses* is salient, while *bring* and *break* facilitate a counting reading of *three glasses of wine* in which the individual glasses of wine are salient. All speakers agree that (28a), the individuating context, is infelicitous. If (28a) has the structure in (16), *glasses* is the head of the phrase and *three* is a determiner. The infelicity is predicted, since *expensive* cannot appear higher than the determiner. In contrast, speakers find (28b/c) acceptable. If *three glasses* and *three teaspoonsful* are measure predicates, then it is expected that they can come under the scope of the higher modifier *expensive*.

(28) a # The waiter brought/broke an expensive three glasses of wine!
       b You drank/spilled an expensive three glasses of wine!
       c She added an expensive three teaspoons(ful) of cognac to the sauce.

The converse argument also holds. If a classifier like *glasses* is a nominal head taking a complement, then it should be independently modifiable by an adjective, but not if it is part of a measure expression. So an individuating context should favour direct modification of the classifier, and the measure reading should disallow it. The examples in (29) support this:

(29)   a # She added three expensive glasses of cognac to the sauce.
       b   The waiter brought three expensive glasses of cognac.

Note that an adjective can modify the measure head when it gives a property of the unit or measure, as in *a heaped/flat/scant teaspoon of sugar*.[2]

So far, our examples involve measuring along the dimension of volume and weight, but measure expressions relating to other dimensions have the same grammatical properties. In (30) *ten seconds* is used to measure a stretch of time, and occurs under the scope of an evaluative modifier as in (28b/c):

(30)   An expensive ten seconds of silence on the international telephone line followed. (Sarah Caudwell, Thus was Adonis Murdered, London: Penguin Books)

Despite the clear evidence that counting and measuring interpretations of classifiers can be distinguished, the syntactic support for the structures in (16) and (23) is not strong.[3] We now turn to numerical constructions in Modern Hebrew, where there is much stronger evidence that structures like (16) and (23) are associated with counting and measuring interpretations, respectively.

3.3   COUNTING AND MEASURING IN MODERN HEBREW

3.3.1   The Data

Rothstein (2009) gives an analysis of classifier constructions in Modern Hebrew, which supports this analysis of measure and

---

[2] 'Cookbook writers it seems to me fail to imagine the time a punter takes holding up a trembling tablespoon and wondering if its piled contents are better described as "rounded" or "heaped"': Julian Barnes, The Pedant in the Kitchen.

[3] Landman (2015) points out that, despite the data in (11), verbal agreement in measure constructions is usually with the measure head as in (i):

(i)   a Two teaspoons of sugar were added to the sauce.
       b 12,000 kilo   aardappels   rolde   over   de   weg.
          12,000 kilo.SG   potato.PL   rolled.SG   over   the   road
          '12,000 kilos of potatoes rolled over the road.'

Landman argues that (i) is evidence that *teaspoons* and *kilo* are the syntactic heads of these phrases, and suggests that, in English and Dutch, there is a mismatch between the syntactic structure and the semantic operations involved in interpretation. However, this does not explain why there is a flexibility with respect to agreement in measuring contexts which is absent in the counting context.

counting constructions. This section summarizes the analysis and discusses its implications for a general theory of counting and measuring. A more detailed analysis appears in the original paper.

Hebrew is a mass/count language. Cardinal numerals (except for *exad* 'one') precede the count nouns they modify, unlike ordinary adjectives and *exad*, which follow the modified noun:

(31)   šaloš   smal-ot   adum-ot
       three.F   dress-F.PL   red-F.PL
       'three red dresses'

Cardinals agree in gender as in (32). Nouns modified by numerals greater than one are usually marked as plural (although there are some exceptions for high round numbers). Mass nouns may not be directly modified by numeral expressions, as in (33).

(32)   a šloša   bakbuk-im
          three.M   bottle-M.PL
          'three bottles'
       b šaloš   smal-ot
          three.F   dress-F.PL
          'three dresses'

(33)   #šloša/šaloš   kemax
       three.M/three.F   flour.M

Numerical modification of mass nouns requires a classifier. There are two standard classifier constructions, the free genitive construction (FG) and the construct state phrase (CSP):

(34)   a šloša bakbuk-im   šel yayin   (FG)
          three bottle-M.PL   of wine
       b šloša bakbuk-ey   yayin   (CSP)
          three bottles-CS.M.PL wine
          Both: 'three bottles of wine'

In the free genitive in (34a) the noun *bakbukim* 'bottles' has the usual masculine plural suffix *-im*, the complement is headed by the preposition *šel*, and the PP complement is optional (as in (32a)).

(34b) is a construct state phrase. Constructs are a widespread phenomenon in Modern Hebrew (see, e.g., Ritter 1988, 1991; Borer 1999; Siloni 2001; Danon 2008; Rothstein 2012; and many others). They are phrases which form prosodic words (Doron & Meir 2013a). Crucially, they can be distinguished from lexical compounds which superficially seem to have the same form (Borer 1989, 1999, 2009). They can be headed by different categorical heads (Siloni 2001) and come in a variety of semantic types (Borer 2009; Rothstein 2012). They all share the same mor-phosyntactic characteristics illustrated in (34b): the head has construct state (CS) masculine plural morphology, i.e. *bakbuk-ey* in place of *bakbuk-im*, the complement is obligatory, and no lexical item intervenes between the head and the complement. Thus, in (34b), there is no preposition marking the relation between the head *bakbuk-ey* and its complement. The bare head and its nominal complement are bound together phonologically to form a 'phrasal word'. A fourth characterizing property is that definiteness is marked only on the complement, but percolates syntactically and semantically to the whole phrase. In the free genitive in (35a), definiteness is marked on the head *bakbukim* by the definite clitic *ha-* as well as on the complement. However, in the construct state construction in (35b), the definiteness can only be marked by cliticizing *ha-* to the complement. The interpretation is 'the bottles of wine' or 'the bottles of the wine', depending on the context.

(35) a ha- bakbuk-im   šel (ha)-yayin   (FG)
         DEF- bottles-M.PL   of (DEF)-wine
         'the bottles of (the) wine'
      b (#ha)- bakbuk-ey   ha-yayin   (CSP)
         (#DEF) bottles-CS.M.PL DEF-wine
         'the bottles of (the) wine'

Though the two NPs in (35) look very similar, they are not semantically equivalent. The free genitive construction, which looks like a word-for-word translation of the English *the bottles of wine*, has only the counting interpretation, while the construct state phrase is ambiguous between a counting and a measuring interpretation. In contexts in which only the measure interpretation is plausible, the free genitive is infelicitous. The following examples show this.

Suppose I ask a waiter to bring me and two friends each a glass of water, then I can use either the free genitive or the construct as illustrated in (36a,b).[4] But, if the same expression is used to denote water to a certain amount, then the construct must be used. The context in (37a) makes this clear: if Dani is mixing paint and needs to add two cups of water, then (37b) is the only way to express it felicitously.

---

[4] Note that the regular feminine plural and the construct state feminine plural are morphologically identical. The constructions are nonetheless distinct.

(36) a tavi   lanu **šaloš kos-ot** **šel mayim,** bevakaša! (FG)
   bring.2.M.SG to.us three.F glass-F.PL of water, please
  b tavi   lanu **šaloš kos-ot** **mayim**, bevakaša! (CSP)
   bring.2.M.SG to-us three.F glass-F.PL water, please
   Both: 'Bring us three glasses of water please!'

(37) a dani mexin ceva ve- hu carix le-hosif mayim.
   dani prepare paint and- he need to-add water
   'Dani is mixing paint and he needs to add water.'
  b ten   lo   **šaloš kos-ot** (#šel) **mayim** be-kad
   give.2.M.SG to-him three.F glass-F.PL (#of) water in-jug
   plasti   bevakaša.
   plastic   please
   'Give him two cups of water in a plastic jug please!'

Similarly, if I ask if there is more soup in the pot, then (38a) using the construct state phrase is an acceptable answer, but (38b), which uses the free genitive, isn't: it implies that the actual bowls filled with soup are in the pot. The free genitive is felicitous when used in a context where the bowls are physically present, as in (38c):

(38) yeš   od   marak b- a- sir?
   there-is more soup in-DEF- pot
   'Is there more soup in the pot?'

  a ken, yeš od **šaloš ka'ar-ot marak** b- a- sir. (CSP)
   yes, there-are more three.F bowl-F.PL soup in-DEF-pot
   'Yes there are three more bowls of soup in the pot.'
  b # ken, yeš od **šaloš ka'ar-ot** **šel marak** b- a- sir. (FG)
   yes, there more three.F bowls-F.PL of soup in-DEF-pot
   Intended: 'Yes there are three more bowls of soup in the pot.'
  c ken, yeš od **šaloš ka'ar-ot šel marak** al ha- magaš. (FG)
   yes, there more three.F bowl-F.PL of soup on DEF-tray
   ''Yes, there are three more bowls of soup
   on the tray.'

Recipes will naturally use the construct, since they make reference to quantity (as in 39):

(39) mosifim **štey** **kos-ot** (#šel) **kemax** ve- **šaloš**
   add   two.F cup-F.PL (#of) flour and three.F
   kap-iot   (#šel) **sukar** l- a- batzek
   teaspoon-F.PL (#of) sugar to-DEF- dough
   u-   mearbevim,
   and- mix
   'Add two cups of flour and three teaspoons of
   sugar to the dough and mix'.

The construct form, then, is ambiguous between individuating and measure readings, while the free genitive has only the individuating reading. If only the measure reading is appropriate, the construct form must be used. If either reading is possible, the speaker can show that the counting reading is intended by using the free genitive, following Grice's Maxims of Quantity (Be maximally informative relative to the requirements of the conversation) and of Manner (Avoid ambiguity). Example (40) illustrates this:

(40) **arba'im ve-**   **štaim kufsa-ot (šel) sfar-im**   lo
      forty   and   two   box-F.PL (of) book-M.PL no
      nixnas-ot l-a-madaf-im   šelanu.
      enter-F.PL to.DEF-shelf-M.PL of.us
      'Forty-two boxes of books don't fit on our shelves.'

Both the free genitive and construct state phrases are felicitous, but in different contexts. If I am unpacking my library and contemplating the quantity of books that have to be put on our shelves, the construct state phrase is preferable, since it is the only way of expressing the measure interpretation. If I am filling a storage room with boxes, then the free genitive form would be preferable, since it would only allow the interpretation that there are too many boxes to fit on the shelves.

Explicit measure heads can also be used in constructs, as in (41a). The free genitive (41b) is not totally infelicitous, but, in line with its counting interpretation, suggests that each kilo is in some sense salient. (41c), where this implication is explicitly rejected, is definitely infelicitous. (*Kilo*, like other borrowed measure words, is not usually marked plural, especially in construct state constructions.)

(41) a kani-ti **arba'a kilo kemax** (be-štey sak-iot   šel
          bought-I four.M kilo flour   (in-two.F bag-F.PL of
          šney   kilo).
          two.M   kilo
          'I bought four kilos of flour in 2 bags of 2 kilos.'
      b kani-ti   **arba'a   kilo   šel   kemax**
          bought-I   four.M   kilo   of   flour
          'I bought four kilos of flour.' (implication: in kilo packages)
      c #kani-ti **arba'a kilo šel kemax** be-štey   sak-iot
          bought-I four.M kilo of flour in-two.F bag-F.PL
          šel   šney   kilo.
          of   two.M   kilo

So the question is: why does the free genitive construction have only the individuating interpretation while the construct state phrase is ambiguous between a measure and an individuating reading?

3.3.2 The Analysis

We start by giving an interpretation for the construct state phrases (CSPs). I assume, following the analysis in Borer (2009), Rothstein (2009), that the complements of the classifier construct phrases in question are NPs. The semantic relation between the head of a CSP and its NP complement is underspecified (Rothstein 2012).

The simplest classifier CSP, shown in (42a), consists only of a head and complement, and has the structure in (42b):

(42) a bakbuk$_N$ yayin$_{NP}$
        bottle.M.SG   wine
        'a bottle of wine'

     b

         N   NP
      bakbuk   yayin
      bottle   wine

An explicit numeral will be adjoined to NP, and agrees with the head in gender:

(43) a šloša   bakbuk-ey   yayin
        three.M   bottles-CS.M.PL   wine.M.SG
        'three bottles of wine'
     b šaloš   kos-ot   yayin
        three.F   glasses-F.PL   wine.M.SG
        'three glasses of wine'

As we have seen above, examples like (43) are ambiguous between the counting and the measure reading. As in English, in the counting reading, the head, *bakbukey*, is interpreted as a relational nominal and the complement *yayin* supplies the internal argument of the head. The NP complement of a construct state noun is interpreted via NP-incorporation (Rothstein 2009).[5] Semantically, NP-incorporation here is grammaticized as the operation that shifts the sortal interpretation of the noun to the relational one, as in the English cases discussed earlier. Thus,

---

[5] Doron (2003) argues that all indefinite arguments in Hebrew are type $<e,t>$ and interpreted via NP-incorporation. Rothstein (2012) suggests that this may be too general, but offers a semantics for construct state phrases in which the NP complement is interpreted this way. Note that Doron's own analysis of construct state phrases is very different, and she treats the complement as an argument at type e (Doron & Meir 2013b).

the $\langle e,t \rangle$ interpretation of *bakbuk* shifts to the relational interpretation at type $\langle\langle e,t\rangle,\langle e,t\rangle\rangle$:

(44) $\lambda P \lambda x. \text{BOTTLE}(x) \wedge \exists y[P(y) \wedge \text{CONTAIN}(x,y)]$

The counting interpretation for (43a), *šloša bakbukey yayin*, uses the meaning for *bakbuk* in (44). *bakbuk* combines with its complement *yayin* to give (45):

bakbukey (yayin):
(45) $\lambda x. \forall a[a \sqsubseteq_{\text{ATOMIC}} x \to \text{BOTTLE}(a) \wedge \exists y[\text{WINE}(y) \wedge \text{CONTAIN}(a,y)]]$

This is then modified by the numerical *šloša* 'three', used at the predicate modifier type, as in (46a), which gives (46b):

(46)   a *šloša*: $\lambda Q \lambda x. Q(x) \wedge | x | = 3$
        b *šloša (bakbukey yayin)*:
           $\lambda x. \forall a[a \sqsubseteq_{\text{ATOMIC}} x \to \text{BOTTLE}(a) \wedge \exists y[\text{WINE}(y) \wedge \text{CONTAIN}(a,y)]$
           $\wedge | x | = 3]$

This denotes the set of pluralities of bottles consisting of three atomic bottles each containing wine. In argument position, this raises to the generalized quantifier type in (47).

(47) $\lambda P. \exists x[\forall a[a \sqsubseteq_{\text{ATOMIC}} x \to \text{BOTTLE}(a) \wedge \exists y[\text{WINE}(y) \wedge \text{CONTAIN}(a,y)]$
        $\wedge | x | = 3 \wedge P(x)]$

Like the English counting interpretation, the counting interpretation of the construct state classifier phrase is headed by a relational nominal, and is a right-branching construction. The head combines with the complement to give an NP which is modified by the numerical. The major difference between the constructions is that the head in the Hebrew phrase takes a bare complement while in English *of* assigns case.

The measure interpretation of *šloša bakbukey yayin* is also simple to derive and parallels the interpretation of the English example. The head *bakbukey* denotes a measure function which applies to a numerical at type n, as in (48a), giving a measure predicate, the property of having a volume of *n*-bottles (48b). This is identical in structure to the measure function denoted by *glasses* in (25):

(48)   a *bakbukey*: $\lambda n \lambda x. \text{MEASURE}_{\text{VOLUME, BOTTLE}}(x) = 3$
        b *šloša bakbukey*: $\lambda x. \text{MEASURE}_{\text{VOLUME, BOTTLE}}(x) = 3$

Since the complement in the construct state phrase is an NP, it is straightforward for this measure predicate to modify it. *šloša bakbukey* shifts to the predicate-modifier type, and applies to the denotation of its complement *yayin* as in (49):

(49)   a   *šloša bakbukey (yayin)*:
         APPLY[λx.MEASURE$_{VOLUME,\ BOTTLE}$(x) = 3, WINE]
       b   λPλx.P(x) ∧ MEASURE$_{VOLUME,\ BOTTLE}$(x) = 3 (WINE) =
         λx.WINE(x) ∧ MEASURE$_{VOLUME,\ BOTTLE}$(x) = 3

This denotes the set of entities that are wine which measure three bottlefuls.

Two factors allow the construct state phrase to be ambiguous.

 (i) The construct state phrase consists of a N NP string, but does not constrain grammatical relations within the phrase. While the first N can be interpreted as a relational noun as in (44), it can also be interpreted as a measure modifier. (Other semantic relations between the N and its adjacent NP are also possible, see Siloni 2001 and Rothstein 2012.)

(ii) The complement in the construct state phrase is a bare NP, and can be analysed either as a complement of N or as a constituent modified by N. In the first case, *šloša bakbukey yayin* has the analysis in (50a) giving the counting reading, and in the second case, it has the analysis in (50b) giving the measure reading.

(50)   (a)

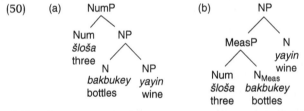

Crucially, the geometry of these two structures parallels the geometry of (16) and (23). The counting structures in both (16) and in (50a) are right branching, while in the measuring structures in (23) and (50b), numerical and measure head combine to form a measure predicate.

This analysis predicts that if, for some reason, one of the structures in (50) is not available, the construct state classifier phrase will unambiguously have the interpretation associated with the second structure. This prediction is correct as is shown by the unambiguous counting interpretation assigned to definite numerical classifier phrases and the ungrammaticality of definite measure phrases in Hebrew.

A crucial fact about Hebrew is that definite numerical expressions have to be expressed using a construct state phrase.[6] In simple indefinite numerical phrases like (51a), the numerical is a specifier, modifying the head, but in definite numerical phrases like (51b), the numerical must head a construct state phrase and take an NP complement. (51b) has all the morphosyntactic characteristics of the construct state phrase discussed above: the numerical head has special construct morphology, it is immediately followed by a bare N complement, and definiteness is marked only on the complement. If the numerical modifies a definite complex phrase such as *bakbukey ha-yayin* 'the bottles of wine', itself a construct state phrase, then the bound numerical head takes the whole lower phrase as its complement (51c):

(51)   a [šloša   bakbuk-im]
          three   bottle-M.PL (indefinite)
          'three bottles'
       b [šloset   [ha- bakbuk-im]$_{NP}$]$_{CS}$
          three   DEF- bottle-M.PL
          'the three bottles'
       c [šlošet   [bakbuk-ey $_N$ [ha- yayin]$_{NP}$]$_{CS}$] $_{CS}$
          three   bottle-CS.MPL DEF- wine

The construct complement *bakbukey ha-yayin* in (51c) is a phrasal word which must remain a syntactic unit. This means that (51c) must be assigned a right-branching structure like (50a). *bakbukey* cannot be analysed as a measure expression and combined with the numeral to form a complex predicate since this will not allow the embedded construct to be a syntactic unit.

The prediction is that the measure interpretation will not be available either. This prediction is borne out: definite numerical classifier phrases only have a counting interpretation. Indefinite classifier construct state phrases with measure readings lose the measure interpretation if they are marked definite. While the indefinite in (52) has a measure reading, (53) shows that a measure reading of the same numerical phrase marked definite is impossible.

(52)   yeš   od   marak b- a-   sir?
       there   more   soup in-DEF pot
       'Is there more soup in the pot?'

---

[6] In standard Modern Hebrew, indefinite numericals do not occur in construct states, except for the numerical *šnayim* 'two', which is always in the construct form, apparently for morphological reasons. Moshavi & Rothstein (in press) show that indefinite numerical construct states occur in semantically constrained contexts in Biblical Hebrew.

ken, yeš   od   **šaloš**   **ka'ar-ot**   **marak** b-a-   sir.
yes, there more three.F   bowl-F.PL   soup   in-DEF- pot
'Yes there are three more bowls of soup in the pot.'

(53)   hizmanti esrim orxim ve- hexanti   esrim ka'ar-ot   marak
       I invited twenty guests and I prepared twenty bowl-F.PL soup
       be- sir gadol.
       in- pot big
       'I invited twenty guests and I prepared twenty bowls of soup in
       a big pot.'

       # rak   šiva-asar   orxim higiu, ve- **šaloš ka'ar-ot ha- marak**
       only   seventeen guests came, and three.F bowls-F.PL DEF-soup
       ha- axron-ot   nišaru   b- a-   sir.
       DEF-last-F.PL   remained.PL in-DEF-pot
       'Only seventeen guests arrived, and the last three bowls of soup
       remained in the pot.'

(53) has an interpretation, but it is a counting interpretation and
asserts that three bowls filled with soup are in the pot, as in (38b).
There is no inherent semantic difficulty in constructing definite measure phrases in contexts like (53). The translation shows that 'the last
three bowls of soup' has a perfectly acceptable measure interpretation
in English, but it is not a possible interpretation of the corresponding
definite construct classifier phrase in Hebrew. Since construct state
phrases are the only way to express measure readings in Hebrew,
there is in fact no definite classifier phrase in Hebrew which can
express a definite measure reading.

The second prediction also concerns definite measure phrases.
Suppose a definite construct state phrase (which, as we have seen,
cannot have a measure interpretation) has a head which can only have
a measure reading. This should result in an internal contradiction
which will make the construction ungrammatical. This is exactly
what happens. Indefinite phrases headed by explicit measure heads
such as *kilo* and *litre* are felicitous, as in (53a), but the definite is
completely unacceptable, as (54b) shows. *kilo* requires a measure reading, but the definite construct form makes the measure reading
impossible.

(54)   a xamiša   kilo   kemax
          five.M   kilo.SG   kemax
          'five kilos of flour'
       b #xameš-et kilo   ha-   kemax
          five-CS   kilo.SG   DEF-   flour
          intended reading: 'the five kilos of flour'

These data clearly support the argument that the two structures in (50) are associated with counting and measure interpretations respectively.

Turning now to the free genitive illustrated in (34a), and repeated here as (55), the question is why these classifier phrases have only the counting reading.

(55)   šloša bakbuk-im šel yayin   (FG)
        three bottle-M.PL of wine

We assume the tree in (56):

(56)

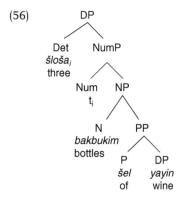

The N *bakbukim* is the head of the phrase and takes a PP complement. The complement of P is a full DP which can contain numeral modifiers (57a), explicit measure phrases (57b), and other modifiers (57c). (57d) shows that it can be definite.[7] When the phrase following *bakbukim* is clearly a DP, *šel* is obligatory and a construct state phrase is unacceptable[8].

(57)   a kaniti   šaloš xavil-ot   #(šel) esrim gul-ot   ve- štey
           bought-I three.F pack-F.PL of   20   marble-F.PL and two.F
           xavil-ot   #(šel) eser   gul-ot.
           pack-F.PL of   10   marble-F.PL
           'I bought three packs of twenty marbles and two packs of ten marbles.'

---

[7] Note that (57d) is not partitive.
[8] Since regular and construct state plurals are morphologically identical in the feminine plural, the presence/absence of *šel* is the only difference between the free genitive and the construct state here.

b kaniti   štey   xavil-ot   #(šel) ma'tayim gram šokolad
  bought-I   two.F pack-F.PL of   200   gram chocolate
  ve-štey   xavil-ot   #(šel) mea gram.
  and two.F   pack-F.PL of   100 gram
  'I bought two packets of 200 grams of chocolate and two packets
  of 100 grams.'
c ani   roca   šaloš   kos-ot   #(šel) mic   meurav/tari.
  I   want   three.F cup-F.PL of   juice mixed/fresh
  'I want three cups of mixed/fresh juice.'
d hizmanti šloša   bakbuk-im #(šel) ha-yayin ha-adom še-
  bought-I three.M bottle-M.PL of   DEF-wine DEF-red that
  ata   ohev.
  you   like
  'I bought three bottles of the red wine that you like.'

Comparing the tree in (56) to the similar structure for the individuating interpretation of *three glasses of wine* for English given
in (16), we see that there is one important difference. While the
English *of* is not semantically interpreted and does not appear in
the tree, Hebrew *šel* is a genuine preposition, and ·heads a PP.
Rothstein (2009) shows that *šel* is a true preposition with
a semantic interpretation. In particular, (i) *šel* is associated with
a limited number of thematic roles, including 'theme', 'posses-
sion' and 'contain', and (ii) *šel* does not occur as a semantically
empty case-marker in partitives and similar constructions. Thus,
in (56), *šel* is a true preposition, mediating the relation between
the head *bakbukim* and its complement *yayin*.

If *šel* is a semantically interpreted preposition, we can immediately
explain why the measure reading is not available for the free genitive. In both English measure constructions and Hebrew construct
state phrases, the measure reading is dependent on being able to
combine *bottles/bakbukey* directly with the numerical and then applying the resulting measure predicate as a modifier to the nominal
complement. In Hebrew construct state phrases, this is possible
because the classifier in the construct state phrase is always followed
by a bare NP. In English, *of* is not a true preposition and does not
appear in the tree. This means that the NP complement *wine* in (23)
can be analysed as an NP predicate and modified by the measure
predicate. In (56), this is not possible. *šel* is a preposition expressing
a relation between its complement and the N head of the phrase,
bakbukim. But then *bakbukim* can only be an N head and cannot be
analysed as a measure expression. Similarly, the DP argument can
only be a DP complement of the P and cannot be a predicate modified
by a measure expression.

The compositional interpretation of (56) treats the head as a sortal as in (58a). *šel* denotes the CONTAIN relation (58b) and combines with *yayin* to give a predicate at type <e,t> (58c).

(58)   a *bakbuk*:   BOTTLE
       b *šel*: $\lambda P \lambda x.\exists y[P(y) \wedge \text{CONTAIN}(x,y)]$
       c *šel yayin* $\lambda P \lambda x.\exists y[\text{WINE}(y) \wedge \text{CONTAIN}(x,y)]$

The PP modifies the sortal noun *bakbuk*, as in (59a). Semantically, pluralization applies to this (59b), and the resulting nominal is modified by the numerical *šloša* as in (59c):

(59)   a *bakbuk šel yayin* $\lambda x.\text{BOTTLE}(x) \wedge \exists y[\text{WINE}(y) \wedge \text{CONTAIN}(x,y)]$
       b *bakbukim šel yayin*
                $\lambda x.\forall a[a \sqsubseteq_{\text{ATOMIC}} \rightarrow \text{BOTTLE}(a) \wedge \exists y[\text{WINE}(y) \wedge \text{CONTAIN}(a,y)]]$
       c *šloša bakbukim šel yayin*
                $\lambda x.\forall a[a \sqsubseteq_{\text{ATOMIC}} \rightarrow \text{BOTTLE}(a) \wedge \exists y[\text{WINE}(y) \wedge \text{CONTAIN}(a,y)] \wedge$
                                    $\mid x \mid = 3]$

(59c) denotes sets of pluralities of bottles with three atomic (bottle-) parts each containing instantiations of the kind *wine*.

To sum up, (56) has only the counting reading because the noun *bakbukim* must be interpreted as the head of the phrase, and the whole expression must then denote a set of bottles, in this case bottles containing wine. The counting structure for English in (16) and the structure in (56) share the property that the nouns *glasses* in (16) and *bakbukim* in (56) are both heads of the phrase. However, in Hebrew, because of the presence of *šel*, (56) is the only possible analysis, whereas in English, because there is no PP node in the tree, an alternative analysis is possible. Despite the fact that *three glasses of wine* and *šloša bakbukim šel yayin* look structurally isomorphic, the English phrase is structurally more similar to the Hebrew construct state phrase because *of* does not project a PP node. Like the construct state classifier phrases, the English string allows two structural analyses and two interpretations.

For completeness, note that there is one other construction, used in higher registers, which expresses measure in Hebrew, illustrated in (60):

(60)   yeš   lanu   šloša   yam-im   xofeš.
       there to.us three.M   day-M.PL   vacation
       'We have three days vacation.'

In (60), the only possible analysis is that the numerical and the measure head form a measure predicate *šloša yamim* which modifies the noun *xofeš*. *yamim* cannot be the head of this phrase. It cannot be

the head of a construct state phrase taking *xofeš* as its complement
since it does not have construct state morphology (i.e *yemey*).
It cannot be the head of a free genitive construction either, since
there is no preposition expressing the relation between head and
complement. The distribution of these measure predicates is much
more restricted than that of construct state phrases, and beyond the
scope of this chapter, but they serve to show that indefinite measure
predicates exist outside construct state phrases, but crucially only
when the numerical and measure head form a predicate modifying
an NP.

3.4 CROSSLINGUISTIC PATTERNS

We have seen that numerical phrases like *three bottles of wine* have two
different interpretations, a counting interpretation in which *three* says
how many bottles of wine there are, and a measure interpretation in
which *three bottles* says how much wine there is. The counting interpretation is sometimes called an 'individuating' reading, because
counting presupposes that atomic bottles of wine can be individuated,
as we will discuss in Chapter 4. I have argued that the two different
readings are associated with two different syntactic structures, reflecting the different semantic operations, and I have supported this with
data from English and Modern Hebrew. In both languages, strings of
the form *Numerical-Classifier-N(P)* are ambiguous because they can be
analysed either as in (61a) or (61b). In (61a), the nominal classifier
bottles is the head of the phrase, and it combines with the NP *wine* to
form an N′ predicate denoting a set of bottles filled with wine. *Three* is
a cardinal modifier which intersects with this set and gives us the set
of pluralities of three bottles filled with wine. In (61b), *bottles* is
a measure head which names a unit of measure, in the same way
that *litre* and *kilo* do. It combines with a numerical at type n to form
a measure predicate which modifies the nominal head *wine*.
The resulting NP denotes the set of entities that are wine which
measure *three bottles* in volume.

(61) a counting configuration: [Numerical [Classifier NP]$_{N'}$]
      b measuring onfiguration: [[Numerical Classifier]$_{MeasP}$ NP]

The contexts in which measure readings are blocked in Hebrew serve
to show us which syntactic properties make measure readings possible. Indefinite construct state phrases are ambiguous because construct syntax does not constrain the internal structure of the phrase.

Definite numerical construct state phrases such as (51c) disallow measure interpretations because the numerical takes a construct state phrase as complement and this forces a right-branching structure like (61a). The free genitive structure in (56) also has a right-branching structure and disallows the measure reading because the noun *bakbukim* 'bottles' takes a PP complement and not an NP complement. The numerical + classifier cannot be analysed as a measure predicate as in (61b), since the measure predicate modifies only an NP and not a PP.

Crucially, a comparison of the Modern Hebrew and English examples shows that the same two basic structures facilitate measure and counting interpretations in both languages, although the morphosyntactic properties which converge to allow or disallow one or other structure in certain contexts are different for each language. In both languages, the counting interpretation is possible when the classifier is a head taking a nominal complement, while the measure interpretation is possible when the classifier and numeral can combine to form a predicate which modifies an NP immediately following the classifier. In Hebrew, the construct state phrase is an independently licensed construction in which such a configuration is possible. In English, the non-thematic properties of *of* make the measure configuration possible in a complex NP construction.

Research into numeral classifier constructions crosslinguistically has shown that the association between the structure in (61a) and the counting interpretation, and the structure in (61b) and the measure interpretation, is not restricted to English and Modern Hebrew, but occurs in a number of typologically unrelated languages. Here are examples from four languages.

3.4.1 Russian

Borschev & Partee (2004), Partee & Borschev (2012) show that constructions like *glass of milk* are expressed in one of two ways in Russian. Either a 'genitive of measure' construction is used, with the complement of the classifier in genitive case as in (62a), or the classifier has a PP complement, with the P taking an argument in instrumental case as in (62b):

(62)   a stakan   moloka
           glass.NOM.SG milk.GEN.SG
           'glass of milk'
      b stakan   s   molokom
           glass.NOM.SG with milk.INST.SG
           'glass of/with milk'

Partee & Borschev show that (62a) is ambiguous between an individuating reading in which *stakan* denotes a container, and a measure reading in which *stakan* denotes a measure of the milk. (62b) has only the individuating container reading. What is striking about this data is that Borschev & Partee (2004), Borschev *et al.* (2006, 2008), Partee (2008) argue that the genitive in Russian (where not assigned as a lexical case by a V head) is a predicate nominal of type <e,t>. If the genitive *moloka* in (62a) is a predicate, (62a) looks very like the Hebrew construct state phrase, where the complement is an NP and both counting and measuring interpretations are available. The individuating structure in (62b) looks like the Hebrew free genitive, with *s* corresponding to Hebrew *šel*. Like *šel*, the preposition *s* is a lexical preposition with semantic content, possibly corresponding to English 'with' as in *kofe s molokom* 'coffee with milk'. If *s* projects a PP phrase like Hebrew *šel*, then the impossibility of the measure reading in (62b) is explained.

3.4.2 French

As shown in Chapter 2, French has a clitic *en*, roughly correlating to 'of it'. *En* is the complement of a quantity expression (either a bare numerical or measure phrase) and is anaphoric to the sortal N which names what is being counted or measured. (63) is repeated from the Chapter 2:

(63) J'en   ai   compté treize.   (Chapter 2: (30a))
      I of them have   counted thirteen
      'I counted thirteen (of them).'

(64a) is a counting context, *en* is the complement of the bare cardinal *deux*, and is anaphoric to the classifier phrase *bouteilles de vin*. In (64b), which makes explicit reference to measures, *en* is naturally the complement of the measure predicate *deux litres* and is anaphoric to the NP *vin* in the previous sentence. My informants tell me that continuing (64b) with *J'en ai acheté deux* is naturally interpreted as 'I bought two barrels', which is of course a counting reading. Note that these example are from Quebec French.

(64) a Il y   avait   peut-être cinquante bouteilles de vin   dans
         there   were   perhaps   fifty   bottles   of wine in
         le magasin. J'en ai   acheté   deux.
         the shop.   I EN have   bought   two
         'There were maybe fifty bottles of wine in the shop. I bought two of them.'

b	Il y avait	cinquante	litres	de	vin	dans	la	cuve.
	there were	fifty	litres	of	wine	in	the	barrel.
	J'en ai	acheté	deux litres.					
	I EN have bought		two litres					

'There were fifty litres of wine in the barrel. I bought two litres of it.'

Brenda Laca (p.c.) pointed out the following contrast, which makes the same point. In (65a) the context favours a measure reading, and *en* is the complement of the measure phrase *deux bouteilles*, dependent on *vin*. In (65b), the verb *casser* 'break' favours the counting interpretation. In this context, the construction parallel to (65a) is infelicitous, since in counting constructions *bouteilles* has to be interpreted as a relational head and not as a measure phrase, and *en* cannot be dependent on *vin*.

(65)	a	Ce	vin	est		très	cher.		Nous	en	avons
		This	wine	is		very	expensive.		We	EN	have
		bu	deux	bouteilles.							
		drunk	two	bottles							

'This wine is very expensive. We drank two bottles of it.'

	b	# Ce	vin	est très cher.		Nous	en avons cassé	deux
		This	wine is	very expensive.		We	EN have broken	two
		bouteilles.						
		bottles						

Intended: 'This wine is very expensive. We broke two bottles of it.'[9]

3.4.3 Hungarian

Schvarcz (2014, in press) shows that Hungarian container classifier constructions like (66) follow the pattern described above. (Note that the noun is in the singular form even when the numerical has a value higher than one.)

---

[9] Fred Landman (p.c.) notes similar effects in Dutch with *er*

(i)	Dit	is	een	hele	dure		wijn.
	This	is	a	very	expensive		wine.

	a	We	hebben	er	twee	flessen	van	gedronken.
		We	have	it	two	bottles	of	drunk

'We drank two bottles.'

	b	#We	hebben	er	twee	flessen	van	gebroken.
		We	have	it	two	bottles	of	broken

Intended: 'We broke two bottles.'

(66)   két   pohár   bor
       two   glass   wine
       'two glasses of wine'

(66) can be disambiguated by adding the suffix *-nyi*, to the classifier. (67) has only a measure interpretation:

(67)   két   pohár-nyi   bor
       two   glass-NYI   wine

Schvarcz argues that the two readings are associated with the two structures in (61), as shown in (68):

(68)   Count reading: [két [pohár bor]]
       Measure reading: [[két pohár] bor]

She supports this with a number of arguments. First, (69a) is an apparent variant of (66). However, unlike (66), (69a) has only the individuating interpretation, and *-nyi* cannot be affixed onto the classifier, as shown in (69b):

(69)   a   két   bor-os   pohár
           two   wine-ATT   glass
           'two   glasses of   wine'
       b # két   bor-os   pohár-nyi
           two   wine-ATT   glass-NYI

If the measure interpretation requires applying the classifier to the numerical, then the obvious explanation of (68b) is straightforward. *Boros* intervenes between the classifier and the numerical, and blocks the formation of a measure predicate. Note that if *boros pohár* is treated as a compound, with the meaning 'two wine glasses', *-nyi* can be affixed to it, as in (70a). But then the meaning is different, with *boros pohár* giving the measure unit as in (70b).

(70)   a   két   [[bor-os   pohár]-nyi]
       b   Két bor-os   pohár-nyi   viz e-t   adtam   a   leves-hez.
           two wine.ATT glass-NYI   water-obj   add.1.SG.PST the   soup-to
           'I added two wine-glass-fuls of water to the soup.'

Schvarcz gives other arguments in support of the structures in (68). In comparatives, when the comparative marker *több* 'more' follows the classifier, the sentence is ambiguous between a counting and a measure reading. (71a) either asserts that János emptied two more bottles than Julia or that the difference between the quantity of wine that the two drank was equal to that contained in two standard bottles. However, if *több* occurs between the number and the classifier, as in (71b), only a counting reading is possible (and the measure suffix -

nyi is infelicitous). The only possible interpretation is that János emptied four whole bottles, while Júlia emptied two.

(71) a János két üveg-gel   több bor-t   ivott-meg   mint Júlia.
         János two bottles-COMP more wine-ACC drank-PERF than Júlia
         'János drank two bottles more wine than Júlia.'
      b János kettő-vel   több üveg-(#nyi) bor-t   ivott-meg   mint
         János two- COMP more bottle -NYI wine-ACC drank-PERF than
         Júlia.
         Júlia
         'János drank two more bottles of wine than Júlia.'

This is explained if *több* precedes and modifies an N: in the measure reading, *üveg* 'bottle' is not a noun but a measure head, and *több* cannot precede it. Adjectival modification is also sensitive to the structural contrast in (68). Modifying *üveg* with an adjective gives an individuating reading (as in (72a)), and the measure suffix cannot be added. In contrast, if the numerical and classifier are under the scope of another adjective, only the measure interpretation is available (as in (72b,c)). These are, of course, the same contrasts that we saw in the English examples (28,29) earlier in the chapter.

(72) a három drága   üveg- (*nyi) gyenge   minőségű bor
         three expensive bottle- NYI bad-quality cheap   wine
      b Egy drága   három üveg(-nyi)   bor   ömöttki.
         an   expensive three bottle-NYI wine spilled
         'An expensive three bottle(ful)s of wine was spilled.'
      c # Egy drága   három üveg(-nyi)   bor-t   volt felbontva.
         an   expensive three bottle-NYI wine-ACC was opened
         'An expensive three bottle(ful)s of wine was opened.'

3.4.4 Mandarin Chinese

As we will discuss in detail in Chapter 6, Mandarin is a classifier language. Unlike so-called 'mass/count languages' like English, no nouns can be directly modified by numericals. Whenever a numerical expression is used, it must combine with a classifier and N as in (73):

(73) a sān   gè   rén
         three   Cl$_{general}$ man
         'three men'
      b liǎng   gōngjīn   píngguǒ
         two   Cl$_{kilo}$ apple
         'two kilos apple'
      c sān   píng   jiǔ
         three   Cl$_{bottle}$ wine
         'three bottles of wine'

(73a) is a counting expression, (73b) is a measure expression, while (73c) is ambiguous (Li 2011, 2013). In (74a), *píng* is used in a measuring context, and in (74b) in a counting context.

(74) a wǒ de   jiǔliàng   shì   sān   píng   jiǔ.
         my   drinking-ability be   three Cl_{bottle} wine
         'My drinking ability is three bottles of wine.'
  b tā   kāi   le   sān   píng   jiǔ.
         he   open PFV three Cl_{bottle} wine
         'He opened three bottles of wine.'

Cheng & Sybesma (1998) point out that *de* can be inserted after the classifier in (75b) and (75c), but not after the classifier in (75a).

(75) a sān   gè   (#de) rén
         three $Cl_{general}$ DE   man
         'three men'
  b liǎng gōngjīn (de)   píngguǒ
         two Cl_{kilo} DE   apple
         'two kilos apple'
  c sān   píng   (de)   jiǔ
         three Cl_{bottle} DE   wine
         'three bottles of wine'

However, when *de* is inserted, the construction has unambiguously a measure interpretation. Inserting *de* in a counting context is infelicitous:

(76) #tā kāi   le   sān   píng   de   jiǔ.
        he   open PFV three Cl_{bottle} DE wine
        'He opened three bottles of wine.'

Li & Rothstein (2012) argue that this is because *de* is a predicate marker which attaches at the right edge of a predicate constituent. When it follows the classifier, it forces Num + Classifier to be analysed as a predicate constituent modifying the noun which follows it. Thus, *sān píng de jiǔ* must be analysed as [[[*sān píng*] *de*] *jiǔ*]. This is, of course, the structure which is associated with the measure interpretation, and so it is no surprise that (75c), when it includes *de*, is unambiguously measure. When *de* is absent, Num + Classifier + Noun can be analysed either as [[*sān píng*] *jiǔ*], in which case it has a measure interpretation, or as [*sān* [*píng jiǔ*]], in which case it has the counting interpretation.

In summary, there is beginning to be a body of crosslinguistic evidence showing that measure and individuating readings of classifier constructions have two different syntactic structures. Individuating or counting readings depend on the classifier being a relational nominal with a complement. Measure interpretations of classifier constructions are possible when the following syntactic conditions hold:

(i) the complement of the classifier can be interpreted as a predicate nominal at <e,t>;
(ii) the numerical and the classifier are adjacent and can be combined into a complex predicate which modifies the NP complement.

3.5 CONCLUSIONS

We have shown that numerical classifier constructions are ambiguous between measure and counting interpretations and have argued that the two readings are associated with two different structures. The data presented in this chapter suggest that similar structural contrasts show up in very different languages, and that the mapping between syntax and semantics follows from very fundamental principles of compositionality (see Rothstein & Treves 2010). We have also shown a new context in which numerals are interpreted as arguments at type n, in addition to those we already discussed in Chapter 2. This raises a number of issues. First, we have seen that nouns like *glass* can shift to a measure interpretation. Under what circumstances is this possible, and what is the relation between the noun and the measure head? Second, while we have distinguished between count and measure interpretations of *three glasses of wine*, Partee & Borschev (2012) argue that this is not fine-grained enough. How many different interpretations of classifier phrases are there and how are they related? Third, are container classifiers the only classifiers which can be used to express measure units? Fourth, what is the status of the syntactic trees in (23) and (50b)? Are the measure trees base-generated with this structure, or is the non-standard syntactic structure the result of reanalysis? I discuss this issue in Rothstein (2016a). Lastly, note that measure expressions such as *kilo* and lexical powers like *hundred* and *thousand* are both are of type <n,<e,t>>, combining with a numerical to give a predicate. This raises the question of what these 'quantity heads' have in common, and in what ways they differ. We will discuss most of these issues (though not the last two), later in the book.

Before that, however, we will explore further the difference between counting and measuring. And, in preparation for this, the next chapter will discuss a fundamental aspect of the grammar of counting – namely, the contrast between mass and count nouns.

3.6 QUESTIONS FOR FURTHER DISCUSSION AND INVESTIGATION

1 For any language that you have access to, explore the expressions of counting and measuring. Is there a distinction between counting and measuring? If there is, then how is it expressed? How is the particular form of the distinction determined by the morphosyntactic properties of the specific language? What lexical measure words are there?

2 The classifiers that we have talked about are all container classifiers. Are there other nouns which can be used in measure constructions?

3 English has two suffixes which indicate that an N is being used as a measure head, illustrated in (77). What are the constraints on these suffixes?

(77)   a He collected a hatful of mushrooms.
       b She bought five dollars-worth of oil.

4 Schvarcz (2014) shows that Hungarian *-nyi* doesn't correspond exactly to either of the English suffixes in (77). For any language that you have access to, investigate whether there are measure suffixes. If so, what are the constraints on using them?

4   The Mass/Count Distinction

'Literatur ist ein Plural Begriff' ('Literature is a plural concept')
Gunter Grass, *Writing Against the Wall*, Interview with
Marc-Christoph Wagner, August 2013

4.1   INTRODUCTION

In the previous chapter, I established a distinction between counting
and measuring interpretations of classifier constructions like *three
glasses of wine*, and the counting and measuring operations needed to
build the semantic interpretations. Each reading used a different
interpretation of the numerical: in the measuring interpretation the
numerical is interpreted at type n, while in the counting interpretation it is a predicate interpreted at type <e,t>. However, a more
frequent context in which counting is discussed is not the count/
measure distinction, but the countable/non-countable distinction,
and in particular the contrast between *count nouns*, which can be
modified by cardinal numericals and so must denote sets of countable
entities, and *mass nouns*, which cannot be modified by cardinal numericals and so seem to denote sets of non-countable entities. *Cats* and
glasses are count predicates as in *two cats / three glasses*, while *wine* and
mud are mass predicates since #*two muds* and #*three wines* are generally
considered to be infelicitous. (We ignore for the moment the reading
where *three wines* denotes either three kinds of wine or three standard
servings of wine.) While it is intuitively clear that cats are objects and
thus countable and mud is stuff and not countable, a definition of
countability or objecthood which can support this distinction is elu-
sive. One problem is the existence of so-called 'object mass nouns', or
naturally atomic mass nouns, like *furniture*, which seem to denote sets
of countable objects. Another problem is crosslinguistic variation
with respect to the count or mass status of nouns. If countability or
objecthood is a pre-linguistic concept and the mass/count distinction

is a reflection of the cognitive distinction between (countable) objects and (non-countable) non-objects, then we would not expect the division of nouns into countable/non-countable to vary from language to language. But there is a great deal of crosslinguistic variation.

Linguistic theories looking for an account of the mass/count distinction have made many attempts to relate the grammatical contrast to an ontological or perceptual distinction framed in terms of countability or objecthood. In the next two chapters, I am going to argue that the countability of count nouns and the distinction between count and mass nouns are better understood in the context of the contrast between counting and measuring. Ultimately, mass nouns denote mass objects which can be measured and count nouns denote sets of individuated entities which can be counted. The object/non-object distinction is related to this, since collections of objects naturally lend themselves to quantity evaluations in terms of number of individuable parts, while mass objects do not. We naturally evaluate quantities of cats by counting how many individual cats make up the quantity, while we naturally evaluate quantities of mud in terms of volume or weight. However, as we will see, quantity evaluations do not have to work this way, and in many languages they don't.

This chapter will begin by reviewing the mass/count contrast and some of the more central semantic theories which try to explain it. I shall argue that linguistic countability is a grammatical property, which involves a grammatical encoding of countability, as proposed both by Krifka (1989) and Rothstein (2010) (though the two papers encode countability in different ways). Grammatical countability is distinct from the perceptual or cognitive notion of objecthood. In Chapter 5, I will discuss in depth the semantics of object mass nouns like *furniture* and so-called 'flexible pairs' like *stone/stone(s)*, and based on this I will show that mass nouns denote sets of entities that can be measured, while count nouns denote sets of objects that can be counted. Chapter 6 looks at some crosslinguistic case studies in the light of the count/measure distinction, and Chapter 7 look briefly at the Universal Grinder.

4.2 WHAT IS THE MASS/COUNT DISTINCTION?

A mass/count language is a language which distinguishes between nouns which, out-of-the-blue, can be directly modified by cardinal numerical predicates – *count nouns* as in (1a) – and those which cannot, the *mass nouns* illustrated in (1b). Chierchia (2010) calls the property of being modifiable by a cardinal numerical the 'signature property' of count nouns:

(1)   a   one cat, three cats, five flowers, twenty-two butterflies
       b   #one mud, #two ink(s), #twenty sand(s)

The plural noun phrases in (1a) denote pluralities of individual entities, and the noun phrases in (1b) are infelicitous. Not all languages have a mass/count distinction of this kind. For example, Mandarin, which we will discuss in Chapter 6, is a classifier language in which no nouns can be directly modified by numericals. For an overview of crosslinguistic variation in how countability can be expressed, see Doetjes (2012).

The contrast indicated in (1) raises the question of whether the mass/count distinction is a grammatical distinction or a reflection of 'real-world' properties of the noun denotations. Sometimes, linguistic infelicity does follow from the properties of the objects that words denote. For example, *black cat* is felicitous while *red happiness* is not, because *cat* denotes a concrete entity which can have colour, while *happiness* is an abstract noun which can only denote colourless stuff. So maybe *three muds* is infelicitous in the same way. Soja, Carey & Spelke (1991) showed that the ability to distinguish perceptually between objects and stuff is pre-linguistic, and more recently it has been shown that infants as young as 2.5 months can make this perceptual distinction (Carey & Xu 2001; Huntley-Fenner, Carey & Solimando 2002). Given that, we might suppose that, in the same way that *cat* contrasts with *happiness* in terms of abstractness, affecting the felicity of modification with colour words, *cat* also contrasts with *happiness* and *mud* in terms of individuability, affecting the felicity of modification with numericals. *Two muds* would then be infelicitous because *mud* does not denote entities or objects which can be counted, just as happiness does not have colour. If this is the case, then the mass/count distinction is not a grammatical distinction but the result of pragmatic appropriateness constraints.

Against this view, there are two kinds of arguments. The first is grammatical. In a mass/count language, a cluster of grammatical properties are sensitive to the mass/count distinction and these cannot all be explained in terms of pragmatic appropriateness. Compatibility with cardinals often goes together with singular/plural marking, while mass nouns do not usually pluralize.

(2)   a   # At the Dead Sea there are two muds/sands.
       b   # I polished that with two greases.
       c   # John bought two furnitures.

Some mass nouns do pluralize. These have shifted to a count reading in which they denote (usually) standard servings or sets of kinds. In (3a), *two waters* and *two coffees* denote two standard servings of water and coffee, while the context in (3b) favours interpreting *two wines* as 'two kinds of wine'.

(3)   a She ordered two waters and two coffees.
        b We had two (different) wines with dinner, a Chablis and a red Beaune. We drank two glasses of each.[1]

Count nouns do not normally occur in the singular with classifiers, while mass nouns do, as in (4):

(4)   a #three pieces/items of chair, #three kilos of chair, # three units of flower
        b three pieces of furniture, three kilos of flour

Determiners are sensitive to the mass/count distinction. Some determiners select only count nouns, as in (5a); some select only mass nouns, as in (5b); some select for mass and plural nouns as in (5c), while others are unrestricted (5d):

(5)   a each/every/a book; several/few/many books; #every/#several furniture(s)
        b little/much water; #little/#much book(s)
        c a lot of / plenty of wine; a lot of / plenty of books; #a lot of / #plenty of book
        d the/some book(s); the/some water

Determiners are also sensitive to mass/count in partitive constructions, as in *many of the books* / *#many of the literature* vs *much of the literature* / *#much of the books*. Distributives are also sensitive to the mass/count distinction, and (in English) take only plural count nouns as antecedents:

(6)   a The chairs / pieces of furniture were stacked on top of each other.
        b #The furniture was stacked on top of each other.

---

[1] Recent results have shown that some mass nouns may pluralize without becoming truly count (i.e. the plural mass noun may not be modified by a cardinal), as in *rain/rains*. The interpretation depends on the lexical item, the context and the constraints of the particular language. Some plural mass nouns get what is called an 'abundance reading', meaning 'a lot of N' (Corbett 2000; Doron & Müller 2013). However, other, readings may be available. See Tsoulas (2006) for Greek, Ghaniabadi (2012) for Persian, Epstein-Naveh (2015) for Modern Hebrew. Abstract nouns may also pluralize and/or occur with indefinite determiners, without being able to occur with cardinals, as in *an admiration* / *#three admirations*.

These kinds of selectional restrictions are difficult to ascribe to pragmatics, especially since not all languages show all these properties. In general, beyond the core signature property, there is cross-linguistic variation in how the mass/count distinction is marked grammatically. For example, *how much* and *how many* in English are sensitive to the distinction between mass and count nouns, as are the Hungarian equivalents *mennyi* and *hány*. However, in French and in Hebrew respectively, *combien* and *kama* express both *how much* and *how many*. Another example is distributives. As we will see below and in Chapter 5, in contrast to (6), distributives cannot be used to distinguish between count and mass in either European or Brazilian Portuguese. When the same grammatical property does distinguish between count and mass in different languages, it need not do so in the same way. Chapter 6 shows that plurality in Hungarian works very differently from plurality in English, although it ultimately distinguishes between mass and count nouns in both languages.

The second bunch of arguments against positing a perceptual basis to the mass/count syntax contrast all stem from the fact that, on closer examination, the mass/count distinction does not mirror any plausible stuff/object distinction. The evidence can be organized into three kinds of data.

(i) *Mismatches between the mass/count distinction and the stuff/entity contrast.* If the mass/count distinction mirrors some perceptual distinction, we might expect a near-perfect match between count nouns and object-like denotations. However, some mass nouns denote sets of entities which are just as object-like as the entities denoted by count noun denotations. These are called 'object mass nouns' in Barner & Snedeker (2005), 'naturally atomic mass nouns' in Rothstein (2010), 'fake mass nouns' in Chierchia (2010), and 'neat mass nouns' in Landman (2011a, 2016). The classic example is *furniture. The furniture in this room* may well denote a collection consisting of a table, four chairs, a sofa and an armchair. These are all objects, but, nonetheless, *there are six furnitures in this room* is completely ungrammatical. Furthermore, the same six objects can be referred to by *the six pieces of furniture in this room*. The objects have remained the same, but now a count NP, *pieces of furniture* is used to refer to them. In English, *jewellery* and *footwear, literature* and *equipment* are all examples of object mass nouns. Various pieces of research in the last decade have shown that although these nouns have the morphosyntactic properties of mass nouns, the grammar is sensitive to the fact that they denote sets of individual or atomic entities. Rothstein (2010) and

Schwarzschild (2011) independently point out that some adjectives, which Schwarzschild calls 'stubbornly distributive adjectives', when modifying an object mass noun, distribute over the atomic entities in the denotation of the object mass noun. In (7), the stubbornly distributive adjective *big* distributes over the individual entities in the denotation of *furniture* and the examples can only mean that the individual pieces of furniture are big (Rothstein 2010: (17)):

(7) a The furniture in our house is big.
     b Please carry the big furniture downstairs first.

Object mass nouns pattern with count nouns, where *big* must also be distributive (as in 8a), and contrast with substance mass nouns, where the stubbornly distributive predicates are not felicitous (as in 8b):

(8) a The books on the table are big.
     b #The mud on that floor is big.

Predicates like *heavy* can be predicated of object mass nouns and count nouns either distributively or collectively, but can only apply to the total quantity when modifying a substance mass noun. In (9a) and (9b), *heavy* is a property either of the individual pieces of furniture or individual books or of the sum of the furniture or the books, while (9c) has only the reading in which the whole sum is heavy. (9d,e) shows how context can favour the collective or the distributive reading with object mass nouns.

(9) a The furniture is heavy.
     b The books are heavy.
     c The mud is heavy.
     d The furniture (on that trolley) is heavy, so push the trolley carefully.
     e The furniture (in this room) is heavy, so carry it down one piece at a time.

Experimental results from Barner & Snedeker (2005) showed that object mass nouns are perceived as denoting sets of individuable objects. Subjects were shown pictures representing two quantities of N and were asked 'Who has more N?'. When N was a count noun like *shoe*, subjects compared the number of atomic instances of N in each group (three small shoes are more than one big shoe). When N was a substance mass noun like *toothpaste*, they compared overall volume, no matter how many separate quantities were pictured (one big blob of toothpaste was more than three small blobs). Object mass nouns like *silverware* consistently patterned like count nouns, with three small pieces of silverware being judged 'more' than one large piece, even if the volume of the large piece was greater than the combined volume of the smaller pieces.

Together these results indicate that we perceive collections in these cases as a collection of objects even while referring to them with a mass noun. So we cannot be relying on our perceptions to establish a grammatical correlation between collections of objects and count nouns.

(ii) *(Near-)synonyms and flexible nouns.* A related problem is that many languages have near synonyms for the same objects, one mass and the other count. These need not be lexically related, as in *shoes/footwear*. They may, however, be derived from the same root, possibly by a semi-productive rule, e.g. *carpet(s)/carpeting, curtain(s)/curtaining*. A similar example is *rehit(im)/rihut* (Modern Hebrew), *meubel(s)/meubilair* (Dutch), which are the count and mass correlates of *furniture*. The extreme case of this is seen in nouns which have both a mass and count form, as in *stone/stone(s), brick/brick(s)*. The latter are called 'flexible' nouns by Barner & Snedeker (2005). Pires de Oliveira & Rothstein (2011) argue that, in Brazilian Portuguese, all count nouns are flexible. Brazilian Portuguese clearly has a mass/count distinction, with count nouns distinguished from mass nouns in the standard ways. Count nouns such as *minhoca* 'earthworm' can be modified by numericals – *uma minhoca / duas minhoca(s)* 'one earthworm / two earthworms' – and count nouns pluralize as in *minhoca/minhocas*. Mass nouns such as *ouro* 'gold' have neither of these properties. However, count nouns can also occur as bare singulars. (10a) and (10b) show singular and plural uses of a count noun, and (10c) illustrates the bare singular:

(10)   a Uma minhoca   cava   buraco.
          an earthworm.SG   dig.PRS.3SG   hole.SG
          'An earthworm digs holes.'
       b Minhoca-s   cavam   buraco-s.
          earthworm-PL   dig.PRS.3PL   hole-PL
          'Earthworms dig holes.'
       c Minhoca   cava   buraco.
          earthworm.SG   dig.PRS.3SG   hole
          'Earthworms dig holes.'

Pires de Oliveira & Rothstein (2011) argue that the bare singular is in fact a mass noun. (We will look at the arguments in detail in Chapter 5.) If this is the case, then all count nouns in Brazilian Portuguese have a mass synonym and are flexible nouns, just like *stone/stone(s)* in English, and anything which can be referred to by a count noun can also be the denotation of a mass noun. But then, mass or count syntax cannot be a direct reflection of the entities or objects themselves, or, as Chierchia (1998a) puts it, the mass/count distinction cannot be determined by the properties of matter.

(iii) *Crosslinguistic variation.* The third problem is crosslinguistic variation. If the count/mass distinction is a direct reflection of pre-linguistic perceptions, we would expect the categorization of nouns as mass and count to be crosslinguistically stable. However, this is not what we find. There are many examples of this: *jewellery* is mass in English, but the correlate *taxšit/taxšit-im* is count in Hebrew. *Evidence, advice* and *encouragement* are all mass in English, but the correlates are count in Hebrew as (11) shows:

(11) a #two encouragements, #three advices, #four evidences
      b šney   idud-im,   šaloš ec-ot,   arba edu-yot
         two.M encourage-M.PL, three.F advice-F.PL, four.F evidence-F..PL

Fruit is mass in British English and count in American English. A systematic study by Kulkarni, Rothstein & Treves (2013) and Kulkarni, Treves & Rothstein (in press), involving a data base of approximately 1,400 nouns in 6 languages shows that, if a language has a mass/count distinction (and not all count nouns are flexible), certain nouns will naturally be only count. These include institutional buildings like *church* and *town hall*, individuals under a professional description like *baker*, and personalized artefacts like *watch*. Beyond this, there is crosslinguistic variation.

Furthermore, not all languages have a grammatical mass/count distinction. In Mandarin Chinese, all nouns show the grammatical properties of mass nouns, and none can be directly counted, as illustrated in (12). On the other side of the spectrum, Lima (2010, 2014) shows that in Yudja, a Tupi language spoken by the Yudja people who live in two areas on the Xingua river in the southern Amazonian basin, all nouns apparently are countable, as in (13):

(12) a liǎng gè   píngguǒ
         two   Cl$_{general}$ apple
         'two apples'
      b #liǎng píngguǒ
         two   apple
         'two apples'

(13) a txabïu ali   wãnã
         three child ran
         'Three children ran'

b yauda awïla   l-apa
   two   honey I-fall
   'Two (drops of) honey fall'

The conclusion on the basis of all this evidence can only be that the mass/count distinction, illustrated in (1), is not a direct projection of the contrast between stuff and individuated or atomic objects, but a grammatical distinction. The question, then, is: what is the basis of this distinction?

4.3 MASS/COUNT AS GRAMMATICAL ENCODING OF A PERCEPTUAL DISTINCTION

The rest of this chapter will discuss theoretical approaches to the mass/count distinction. Many theories of the mass/count distinction have been offered over the years, and they can be classified in different ways. Here I focus on two different approaches to the notion of 'individual' or 'atom'. One approach, represented by Link (1983, 1984) and Chierchia (2010), takes the position that the mass/count distinction is a grammaticalization of the perceptual distinction between stuff and atomic objects. These theories try in different ways to grammaticalize the pre-linguistic concept of atomicity. The second approach, represented in particular by Krifka (1989) and Rothstein (2010), takes the position that the mass/count distinction is an expression of the grammaticalization of countability, and that grammatical atomicity should be defined in terms of countability. We will discuss these two approaches in turn in this and Section 4.4. Section 4.5 will discuss syntactic accounts of mass and count. In the next chapter, Chapter 5, we discuss theoretical and experimental work on the semantics of object mass nouns, and show that they support a theory framed in terms of the semantics of countability.

Link (1983, 1984) formalized the contrast between mass nouns and count nouns in terms of the properties of mass and count predicates. Mass nouns are homogeneous predicates. They are upwardly homogeneous, or cumulative, since they are closed under the sum operation. If two quantities of ink are both in the denotation of the predicate *ink*, the (possibly discontinuous) sum of those two quantities is also in denotation of *ink*. Mass nouns are also downwardly homogeneous, or divisive, since if we split a quantity of ink into two quantities, both will still be ink. This contrasts with the singular count nouns which are characterized as neither cumulative nor divisive. The sum of two entities in the denotation of *cup* cannot itself be in the denotation of *cup* (but only in the denotation of the plural *cups*), while splitting a cup into two more or less equal parts gives you two pieces, neither of which is in the denotation of *cup*. (It is possible to split a cup unequally into, say, a chip and the rest of the cup, and then the larger part will probably still count as a cup, but this contrasts with *ink*, where splitting a body of ink into two unequal divisions gives you two bodies, both of which count as ink.) As Link points out, in contrast to singular count nouns, plural count predicates are like mass nouns in terms of upward and downward closure properties, or homogeneity, discussed in detail in Krifka (1989, 1992), and other papers. *Cups* is upwardly homogeneous (since cups + cups is just more cups) and also divisive down to minimal parts, the single individual cups.

Cumulativity is defined formally in (14). $\sqcup$ is the sum operator:

(14) Cumulativity (upward homogeneity):
      P is a cumulative predicate iff: $\forall x \in$ P $\forall y \in$ P: $x \sqcup y \in$ P
      'P is a cumulative predicate iff when x and y are in P, then the sum of x and y is also in P.'

Divisiveness is defined in (15). $\sqsubseteq$ is the part-of relation, O is the overlap relation, and y and z are required to be to be non-null (i.e. divisiveness cannot be satisfied trivially).

(15) Divisiveness (downward homogeneity):
      If P is divisive then $\forall x \in$ P $\exists y \in$ P $\exists z \in$ P[$y \sqsubseteq x \wedge z \sqsubseteq x \wedge \neg O(y,z)$].
      'P is a divisive (homogeneous) predicate if for every x in P, there is a way of splitting x into two non-overlapping parts, both of which are also in P.'[2]

Link (1983) proposes that homogeneous and non-homogeneous singular predicates have their denotations in different domains, reflecting the fact that they denote different kinds of entities. Homogeneous singular predicates, i.e. mass nouns, have their denotations in a non-atomic domain, and denote non-atomic Boolean semi-lattices. Non-homogeneous singular predicates, i.e. singular count nouns, have their denotation in an atomic domain and denote sets of atoms. Plural count nouns denote Boolean semi-lattices, the closure

---

[2] This is weaker than some formulations of downward homogeneity, which propose that if P is homogeneous and $x \in$ P, then for every way of splitting x into y and z, $y \in$ P and $z \in$ P. This obviously is too strong, since we should be able to split water into hydrogen and oxygen.

of the denotation of the corresponding singular count noun under sum. Mass nouns and plural count nouns are homogeneous since they both denote Boolean semi-lattices (see the discussion of Link in Landman 1991). The fact that plural count nouns are divisive down to atomic parts while mass nouns are fully divisive follows from the fact that they have their denotations in different domains. In support of the double-domain hypothesis, Link offers an explanation for paradoxes like the following:

(16)   This is a gold ring. The ring is new but the gold is old.

If r is the object which satisfies *a gold ring*, it is both an object in the denotation of *ring* and an object or chunk of stuff in the denotation of *gold*. But then (16) leads to a contradiction since OLD(r) and NEW(r) are apparently both true. Link argues that if *ring* as a count noun has its denotation in the atomic count domain, while *gold* has its denotation in the non-atomic mass domain, the paradox can be resolved. Atomic entities in the count domain are constructed out of stuff in the mass domain, and related by a CONSTITUTES relation. (16) then has the non-contradictory interpretation in (17):

(17)   RING(r) $\wedge$ NEW(r) $\wedge$ $\exists$x[GOLD(x) $\wedge$ CONSTITUTES (x, r) $\wedge$ OLD(x)]
          r is a ring, and r is new and there is some gold x out of which r is constituted and x is old.

On the assumption that r and x are two different entities from two different domains, this is no longer contradictory.

Link's model captures the distinction between objects and stuff as an ontological distinction between two different kinds of things. It posits two different semantic domains representing two different kinds of entities related by the physical relation of material constitution. The analysis has been highly influential, but leaves many questions unanswered.

First, are mass nouns truly downwardly homogeneous? While *milk* and *salt* are intuitively divisive, there are quantities of milk and salt too small to be further divided into quantities of milk and salt. As Landman (2011a) points out, individual molecules of salt count as *salt*, but cannot be split into two portions, both of which count as salt.

Object mass nouns such as *furniture* and *footwear* raise a different issue, since they have clearly defined atomic parts. A shoe is in the set denoted by *footwear*, but a piece of shoe is not footwear, any more than a piece of a jacket is a jacket. Further, these object mass nouns pattern in some ways semantically like count nouns, as we saw in (7)–(9) above, suggesting that they denote the same sort of objects.

As Landman (2011a) also points out, if divisiveness were a property of mass predicates, we might expect there to be a count predicate *salt* denoting a set of atomic salt molecules, while *one salt* could denote a single molecule of salt, but this is not the case.

The ontological distinction between stuff and objects is also problematic. As Chierchia (1998a) and others show, Link's analysis predicts that near-synonyms like *carpets* and *carpeting* denote different kinds of objects, which is implausible, given that it is possible to point at a single pile of material and describe it as 'that carpeting' or 'those carpets'. Rothstein (2010) also pointed out that the Gold Paradox in (16) can be replicated with pairs of mass nouns as in (18a) and pairs of count nouns as in (18b):

(18)   a The jewellery is new, but the gold it is made of is old.
       b The wall is new, but the bricks it is made of are old.

This means that the paradox in (16) and the solution in (17) cannot be used as support for Link's two-domain theory, since the problem underlying the paradox is more general and can be replicated within a single domain.

A different approach to the mass/count distinction which explicitly tries to ground it in a cognitive distinction is proposed by Chierchia (2010). Chierchia argues in two papers (Chierchia 1998a, 2010) that mass and count nouns have their denotation in the same domain, and that there is no ontological distinction between them. Instead, the difference depends on the vagueness of the atomic elements in their denotations. Chierchia (1998a) proposed that a singular count noun denotes a set of atoms, while the plural count noun denotes the closure of that set under sum. Mass nouns are inherently plural, and thus denote sets of atoms closed under sum. Crucially, what counts as an atom is vague, and thus the set of atoms generating the plural set cannot be specified. So, for a mass noun N, there is no simple lexical item denoting the set of atomic parts of N. This is illustrated with the Boolean semi-lattice in (19). *Carpet* denotes the set of atomic carpets {a,b,c}, *carpets* denotes the set closed under sum (i.e. the whole semi-lattice)[3], and *carpeting* has the same denotation as *carpets*, except that

---

[3] Chierchia (1998a) argues that plural predicates denote the set closed under sum minus the atoms, and thus plurals and mass nouns have different denotations. In his (2010) paper, he takes a more conventional approach to the semantics of plurality, in which the atoms are also members of the plural set. This correctly

this is its lexical meaning, and is not derived from a semantic pluralization operation triggered morphologically.

(19)

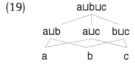

The words *carpet/carpets* presuppose a set of identifiable atomic elements, whereas *carpeting* allows for unclarity or vagueness in what counts as an atomic piece of carpeting. Object mass nouns have a natural place in this theory. Vagueness comes in degrees. Prototypical mass nouns like *mud* and *water* have a high level of vagueness, and the sets they denote are generated by a completely underspecified set of atoms. In contrast, object mass nouns like *carpeting* and *furniture* are not as vague as prototypical mass nouns, and the sets of their atomic parts are at least partially specified.

In Chierchia (2010), vagueness plays a different and much more developed role. The explicit goal of the paper is to develop a grammatical notion of mass/count which grounds the grammatical distinction in the conceptual distinction between individuated object and undifferentiated stuff. Chierchia writes: 'A noun is count if there are at least some things it applies to that are clearly atomic ... A noun is mass if *all* of its *minimal* instances/manifestations fall in the vagueness band (and can be construed as atomic or not depending on how we choose to make things more precise)' (2010: 146). A consequence is that, for a given plurality of stable atoms (children or cats or chairs), the Boolean structure of the plurality is transparent and we can reconstruct the unique way in which the plurality is constructed from its atomic parts. In contrast, faced with a quantity of mud, there is no unique way of representing it as a sum of mud atoms, since there is no unique way of characterizing its atomic parts. Thus, Chierchia brings back the mass/count distinction to our perceptions that some kinds of things have at least some inherently individuable atomic entities in their denotation, while others do not.

---

predicts that (i) is a felicitous piece of discourse, and (ii) is not. The 1998 theory incorrectly predicts that (i) is infelicitous and (ii) felicitous.

(i)   'Do you have children?' 'Yes, one'.
(ii)   'Do you have children.' 'No, only one'.

The theory is built on two distinct concepts; vagueness in predicate meaning (what counts as an instance of P), and vagueness or instability in atomicity (what counts as a single instance of P). For example, the meaning of the predicate *child* is vague because it has vague borders, since it may be unclear what counts as a child in a particular context. However, given a definition of what is meant by *child*, what counts as an atomic child is clear, and given a plurality of children, it is usually clear what the atomic children are. Thus its atoms are stable. A predicate like *mud* may also have fuzzy borders, since what counts as 'mud' may change from context to context. But, *mud* is also atomically unstable: a body of mud can easily be seen as a sum of smaller bodies of mud, but what counts as an atomic body of mud is not defined.

The two kinds of vagueness interact. A count predicate like *child* is associated in a base context c_b with a partial function which has a positive extension, the things which definitely count as an instance of *child*; a negative extension, those things which are definitely not children; and a vague band for which the value is undefined. A mass predicate like *mud* does not necessarily have a positive extension in the base context. Vagueness is resolved for all nouns step-by-step through a precisification function (see Kamp 1975; Landman 1991). Assume a partial function $f_c(N)$ giving the positive and negative interpretations of a noun N in context c. The precisification function $P_{c'}$ applies to $f_c(N)$ and gives the interpretation of N in context c', a context in which part of the unclarity about its meaning in context c is resolved. In this way, the vagueness band is diminished, until the function has become total. (There may be different ways of sharpening the definition and so different ways of making the function total. What counts as a child for a reduced bus-fare is not the same as what counts as a child for income tax submissions.) Crucially, if a predicate is stably atomic, the atomic structure is preserved through each precisification step, and what counts as a child in c, will count as a child in any precisification of c. An essential part of guaranteeing this is the fact that the positive extension of the predicate in the base context is not empty. If a predicate is not stably atomic, like *mud*, preservation of atomic structure through precisifications is not guaranteed.

Chierchia represents the domain U of N denotations as in (20) (Chierchia 2010: (40), p. 121). Singular count nouns denote sets of stable atoms, plural count nouns denote stable sums (i.e. sums of stable atoms) and mass nouns denote partial sums, or sums of unstable atoms.

(20)   The structure of the domain U

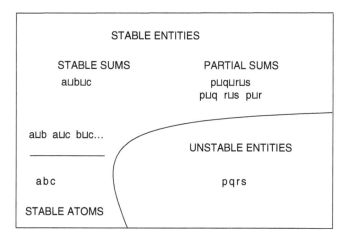

Count predicates can be counted because they are identified with a set of stable atoms, while mass nouns are not countable because their minimal parts are unstable, and thus not well enough defined to be countable. It is possible to tell at least in some cases what counts as one (atomic) cat, and so *cats* can be modified by a cardinal, but since it is not possible to tell what counts as one (atomic) rice, counting rice is impossible.

Many questions are raised by this theory, in particular involving the relation between the context-dependence of atomic structure and non-countability. In general, the issues are the same as those that we raised at the beginning of the chapter: how does a theory which grounds the mass/count distinction in a perceptual distinction between inherently individuable entities and stuff deal with the mismatches, both within a language and crosslinguistically? How convincing one finds Chierchia's theory depends ultimately on how well one thinks he has answered this question. The three issues I shall raise here are homogeneous count nouns, 'furniture' nouns and flexible nouns.

(a) **Homogeneous count nouns.** As Mittwoch (1988), Krifka (1992) and Rothstein (1999, 2010) have all pointed out, not all count nouns are stably atomic in the same way that *child* is, and this calls into question Chierchia's claim that count nouns must apply to at least some things which are atomic. Thus, Mittwoch (1988) points out that mathematical predicates such as *line* and *plane* are divisive, since both a line and a plane can be bisected into two lines and two planes. Krifka discusses predicates such as *sequence of numbers* and *twigs* (most sequences of numbers have subparts which are also sequences of numbers, and twigs can be broken into other twigs). Rothstein (1999, 2010) generalizes the problem of homogeneous count nouns to a wider range of predicates including *fence* and *wall*, and argues that in a particular context it may be underdetermined what the atomic entities are. If the owners of two adjoining houses each build a fence between their front yards and the street, meeting at the point at which the properties join, then the resulting stretch of fencing can count as either two adjoining fences (each one built by a different person) or one fence (which the two of them jointly built), and the number of fences cannot be counted without an explicit decision as to what counts as an atomic fence. Chierchia discusses similar examples, in particular how to individuate entities like mountains, which are usually not spatially discrete. He treats homogeneous count nouns in a similar way to *quantity of N*, which denotes a contextually salient partition on the mass domain into contextually relevant quantities of N which count as atomic in a particular context.[4] *Quantity of water* denotes a partition on the denotation of *water* into a contextually salient set of individuable quantities. *Fence* can be thought of as denoting a contextually salient partition on the denotation of *fence*. Chierchia argues that these count nouns are 'horizontally vague'; in other words, if in context c a particular atomic division into fences has been established, any precisification of *fence* will have to preserve that initial classification into atoms. He claims that this contrasts with mass nouns which are 'vertically vague', since 'the generating elements may be split into components more than one way' (p. 122).

It is difficult to see, though, how this explains the basic conceptual contrast between mass nouns and count nouns. Homogeneous count

---

[4] A partition on a set is a division of a set into non-overlapping blocks. (See, e.g., Landman 1991 for details.) Strictly speaking, the blocks of a partition are subsets: when Chierchia proposes that *quantity of N* denotes a partition on the denotation of N, the concept he uses is that of a set of sums of members of a partition on X. Assume that $\Pi(N)$ denotes a partition on N, i.e. a set of non-overlapping subsets of N such that for any $x \in N$, there is some $X \in \Pi(N)$ such that $x \in X$. Then *quantity of N* denotes the set of plural entities which are the sums of the blocks of the partition, i.e. $\{x: \exists X \in \Pi(N): x = \sqcup X\}$.

nouns are treated as stably atomic in a particular base context and the precisifications of this context, and are thus countable, while this is impossible for rice or wheat, no matter what context we choose. Suppose we set up a context in which the grains of rice are the stable atoms. For example, in the famous chessboard story, a sage (in some versions, the sage who invented chess) is asked to choose his own reward. He asks for one grain of rice on the first square of the chessboard, two grains on the second square, four grains on the third square and so on. It is difficult to think of a context in which the grains could be more stably atomic. But, even in this case, we cannot talk about *one rice, two rices, four rices, 2^n rices* and so on.

Obviously, we can claim that grains of rice are not usually counted or salient for counting, and thus it is very natural to treat them as mass, but this begs the question of what it is to treat a noun as mass. Count nouns like *fences* show that stable atoms can be context-dependent, and that the line distinguishing unstable minimal parts from the rest of the domain in (20) is not fixed. That being so, it is difficult to see why this dividing line cannot be moved in a context in which we are focusing on, say, individual grains of rice, and why we cannot, in that context, treat *rice* as a count noun.

(b) **'Furniture' nouns.** If the first problem for Chierchia's theory is homogeneous count nouns, the second is the converse, namely non-homogeneous mass nouns, object mass nouns which have individuable entities in their denotations. Here, Chierchia backs off from his position in his 1998a paper that furniture-nouns are the prototypical mass nouns, since this is clearly incompatible with the claim that mass nouns denote sets of unstable atoms. Instead, in his 2010 paper, Chierchia treats these nouns as 'fake mass nouns'. He first suggests that singular morphology on all mass nouns should be semantically interpreted, and proposes that mass nouns universally denote singleton properties true of the totality of (atomically unstable) instantiations of a property. *Water*, for example, will denote $\lambda x.x = \text{WATER}_{\text{MAX},w}$, the singular entity which is the sum of all (unstable) water parts in a world w. Mass quantifiers such as *most* will apply to the set of parts of the singular property (Chierchia 2010: 136). Fake mass nouns like *furniture* result from a sort of 'copycat' effect: they have count-like denotations but are listed in the lexicon as singleton properties which apply to the sum of all entities in the N denotation. A possible format for these lexical entries is (21) (Chierchia 2010: (78), p. 139):

(21)   <furniture, λx.x=⊔FURNITURE>

Such a listing would make the core property meaning λx.FURNITURE(x) and its pluralization unavailable.

Chierchia's account of furniture-nouns amounts to the following: the mass/count distinction is a reflection of the distinction between properties with unstable minimal parts and properties with stable minimal parts. However, there exists a set of exceptions which must be stipulated on an *ad hoc* basis and listed in the lexicon. *Furniture* and *footwear*, on this account, are fake because they have the grammatical properties of mass nouns, but are conceptually atomic, just like count nouns. They also have some of the semantic properties of count nouns, for example, they allow stubbornly distributive predicates (see Section 4.1, above).

If there were only a few object mass nouns, treating object mass nouns as stipulated exceptions might be plausible. However, given the extent of the phenomenon, the existence of object mass nouns clearly weakens the claim that mass nouns are mass because of the instability of their atomic parts.

(c) **Flexible nouns**. Fake mass nouns connect to the third problem for Chierchia's theory, the issue of flexible nouns, which have a mass and a count usage. Chierchia posits two sorts of flexible nouns, one of which is inherently count, and can be shifted into a mass reading, and another which is inherently mass and can be shifted into a count reading. The first kind is illustrated by example (22), where the count predicate *rabbit* is given a mass interpretation, in which it denotes an unstable set of rabbit parts.

(22)   There is rabbit in the soup.

This reading is the result of an operation often called the Universal Grinder,[5] which maps the set of atomic elements in the denotation of a predicate onto a set of parts of the atomic elements.

The second kind of flexible noun is illustrated by nouns like *stone/ stone(s)*, *rope/rope*, *beer/beer(s)*. These are often seen as illustrating the reverse operation to the Universal Grinder, namely the operation which packages stuff into individuable units via the Universal Packager. Chierchia suggests that, in these flexible pairs, the nouns are basically mass, denoting sums of unstable atoms. The count

---

[5] The term 'Universal Grinder' was invented by David Lewis and popularized by Pelletier (1979). The origins of the term 'Universal Packager' (see below) are less clear. See Chapter 7.

reading is derived by an operation which imposes a contextually salient partition on the mass denotation. Chierchia (2010: (59), p. 129) proposes an operator *F* which picks out the most salient partition in a context, as defined in (23).

(23)   For any model M, any c ∈ C and any P ∈ $D_{<e,t>}$,
        $F(\Pi_{ST})(c)(P)$ is the partition for P most salient in c (the standard S-partition).

According to (23), the count nouns *beer* and *stone* denote contextually relevant partitions on the denotation of the mass noun. In practice, the partitions are not only contextually salient, but are determined by normative constraints. This is shown by the contrast between (23) and the partition introduced by *quantity of N*. For $stone_{count}$ what determines the contextually salient partition is what counts as one individuable, stable atomic piece of stone. Even if two stones are stuck together and constitute a contextually stable object, they cannot count as one entity in the denotation of $stone_{count}$. *Three stones* must be three atomic stones. This contrasts with *three quantities of stone*, where the partition introduced by *quantity* is into atomic quantities, each of which may be constituted from multiple atomic stones. In pairs such as *brick/brick(s)*, what counts as an atom in $brick_{count}$ is even more constrained: bricks are blocks of brick of a particular size, for example, 8cm by 8cm by 20cm. A part broken off such a block will be in the denotation of $brick_{mass}$ but not in the denotation of $brick_{count}$. In *three beers*, the quantities of beer introduced by the partition in (23) are standard servings, individuated by the standard container for serving. As Landman (2011a) points out, *three beers* cannot denote a bottle of beer, a saucer of beer and a teaspoon of beer. However, *three quantities of beer* can denote just that. Chierchia suggests that the constrained status of the partition induced by true flexible nouns such as *stone* or *brick* follows because the partitions are particularly salient: '[B]ounded instances (often with a uniform, recognisable function) occur frequently enough to constitute a particular partition salient enough for lexicalization' (2010: 128).

   This raises again the same question that we asked above: what prevents us from packaging any mass noun via (23)? Chierchia would respond that these partitions are conventionalized, but relying on conventionalization moves us further away from the hypothesis that mass/count distinction is a grammatical reflection of a perceptual distinction.

   A further issue is that Chierchia gives completely unrelated accounts of object (or fake) mass nouns and flexible nouns.

However, crosslinguistic variation suggests that the phenomena are related. Specifically, nouns which are 'fake mass' in one language may be flexible in another. The English 'fake mass' *furniture* correlates with the Dutch flexible pair *meubel(s)/meubilair* and Hebrew *rehit(im)/rihut*. *Footwear* correlates with the Hebrew flexible pair *na'al* 'shoe' / *han'ala* 'footwear' and so on. In Brazilian Portuguese, it seems that all count nouns are part of a flexible pair. We already saw in (10) that in Brazilian Portuguese all count nouns have a bare singular form, which Pires de Oliveira & Rothstein (2011) argue is a mass noun (for detailed arguments, see Chapter 5). (24) gives another example with *criança* 'child'.

(24) Criança   (nessa idade)   pesa   20 kg.
      child.SG   (at.this age)   weigh.PRS.3SG   20 kg
      'Children (at this age) weigh 20 kg.'

If the bare singular is mass, then all count nouns in Brazilian Portuguese are flexible, and are paired with a mass noun.[6] In Chierchia's analysis, this means that all count nouns should be derived via partitions on a non-stably atomic domain. But it is difficult to see how the count noun *criança* 'child' can be derived from a partition on a non-stably atomic domain, or how its denotation could be any the less stably atomic than its English counterpart *child*. The mass counterpart of *criança* must be an object mass noun, and the distinction between the mass and count denotations of *criança* cannot be in terms of the stability of its atoms.

Flexible nouns such as *stone/stone(s), criança/criança(s), meubilair/ meuble(s)* suggest that that in some cases (and, in Brazilian Portuguese, in many cases), languages allow the same set of objects to be denoted by both a mass and a count noun; put differently, that a mass perspective and a count perspective are available for the same set of objects. In this context, it seems that fake mass nouns are nouns which allow only a mass perspective on some set of objects. This brings us back to the central question of what a 'mass perspective' is, since, at this point, stability of atomic structure seems not be involved. We will discuss this question in Chapter 5.

I have discussed Link (1983) and Chierchia (2010) in detail as examples of theories which try to ground the mass/count distinction in the difference between the denotations of mass and count nouns, and in particular the difference between the properties of the minimal parts in the mass and count domains. Link hypothesized non-atomic vs

---

[6] Schvarcz & Rothstein (in press) argue the same for Hungarian. See also Chapter 6.

atomic domains, while Chierchia hypothesized a division of the domain of reference into stable vs unstable atoms. The test for these theories will be how they deal with mismatches, both mismatches within a single language and crosslinguistic variability. The specific problems include object mass nouns such as *furniture*, non-homogeneous count nouns such as *fence*, and flexible nouns, including the English pairs such as *stone/stone(s)* and Brazilian Portuguese count nouns which also have a mass interpretation. Flexible nouns, in particular, strongly suggest that the difference between mass and count lies not in the naturalistic properties of the sets denoted by these nouns, but in the grammatical properties of the nouns which refer to the sets, and how they encode or represent the properties of the objects they denote.

We now turn to theories which take this approach to explaining the mass/count distinction.

4.4   MASS/COUNT AND THE SEMANTICS OF COUNTING

The second group of theories that we will discuss sees the mass/count distinction as resulting not from differences in the objects that nouns denote, but from the semantic properties of the expressions which denote them. This contrasts with Link and Chierchia, who assume that mass nouns and count nouns are both predicates of type <e,t> and that the difference between them lies in the properties of the minimal x objects in their denotation.

Gillon (1992) was one of the first to propose that mass nouns and count nouns have their denotations in the same domains. He argues that mass nouns denote aggregates, singularities built out of the same stuff as the count denotations. Mass nouns and count nouns have different features, and are marked [−CT] and [+CT] respectively. While a [+CT] feature allows for either a singular or plural denotation, it requires the predicate to be true of all the minimal parts of the denotation. [−CT] nouns are obligatorily singular, and denote a singleton set, whose sole member is the greatest aggregate of which the noun or noun phrase holds. Thus *the carpets* and *the carpeting* pick out the same object (in a particular context). However, *carpets* denotes the Boolean set of atomic carpets closed under sum, and *carpet* is true of all the minimal entities in the set. *Carpeting* denotes the singleton set containing the aggregate of all the carpets in the relevant context. Gillon's theory explains some important differences between mass and count nouns, in particular (25):

(25)   a The carpets and the curtains resemble each other.
        b The carpeting and the curtaining resemble each other.

(25a) is ambiguous between the reading in which the sum of curtains resembles the sum of carpets and vice versa, and the reading in
which all the individual carpets and curtains resemble all of the
others.[7] (25b) has only the first reading. Gillon argues that this is
because the mass nouns *carpeting* and *curtaining* denote singleton sets
containing the aggregate of all the carpeting and the aggregate of all
the curtaining respectively, and thus the individual carpet and curtain
atoms are not available as the antecedents for *each other*. Gillon's
account explains the *contrast* between mass and plural count nouns,
treating mass nouns as singleton sets, but misses the *analogies*
between them. These analogies suggest that mass nouns denote plural
sets and not singletons. For example, (26a) is parallel to (26b): both
assert that all the contextually relevant parts of the sum of wine parts
and the sum of shirts are either red or white. If *wine* was a singleton,
denoting a single aggregate, one might expect the reading that either
the whole quantity is white or the whole quantity is red.

(26)   a All the wine is either red or white.
        b All the shirts are either red or white.

Krifka (1989) and Rothstein (2010) approach the question from
a different point of view. They start from the assumption that count
nouns denote sets of objects which are countable, and they ask how
countability is grammatically encoded. They both answer that mass
nouns are more basic, and that count nouns are derived from them in
an operation which adds the 'countability' property to the basic
N meaning, but they do this in different ways.

Krifka (1989) argues that mass nouns are predicates of type $\langle e,t \rangle$
applying to a plural domain which is the closure under sum of a set of
partially specified minimal elements, e.g. WATER. In contrast, count
nouns are two-place relations between numbers and entities which
incorporate a classifier meaning.[8] The interpretation of count nouns

---

[7] There may be also intermediate readings, but we will ignore those here.

[8] Krifka (1995) suggests that the classifier meaning in English is built into the
numerical and not the noun. If this is the case, it implies that: (i) there are two
sorts of numericals in English, those that include classifiers and those which
combine with measure classifiers such as *kilo*; (ii) the numericals which include
classifiers select only for count nouns, and thus presuppose a different theory of
the count/mass distinction from the one presented here. Bale & Coon (2014)
suggest that in Mi'gmaq (Algonquian) and Chol (Mayan), some numericals
include classifiers. Khrizman (2015) argues that Russian collective numerals

is modelled on classifier expressions such as *five head of cattle*. *Cattle* is analysed as a mass predicate denoting CATTLE, the function associated with the Boolean semi-lattice representing the set of individual cattle closed under sum.[9] The classifier *head of* is a measure head modelled on measure expressions like *kilo*. Krifka assumes that *kilo* expresses a relation between a number n and a quantity of P expressed in terms of kilo units (this was the account of *kilo* that we adopted in Chapter 3). *Head of* has an analogous interpretation, denoting a measure relation between its complement and a number n. The measure relation is in terms of natural units, or **NU**. *Head of* denotes the expression in (27a). It applies to *cattle* to give (27b). This in turn applies to a number like 5, to give (27c):

(27) a $\lambda P\lambda n\lambda x.P(x) \wedge \mathbf{NU}(P)(x) = n$
      b $\lambda n\lambda x.\text{CATTLE}(x) \wedge \mathbf{NU}(\text{CATTLE})(x) = n$
      c $\lambda x.\text{CATTLE}(x) \wedge \mathbf{NU}(\text{CATTLE})(x) = 5$

(27c) gives the set of pluralities of cattle which are sums of five 'natural' individuals.

Krifka (1989) proposes that in count nouns the classifier meaning is built into the meaning of the head noun. Count nouns are derived from an abstract mass noun via a 'count' operation. This operation applies to a predicate at type <e,t>, and gives an expression analogous to (27b) at type <n <e,t>>. For example, the count noun *cow* has the meaning in (28a). It is derived from the abstract mass predicate COW. The relation between COW′ and the abstract predicate COW is given in (28b):

(28) a $\lambda n\lambda x.\text{COW}'(x,n)$
      b $\text{COW}'(x,n) \leftrightarrow \text{COW}(x) \wedge \mathbf{NU}(\text{COW})(x) = n$

The count noun *cow* in (28a) either combines with a numerical or the n argument is existentially quantified. *One cow* or *a cow* denotes (29a), *five cows* denotes $\lambda x.\text{COW}'(x,5)$ as in (29b), and the bare plural *cows* denotes (29c).

(29) a $\lambda x.\text{COW}'(x,1)$
      b $\lambda x.\text{COW}'(x,5)$
      c $\lambda x.\exists n[\text{COW}'(x,n)]$

---

incorporate a classifier as Krifka (1995) suggests, but in contrast to 'ordinary' cardinal numericals which do not.

[9] In fact, *cattle* is not a mass noun in English, but this is irrelevant to the discussion here.

By this point, the count noun is again at type <e,t>, the same type as the mass noun, and it can combine with a determiner as in *some cows*, *the cows*, or shift to the bare plural argument type.

In sum, count nouns differ structurally from mass nouns since they are born at type <n,<e,t>>, while mass nouns are born as predicates at type <e,t>, but the typal difference is not accessible above the N level. Singular count nouns are not semantically distinguished from plurals, but are simply functions from the number 1 to sets of singleton cows. Plural marking, the contrast between *cow* and *cows* is a matter of agreement: *one* or *a* induce singular morphology on the head noun, while *five* induces plural morphology on the head noun.

Krifka's account treats counting as a special kind of measuring, and count nouns as measure operations from a number n to sets of plural individuals in N with cardinality n. It expresses the intuition that counting presupposes individuating atomic entities by incorporating a 'natural unit' measure into the meaning of the count noun. **NU** is assumed to be as general as possible, '[W]e can assume that **NU** yields the same measure function for entities of a similar kind ... **NU**(CATTLE) and **NU**(GAME) should denote the same measure function' (Krifka 1989: 84). In more recent work, Krifka notes, following observations in Rothstein (2010), that the **NU** function must be at least partially context dependent in order to deal with context-dependent choices of atoms with nouns like *fence, wall* and so on.

An important point about Krifka's theory is that the distinction between mass nouns and count nouns is lexical. Mass nouns are <e,t> predicates and count nouns are <n <e,t>> relations, but this lexical distinction is neutralized as soon as a noun is inserted into a nominal phrase, as shown in (29). The typal difference is not projected higher up into the nominal phrase. But, as we saw, determiners such as *every* do distinguish between count and mass nouns, and other operations require us to distinguish between count and mass NPs and DPs. Gillon's examples in (25) illustrate this for reciprocals, as do the examples in (30). Partitivity is also sensitive to the mass/count distinction, as in (31):

(30)   a   #The furniture was piled on top of each other.
         b   The pieces of furniture / chairs were piled on top of each other.

(31)   a   Much/#many of the furniture was new.
         b   Many/#much of the pieces of furniture / chairs were new.

The second point that Krifka's theory raises is conceptual as well as structural. Krifka proposes that we treat counting as a form of measuring. *Five kilos of flour* denotes a quantity of flour that measures five kilos, while *five cows* denotes a quantity of cows that measures five natural units (**NU**), and *one cow* denotes a quantity of cows which measures one **NU**. A classifier like *unit/ piece* denotes the **NU** measure head, and *five pieces/units of furniture* denotes a quantity of furniture which measures five units. The neutralization of the typal difference between mass and count nouns at the NP level reflects the fact that *five cows* and *five kilos of flour* are both measure expressions.

However, as we have seen in Chapter 3, there is good evidence that counting and measuring are two different operations, which are associated with two different grammatical structures. Counting is putting individual entities in one-to-one correspondence with the natural numbers, while measuring is assigning a measure value to a quantity on a dimensional scale independent of the internal structure of the quantity. Individuating classifiers cannot be assimilated to measure classifiers since, as we saw in Chapter 3, they have a very different semantic function. Individuating classifiers like *bottle of, glass of* (as well as other non-container classifiers like *piece of*) pick out the relevant individual entities which are to be counted, while measure classifiers, like *kilo, litre* and *glass* (on its measure reading), specify the unit in terms of which a dimensional scale is calibrated. Thus, analysing count nouns as covert measure expressions is to miss something fundamental about the contrast between counting and measuring. Count nouns may include a covert classifier, but the results from Chapter 3 suggest that this should be a counting classifier, and that counting classifiers and measure classifiers are of different types.[10]

Rothstein (2010) gives an analysis which shares some insights with Krifka's account but which stresses the difference between counting and measuring operations. Rothstein (2010), like Krifka (1989), treats counting as counting with respect to a specific N. Counting is always counting N of a certain kind, and it does not make any sense to ask 'How many are there?', but only 'How many N are there?' (see

---

[10] In Chapter 3, measure classifiers combine with numbers to form predicates which modify mass nouns, while individuating classifiers combine with NPs to form nominal predicates. In Krifka's (1989) account, the **NU** measure head is a function of type $<<e,t>,<n,<e,t>>>$, though in his (1995) paper he suggests that the measure head is incorporated into the numeral (see footnote 8), which makes the numeral equivalent to the measure predicate.

Chapter 2: examples (28,29). This explains why counting across N conjunctions is highly restricted. If I have four cups and two saucers, the question 'How many cups and saucers are there?' is unlikely to produce the answer 'six', since *cups and saucers* is not a N predicate denoting a set of objects of the same kind. Counting across conjunctions is possible if N *and* N can be interpreted as instances of a more general (countable) kind, as when 'How many girls and boys are there in the class?' is interpreted as 'How many children are there?'. It is also possible when 'How many N and N' is understood as a question about non-overlapping (Cartesian) pairs. 'How many cups and saucers do we need?' might get the answer four' if there are four guests, and we need cup-and-saucer pairs to give them all tea.

While counting always presupposes a predicate defining the sort of entity to be counted, it also presupposes that the predicate is atomic and that disjoint minimal entities in the denotation of N can be individuated. Count nouns provide both these kinds of information: they determine what kind of object is being counted and encode the atomic structure of this set, thus enabling counting to take place.

Rothstein (2010) argues grammatical atomicity is grammatically encoded in count noun denotations. Like Krifka (1989), the theory derives count nouns from mass nouns. However, while Krifka treats counting as a form of measuring, Rothstein (2010) makes explicit the differences between the two operations. The starting point of the paper is the observation that what counts as a single countable atomic unit in the denotation of a count noun is often context-dependent, since not all count nouns denote sets of inherently individuable objects. As we already mentioned, nouns such as *place, fence, wall, hedge* and *lawn* require a context-dependent decision as to what counts as one item. Rothstein (1999, 2010) gives as an example a situation such as (32), in which four farmers enclose an open space, each one building a stretch of fencing along the side of the space bordering her land.

(32)

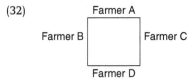

If we ask how many fences were built, the answer depends on our choice of what counts 'as one item. If each farmer built a fence, four fences were built. If the farmers together built a fence, then one fence was built. If one bank financed the work done by A and B and another the work done by C and D, then arguably the answer is two fences. Similarly, if I ask how many places you visited in England last year, you might answer 'Three – Oxford, Cambridge and London'. But you might also answer: 'About ten: the Tower of London, the National Gallery, Greenwich Observatory and Westminster Abbey in London, two colleges and a museum in Oxford, and two or three colleges in Cambridge'. It depends on what, in context, counts as a place (see Rothstein 2000 for discussion of the semantics of *place*). These examples show that count nouns are not necessarily associated with sets of inherently individuable or disjoint objects.

Rothstein (2010) suggests that, grammatically, atomicity is always atomicity relative to a context, and that this contextual dependency must be grammatically encoded in the meaning of the count noun. Count nouns are derived by an operation which applies to a mass noun meaning N_{mass}, and gives as an output a set of elements in N which count as one N (an atomic instance of N) relative to a particular context k. These are the atoms of N relative to context k. The singular count noun is indexed for the context k in which its members count as atoms. As a result, count nouns and mass nouns are typally different. A mass noun denotes a set of (plural) entities and is of type $<e,t>$. Count nouns denote sets of indexed entities e_k where e is an entity and the index k indicates the context in which e counts as atomic. Count nouns, then, are of type $<e\times k,t>$. This typal difference is preserved as NP structure is built up, and allows DPs headed by count nouns to be distinguished from DPs headed by mass nouns. *The* $+N_{mass}$ is an expression of type e, while *the* $+N_{count}$ is an expression of type $e\times k$. Since we will be using this theory in the chapters that follow, we will describe it briefly (for details, see the original paper).

Nominal interpretation is relative to a complete Boolean algebra M, ordered by the part of relation $\sqsubseteq_M$. Intuitively, M is the mass domain. $\sqcup_M$, the sum operation on M, is the complete Boolean join operation, i.e. for every $X \subseteq M$: $\sqcup_M X \in M$. All nominals are associated with an abstract root noun, $N_{root,}$ which denotes a generated ideal in M: $N_{root} = \{m \in M: m \sqsubseteq \sqcup N_{root}\}$. (The ideal generated by x is the set of all x's parts.) This means that root nouns have the structure that Link assigns to mass nouns and plural. We assume that mass nouns are root nouns, thus $MASS(N_{root})$ is the identity function on N_{root} as in (33).

(33) $MASS(N_{root}) = N_{root}$

We will assume that M includes a set of atoms ATOM. The atoms of M can be natural atoms, i.e. salient individuable entities, or vague, non-stable entities.

> Let **min**(N) = {m ∈ N: ∀n ∈ N: if n ⊑ m: then n = m}.
> Root noun N_{root} is atomic iff:
> **min**(N_{root} − {0}) ⊆ ATOM. $ATOM_{Nroot}$ = N_{root} ∩ ATOM

Atomic root nouns have the structure that Link and Chierchia assign to plural nouns: they are provably the closure under sum of their set of atoms.

(34)   For atomic root nouns: N_{root} = *$ATOM_N$,
>   where *X = {m∈ M: ∃Y⊆X: m = ⊔$_M$Y} (Link's operation of pluralization).

I will assume that mass nouns like *furniture* denote atomic root nouns.
    Root nouns are the input to operations deriving N_{mass} and N_{count}.

Mass nouns can be fully naturally atomic, if all their atoms are naturally disjoint, or non-naturally atomic. Natural atomicity is a gradable property, thus allowing a mass noun to be generated by a set of atoms of which only a subset are naturally atomic.

(Singular) count nouns denote a set of **semantic atoms** derived from the root noun relative to a particular context. They presuppose a context-dependent choice as to what counts as one entity. This choice is encoded in the notion of (counting) context k, which intuitively collects together the entities which count as atoms in k. We define an (atomic) context k as in (35). The idea is the following: semantic atoms are objects that are chosen as semantic in context k. They are not necessarily themselves atoms in M, it is k that makes them into atoms. In what follows, we use a for objects chosen as semantic atoms by k:

(35)   A **context** k is a set of objects from M, k ⊆ M; K is the set of all contexts.
>   The set of count atoms determined by context k is the set
> A_k = {<a,k>: a ∈ k}

Singular count nouns are derived from root nouns by a count operation $COUNT_k$ which applies to the root noun N_{root} and picks out the set of ordered pairs {<a,k>: a ∈ N_{root} ∩ k}. We assume that contextual disjointness is a condition on k. (Thus, k is a local context.)

This means that k is taken contextually to be a disjoint set. This is necessary since the Boolean structure generated from k must have the structure of a complete atomic Boolean algebra with k as its set of atoms, otherwise the count operation will not be defined properly. Singular count noun denotations are taken to be sets of disjoint elements in k. This means that we will need to be pragmatically flexible and allow more than one counting context in a discourse when necessary – for example, if we want to talk about individuals and their body parts, or walls and the bricks they are constructed from. But this fits with our sense that when we count walls and when we count bricks, we are individuating objects at different levels of finegrainedness, expressed by different choices of counting contexts. For discussion of these and more complex cases, see Landman (2011a).

$COUNT_k$ (N_{root}) then gives the set of entities in N_{root} which count as one in context k, or the set of individuals in the intersection of N and k, indexed for k. This is a set of semantic atoms.

(36)   For any $X \subseteq M$: $COUNT_k(X) = \{<a, k>: a \in X \cap k\}$

The interpretation of a count noun N_{count} in context k is: $COUNT_k(N_{root})$. We use N_k as short for $COUNT_k(N_{root})$, the interpretation of a count noun in context k.

We illustrate this with a flexible noun, *stone*:

(37)   a ⟦stone$_{mass}$⟧ = MASS(STONE$_{root}$) = STONE$_{root}$ = {x: x ∈ STONE$_{root}$}
         b ⟦stone$_{count}$⟧ = $COUNT_k$(STONE$_{root}$) = {<a, k>: a ∈ STONE$_{root}$ ∩ k}

So *stone*$_{mass}$ denotes a set of stone-mass entities, while *stone*$_{count}$ denotes a set {<a, k>: a ∈ STONE$_{root}$ ∩ k} of type < e×k, t>, i.e. the set of indexed entities which count as one in context k.

Crucially, COUNT may, but need not, apply to a naturally atomic set, and it will always yield a set of semantic atoms. Unlike natural atomicity, semantic atomicity is not gradable. However, count nouns will differ in how context-dependent the choice of atoms is. If COUNT applies to a naturally atomic set, then, for a particular domain M, the value will be constant, independent of the choice of k. Thus, COUNT(child$_{root}$) will denote the same count set, independent of choice of k.[11] However, if COUNT applies to a non-naturally atomic predicate such as *fence*, the choice of context k will result in possibly different sets of atoms, as illustrated in (32).

Plural count nouns are derived by applying the standard plural operation * to the first projection of N_k. *(N_k), the plural of the set of ordered pairs denoted by N_k, is the set of ordered pairs whose first

---

[11] We are ignoring here vagueness as to what counts as a child. As discussed above, this may vary according to context (child with respect to bus fares, child with respect to legal rights, etc.). But this is orthogonal to the choice of k.

projection, $\pi_1(N_k)$, is the plural set derived from the first projection of N_k, and whose second projection, $\pi_2(N_k)$, is the (same) value k.

(38)   Assume: $\pi_1(N_k) = \{a: \langle a,k \rangle \in N_k\}$
    $\pi_2(N_k) = k$
    In default context k: $PL(N_{count}) = {}^*N_k = \{\langle d,k \rangle: d \in {}^*\pi_1(N_k)\}$

The value of a plural set will depend on the context-dependent choice of semantic atoms. This means that, in a single domain, the mass noun *carpeting* will not necessarily denote the same set of real-world items as the plural count noun *carpets*. The singular count noun *carpet* is derived from the mass noun via the COUNT operation and denotes the set of k-indexed atomic carpets which count as one in context k, as in (39b). *Carpets* denote the pluralization of this set.

(39)   a ⟦CARPETING⟧ = CARPET$_{root}$
    b $COUNT_k(CARPET_{root}) =$ $CARPET_k = \{\langle a, k \rangle: a \in CARPET_{root} \cap k\}$
    c ⟦CARPETS$_k$⟧ = $\{\langle d,k \rangle: d \in {}^*\pi_1(CARPET_k)\} =$
    $\{\langle d,k \rangle: d \in {}^*CARPET_{root} \cap k\}$

But $COUNT_k(CARPET_{root})$ need not contain all the minimal parts of CARPET$_{root}$. Suppose CARPET$_{root}$ (the meaning of the mass noun *carpeting*), contains the following minimal parts: a,b,c. However, c is too small to count as a carpet, since it is only a piece cut from a bigger carpet to make the latter fit in the room. In this situation, $COUNT_k$ (CARPET$_{root}$) will be the set $\{a_k, b_k\}$. The plural *carpets* will denote the pluralization of this set $\{a_k, b_k, a_k \sqcup b_k\}$, while the *carpeting* will denote **all** the minimal pieces of carpets and their sums: $\{a,b,c, a \sqcup b, a \sqcup c, b \sqcup c, a \sqcup b \sqcup c\}$. This seems to be the right result, since we do not in everyday speech expect the denotation of *carpets* and *carpeting* to be the same. This is shown in (40):

(40)   a Please pack all the carpets!
    b Please pack all the carpeting!

Arguably someone who packs all the full-size carpets in response to (40a) and ignored the small pieces piled in the corner has fulfilled the instructions in (40a), but they have not fulfilled the instructions in (40b).

This account of the mass/count distinction has a number of advantages. Count nouns and mass nouns are of different types, so the sensitivity of grammatical operations to the mass/count distinction is explained by selectional restrictions. We make a typal distinction between mass and count NPs and between mass and count DPs. Hence we have a compositional account of the mass/count distinction, in which the distinction applies to complex NPs, like partitive constructions, and DPs, allowing, for instance, an account of reciprocal VP predicates, which require a count DP subject.

Mismatches between the count/mass distinction and the object/stuff distinction are explained by the non-isomorphism between natural atomicity and semantic atomicity. Naturally atomic predicates are mass or count predicates which denote sets of individuable entities. Semantically atomic predicates are count predicates in which context-dependent atomicity is grammatically encoded. Rothstein (2010) argues that counting is restricted to count nouns since cardinal numerals only modify predicates at type $<e \times k, t>$.

Instead of denoting $\lambda x.|x| = 3$, *three* denotes the predicate in (41), where x is a variable of type $e \times k$ and P_x is a predicate of type $<e \times k, t>$:

(41) $\lambda x. |\pi_1(x)|_k = 3$

(41) denotes the property that a k-indexed entity has if it has exactly three minimal parts that count as atoms in context k. It shifts to the modifier type $<<e \times k, t> <e \times k, t>>$, as in (42), and thus applies only to count nouns.

(42) $\lambda P_x \lambda x.P_x(x) \wedge |\pi_1(x)|_k = 3$

At first, it looks stipulative to rule out #*three furnitures* by type mismatches. However, the typal restriction on (41) is an expression of the important point that we made earlier, that counting is always relative to a context-dependent decision about what counts as 'one N'. The k index on the numerical in (41) and (42) expresses the fact that counting is parameterized, and that out of the blue 'I counted three' is unverifiable without information about what kind of N-object was being counted and what, in context, the countable atomic entities in N are.

In sum, natural atomicity is neither a necessary nor sufficient condition of being a count noun. *Water* and *mud* are not naturally atomic mass nouns, while *furniture, cutlery, jewellery* and *company* are naturally atomic and mass. Many, but not all, count nouns are naturally atomic: *boy* and *cat* are, but *fence, wall, lawn, sequence, line, plane, twig* are not. Count nouns are associated with a grammatically encoded set of atoms, indexed for the context in which they are atomic, and it is this context-dependent encoded atomicity which makes them countable. $COUNT_k$ is a lexical operation deriving count nouns from mass nouns. It can be seen as an implicit classifier incorporated into count noun denotations, but crucially it is a count classifier and not a measure head, and it is part of the lexical meaning of the count noun.

I shall use a (simplified) version of Rothstein (2010) in the rest of this book, but obviously this is not the only framework in which the analysis can be formulated. Landman (2011a, 2016) is a recent account that focuses on the properties of mass nouns. Landman argues that the count/mass distinction is a distinction between predicate denotations grounded in a disjoint base (count predicates) and those grounded in a non-disjoint, or overlapping, base (mass predicates). In his account, there are no atomic predicates, and no atoms. All nouns (and noun phrases) have their denotations in a single domain, and denote pairs consisting of a body and a base, i.e. $[\![N]\!] = \,$<body(N), base(N)>. *Body(N)* is the set of N entities, and *base(N)* is the set which grounds it. For singular nouns, body(N)$\subseteq$ base(N), while, for plural count and mass nouns, body(N) is the closure of base(N) under sum. Countability presupposes disjointness, which may be contextually determined, while mass predicates presuppose non-disjointness or overlap. Landman distinguishes 'horizontal' overlap, which characterizes 'mess' mass nouns like *mud*, and 'vertical' overlap, which characterizes 'neat' mass nouns like *furniture*. The overlap in the case of *mud* is horizontal, since entities in the denotation of *mud* overlap. Overlap in the case of *furniture* is vertical, since individual objects and collections of those same objects can simultaneously count as 'one item' – for example, the items of furniture for sale may include a table, six chairs, or the dining room suite consisting of the table and six chairs. Crucially, the same body may be generated by different bases, and N will be count or mass depending on whether the base is overlapping or disjoint. This is the case with pairs like *carpet/carpeting*. Landman's theory presupposes disjointness in the denotation of count nouns and overlap in the mass domain, while Rothstein (2010) encodes contextual disjointness explicitly via the COUNT operation, and is agnostic as to the properties of the mass domain. But what the theories share is the idea that countability is a grammatical property of N denotations and not a property of objects.

4.5   SYNTACTIC APPROACHES TO THE MASS/COUNT DISTINCTION

There is one more group of mass/count theories to discuss. These theories argue, based on examples like (43), that all nouns are in principle flexible, and that count nouns are derived from mass roots via a null syntactic classifier:

(43)   a He ate chocolate / a chocolate.
       b We ordered three waters and two coffees.
       c After the accident there was dog all over the road.

(43a) and (43b) illustrate cases where naturally mass nouns have count interpretations. The count interpretation of *chocolate* occurs when $chocolate_{mass}$ is embedded under a null classifier, as proposed in Sharvy (1978).[12] Similarly, *three waters / two coffees* are analogous to *three glasses of water / two cups of coffee*, although when the classifier is null, plurality is marked on the noun and not on the classifier. In (43c), a naturally count noun *dog* is used as a mass noun. (43a,b) have been called examples of 'packaging', while (43c) illustrates so-called 'grinding'.

Borer (2005) proposes a theory of mass/count based on the contrasts in (43). She argues that all count nouns are mass nouns embedded under a syntactic classifier. *Two dogs* is analysed as [two [Cl dog_{mass}]], with the meaning 'two animal quantities of dog stuff', and the reading in (43c) occurs when *dog* is not the complement of a classifier. In this framework, the so-called 'universal grinder' readings turn out to be the basic meanings of all nouns. Borer argues that classifiers and number fill the same syntactic head NUM, and so are in complementary distribution. They have the semantic function of introducing a 'dividing' operation, DIV, on the denotation of the nominal predicate, which is a necessary condition of counting. Assume that *water* denotes the mass 'stuff' water. *Waters* is then analysed as the classifier phrase [NUM_cl water], denoting a set of quantities of water, the result of dividing the stuff into contextually relevant units. If NUM is empty, then the noun is interpreted as mass. NUM must thus be empty in the mass reading of (43a) as well as (43c).

Pelletier (2012) offers a different version of this approach. Instead of positing a null classifier, he argues that count nouns and mass nouns are derived in the lexicon by an operation which adds [+COUNT] or [+MASS] to abstract lexical items. Although Pelletier's operation is lexical, it is strictly an operation on features and underspecified semantically. In general, these theories want to build a direct analogy between English-type languages and classifier languages like Mandarin Chinese, arguing that the null classifier or plurality (or

---

[12] In some versions of this approach, both count and mass are derived by separate operations from a root noun. However, since the mass operation is syntactically inert and semantically null, there is no empirical distinction between the two theories.

[+COUNT] operation) fills the same role as the explicit sortal classifier in Mandarin, and explaining the absence of the plural marker.

The proposal that count nouns are derived by applying a null operator to mass noun (or root noun) denotations is not new, as we saw in the discussion of Krifka (1989) and Rothstein (2010) above, nor is the suggestion that this operation is the lexical correlate of the operation expressed by individuating classifiers in Mandarin. However, in contrast to the theories proposed by Krifka and Rothstein, the theories under discussion here argue that the null operator is a general productive operation expressed in a syntactic head and that all nouns have both a count and mass interpretation. Thus, in principle, all nouns should be fully flexible. Examples like (43c) are crucial for these theories, since they provide evidence that what look like pure count nouns also have a mass reading.

I shall discuss the Universal Grinder in Chapter 7, arguing that 'ground' readings like those in (43c) are not the basic mass nouns from which count nouns are derived, but are derived by an independent operation. But, if this is the case, then count nouns like *boy* and *dog* cannot be used as mass nouns, and much of the conceptual support for a Borer/Pelletier-style theory disappears. But, in order to put the properties of the Universal Grinder in context, we first explore the semantics of object mass nouns in English, and then we will consider some case studies in crosslinguistic variation.

4.6   QUESTIONS FOR FURTHER DISCUSSION AND INVESTIGATION

1 For any given language that you have access to, explore whether there is a mass/count distinction, and, if so, what grammatical tests distinguish between mass and count nouns.
2 It is often assumed that only count nouns pluralize as in *boy/boys* vs *rice/#rices*. Standard exceptions are then noted: pluralized mass nouns may have a plurality of kinds reading, as in (44a), and a plurality of servings reading, as in (44b):

(44)   a He bought many different cheeses for the party.
       b We ordered three waters and two coffees. (43b)

However, some mass nouns do take plural markers, in a variety of contexts and with a variety of interpretations. Some plural mass nouns have so-called 'abundance' readings (Corbett 2000; Doron & Müller 2013), and the plural mass noun denotes 'a lot of N', as in *the winds blew*. Ghaniabadi (2012) argues that, in Persian, some plural mass nouns have a definite reading, while indefinite plural mass nouns denote *instances of N*. Epstein-Naveh (2015) shows that *gešam-im/šelag-im*, literally 'rains'/'snows' may denote (among other things) pluralities of events of raining and snowing. What range of meanings may plural mass nouns have In (a) English, (b) any other mass/count language that you have access to?

3 It has often been noted that object mass nouns in English are superordinates, names for 'superkinds'. *Furniture* denotes items which can be classified as chairs, tables, beds and so on. *Jewellery* includes rings, necklaces and bracelets; *mail* includes letters, postcards, newspapers, etc. These nouns have a characteristic grammatical property that they do not allow a plural of kinds reading, and it is impossible to find a grammatical interpretation for *#furnitures* in (45a), though (45b) is felicitous:

(45)   a   #They sell many furnitures in that store.
        b   They sell many kinds of furniture in that store.

This is presumably not accidental, and suggests that subkinds of mass nouns can be identified with interesting grammatical properties. What might be the relation between the semantics of superordinacy and the data in (45)? Can you find other semantic subgroups of mass nouns characterized by grammatical properties? Is is possible to relate the semantic properties of these nouns to their morphosyntactic characteristics?

4 There are almost no crosslinguistic corpus studies of how categorization into mass nouns, count nouns and flexible nouns varies crosslinguistically. How might you go about setting one up? What difficulties might such a study run into? Kulkarni, Rothstein & Treves (2013) describes one such study. What problems does that study run into and how might they be circumvented?

5 Object Mass Nouns, Measuring and Counting

'The next day, when Ali Baba left home, his wife decided she wanted to count the gold coins in the bags that Ali Baba had brought home. There were too many of them to count them one by one, so she decided to weigh them, just as you would weigh out grain.'

Ali Baba and the Forty Thieves, Peter Haddock Publications Ltd

5.1 INTRODUCTION: BARNER & SNEDEKER (2005), BALE & BARNER (2009)

This chapter examines the semantics of object mass nouns. Chapter 4 proposed a semantic analysis of count nouns, arguing that they denote sets of contextually dependent atoms, indexed for the context in which they count as atoms. These sets are derived by a COUNT operation which applies to mass noun denotations. Mass nouns are the 'default case'. They denote Boolean algebras, which either are not generated by a set of atoms, or are generated by a set of atoms which are grammatically inaccessible.

As has become clear in the literature since the mid-1990s, there is more to be said about mass nouns than this. As we already saw, mass nouns naturally divide into two groups. The first group includes nouns like *mud, sand* and *fabric*, which typically denote material, or 'stuff', which does not naturally come in atomic units. These are often called 'substance nouns'. The second group includes nouns which denote sets of naturally individuable units, such as *furniture, kitchenware* and *poultry*. Barner & Snedeker (2005) and Bale & Barner (2009) call these 'object mass nouns', while Rothstein (2010) calls them 'naturally atomic mass nouns' and Landman (2011a, 2015) calls them 'neat mass nouns'. Chierchia (2010) calls them 'fake mass nouns', but as we shall show in this chapter, there is nothing fake about them. As we saw in the previous chapter, the atoms of these predicates are available for certain grammatical operations, as in (1) (= Chapter 4: (7)), where the predicate *big* distributes to the atoms in the denotation of object mass nouns.

(1)   a   The furniture in our house is big.
       b   Please carry the big furniture downstairs first. (from Rothstein 2010)

These nouns are a problem for any theory that tries to ground the mass/count distinction in a conceptual distinction between stuff and objects. They are grammatically mass, but they denote sets of individuable objects which are nevertheless not grammatically countable. This forces us to be precise about the relation between objecthood and countability. I proposed in the previous chapter that countability is grammatically encoded atomicity. Not all naturally atomic predicates encode atomicity semantically, thus leading to object mass nouns. In this chapter, we examine these nouns further. We begin with the very different account of object mass nouns offered in Bale & Barner (2009). They argue, based on the results of Barner & Snedeker (2005), that object mass nouns are semantically count nouns, with the morphosyntax of mass nouns. I will show that this is not supported cross-linguistically, and propose an account which grounds the contrast between object mass nouns and count nouns in the contrast between measuring and counting.

Barner & Snedeker (2005) show experimentally that object mass nouns denote sets of individuable entities. Subjects were shown a number of pictures representing two collections of objects, one consisting of two large objects and the other consisting of six small objects of the same kind. These included a picture representing a group with two large shoes and a group with six small shoes, a picture representing two large blobs of toothpaste as opposed to six small blobs and one representing a large knife and fork and three small pairs of knives and forks. Subjects were then asked *Who has more N?* Predictably, when N was a count noun (*Who has more shoes?*) comparison was by cardinality (six small shoes were more than two big shoes), and when N was a mass noun (*Who has more toothpaste?*), comparison was by overall volume (two big blobs were more than six small blobs). With a flexible noun like *stone*, the syntactic form of the noun determined the basis of the comparison: *Who has more stones?* led to comparison in terms of cardinality, while *Who has more stone?* resulted in comparison in terms of volume.

When N was an object mass noun (*Who has more silverware?*), evaluation of the comparison was by cardinality. Subjects consistently judged the larger number of items to be 'more N' even if the overall volume of the fewer big pieces was greater than the overall volume of the larger number of smaller pieces. This suggests that comparisons involving object mass nouns require comparing the cardinalities of two sets or two quantities of individuable entities, exactly as triggered by count nouns. They suggest that object mass nouns are marked in the lexicon as [+individual], giving them the semantics of count nouns, but the syntax and morphology of mass nouns. Barner & Snedeker's experiments further show that, with flexible nouns such as *stone/stone(s)*, the syntactic form of the nominal determines the comparison mechanism. The count noun in *Who has more stones?* requires comparison in terms of cardinality, while the mass noun in *Who has more stone?* requires comparison in terms of volume. This implies that object mass nouns and mass nouns in a flexible pair are very different semantically.

Bale & Barner (2009) offer a general theory of the mass/count distinction, based on these results. Using comparatives as the test for distinguishing between different classes of nouns, they divide nouns into three main classes:

(i) Count noun such as *boys, girls, books, pens*. These denote sets generated by individuals, and comparative operations always compare in terms of cardinalities, as in (2). There is no reading of (2a) which asserts that the overall volume of boys in your class in greater than in mine. If you teach a class of eighteen-year-olds with three boys in it and I teach a group of five-year-olds with six boys in it, (2a) is just false.

(2) a There are more boys in your class than in my class.
     b There are more girls in the class than boys.

(ii) Object mass nouns such as *furniture, footwear* and *jewellery*. These are also compared via cardinalities as in (3). They must thus have the same kind of denotations as count nouns.

(3) a John has more furniture than Bill = John has more pieces of furniture than Bill.
     b That baby has more footwear than her mother = She has more pairs of shoes than her mother!

(iii) Substance mass nouns which require comparison of overall quantities in terms of volume, weight or some other non-cardinal dimension, as in (4).

(4) a John has more gold than Bill.
     b There is more mud on this floor than on that floor.

In addition, flexible nouns like *stone* are ambiguous between mass and count. In these cases, the count noun behaves as a normal count noun, and the mass noun behaves like a substance mass noun. (5a) compares cardinalities, while (5b) asks for a comparison of overall volume:

(5)   a Which garden has more stones in it?
        b Which garden has more stone in it?

Bale & Barner identify two crucial results:

(I) Object mass nouns like *furniture* pattern with plural count nouns like *boys* and require comparison in terms of cardinality. This indicates that both count nouns and object mass nouns have denotations grounded in sets of individuals.

(II) In a pair of flexible nouns like *stone/stone(s)*, the mass noun cannot be compared in terms of cardinality. It is, therefore, not an object mass noun.

So, an object mass noun has the semantics of a count noun but the syntax of a mass noun, while the mass noun in a flexible pair is always a substance mass noun.

Bale & Barner make the following proposal. Mass nouns and plural count nouns denote Boolean semi-lattices. Semi-lattices can in principle be either individuated or non-individuated. Individuated semi-lattices are generated by a set of non-overlapping individuals – to all intents and purposes, atoms.[1] Non-individuated semi-lattices may be either limited, which means that they are generated by a set of minimal but overlapping parts, or continuous, with no minimal parts. When the denotation of a noun N is an individuated semi-lattice, comparison is in in terms of cardinality, and *Who has more N?* asks which set has more individuals in it. When the denotation of N is not an individuated semi-lattice, comparison via cardinality is impossible. Object mass nouns and plural count nouns must thus denote individuated semi-lattices, while substance mass nouns do not. The mass N in a flexible pair must be a substance mass noun.

This is worked out grammatically as follows. Mass nouns and count nouns are generated from a root noun which denotes a Boolean semi-lattice. The root noun must be embedded under a functional head.

---

[1] Bale & Barner (2009) are careful not to use the term 'atom' or 'atomic lattice', presumably because the individuals generating the individuated semi-lattices, while non-overlapping, may have internal structure, However, the individuated lattices are, in fact, atomic lattices.

There are two functional heads, n, the functional head which combines with a root noun to give a mass noun, and $[n,c]$ which combines with a root noun to give a count noun. n denotes the identity function mapping a semi-lattice onto itself.

Object mass nouns like *furniture* occur when the root noun denotes an individuated semi-lattice. Since n is the identity function, the mass noun also denotes an individuated semi-lattice. Comparison of quantities of furniture will be comparison by cardinality.

The root of substance mass nouns like *water* denotes a non-individuated semi-lattice, and so the mass noun does too. Comparison is by volume (or some other continuous dimension).

Count nouns are derived using the functional head $[n,c]$. $[n,c]$ denotes the partial function *IND* which maps a non-individuated semi-lattice onto an individuated one.[2] Take, for example, the flexible nouns *apple* and *stone*. The roots of these nouns, $stone_{root}$ and $apple_{root}$, denote non-individuated semi-lattices, as do the mass nouns $stone_{mass}$ and $apple_{mass}$. Comparisons like *Who has more stone/apple?* are evaluated only in terms of a continuous dimension.

$Stone_{count}$ and $apple_{count}$ are derived by applying the *IND* function to the non-individuated semi-lattice, and mapping it onto an individuated semi-lattice by selecting a contextually relevant set of minimal elements which do not overlap (a set of atomic stones or apples) and then closing this set under sum. As a result, *Who has more stones?* can be evaluated only by comparing the cardinalities of two sets of stones. Crucially, *IND* can never be an identity function, and its domain is restricted to non-individuated semi-lattices. The judgements in (5) are thus explained.

This theory has somewhat paradoxical results. Object mass nouns, according to Bale & Barner, have the syntax of mass nouns, but the semantics of count nouns. From the other perspective, count nouns have the semantics of object mass nouns, but they are derived by the *IND* function from root nouns which have the semantics of substance mass nouns. While this may just make sense for nouns which are part of a flexible pair like *apple* and *stone*, many count nouns are not flexible. The paradoxical and counter-intuitive conclusion is that the root nouns dog_{root} and $chair_{root}$ and $people_{root}$ must denote non-individuated semi-lattices. It is hard to see what kinds of denotations these are, since we have little concept of what non-atomic dogs, chairs, boys or individual people are. One possibility is that the root noun denotes 'ground' stuff,

[2] $[n,c]$ maps root nouns onto plural count nouns. An independent functional head derives the singular denotation, a set of individuals or atoms.

as in example (6), as Borer (2005) suggests, though I already noted that there is evidence against this, which we will discuss in Chapter 7.

(6)   After the accident, there was dog all over the road.

Here, I note that, whatever the non-individuated denotation of a root noun is, it is surprising that canonical count nouns like *dog, school* and *postman* are derived from non-individuated root nouns, while *furniture* and *jewellery* are derived from root nouns denoting individuated semi-lattices. Object mass nouns in English tend to be superordinates, nouns which denote sets of subkinds rather than sets of individuals, as noted at the end of Chapter 4 (Section 4.6, Question 3). Giving them a semantics which makes them inherently count is rather counter-intuitive.

However, the major point that I want to make does not focus on either of these issues, but on a more important issue: closer inspection indicates that object mass nouns and count nouns do not behave the same way in comparative constructions after all.

5.2   A CLOSER LOOK AT THE SEMANTICS OF OBJECT MASS NOUNS

Barner & Snedeker (2005) and Bale & Barner (2009) claim that object mass nouns are always compared by cardinality and thus must denote sets of individuals just like count nouns. However, there is increasing evidence against this claim, both in the theoretical and experimental literature. Rothstein & Pires de Oliveira (in press) and Rothstein (2016a) show that non-cardinal evaluations are possible when triggered by context, for example in (7a).

(7)   a John has more *furniture* than Bill, so he should use the larger
         moving truck.
       b John has more *pieces of furniture* than Bill.

Suppose that John and Bill are moving house, and John has a grand piano, a large sofa, a double bed and his grandmother's heavy wardrobe (= four pieces of furniture). Bill, in contrast, has four folding chairs, a small table and a rolled-up mattress (= six pieces of furniture). In this situation, (7a) is judged by native speakers to be true, because in the context of choosing a moving truck, the volume of the furniture is relevant and not the number of pieces. (7b) is false, since John does not have more pieces of furniture than Bill (even though, in this context, he has more furniture). (8) contrasts with (7a).

(8)   John has more *pieces of furniture* than Bill, so he should use the larger moving truck.

While informants routinely agree that (7a) is true, their response to (8) is, 'Well, it depends how big the pieces of furniture are!' Further examples illustrating the same point are given in (9):

(9)   a   Who has more jewellery to insure?
        b   John got sick because he ate more fruit than Mary. She ate two apples and three strawberries. He ate a whole watermelon.

(9a) can be compared in terms of pieces of jewellery or in terms of overall value, while in (9b) *more fruit* is naturally interpreted as meaning a greater overall quantity of fruit and not a greater number of pieces of fruit.[3]

Landman (2011a) makes the same point about comparison of object mass nouns using the comparative determiner *most* instead of *more*. Evaluating the truth of *most N are P* involves comparing N∩P with N∩P̄ (the size of the intersection between N and P and the size of the intersection between N and the set of things which are not P). So *most cats purr* is true if the intersection of cats with purrers is bigger than the intersection of cats with non-purrers. When N is count, the truth of *most N are P* depends on the cardinality of N∩P vs N∩P̄. When N is not count, then there is a choice as to how to compare the size of the two intersections. The examples in (10) are based on Landman (2011a).

(10)   a   Most farm animals are chickens.
        b   Most farm animals are cows.
        c   In terms of number, most livestock is poultry.
        d   In terms of volume, most livestock is cattle.
        e   #In terms of volume, most farm animals are cattle.

(10a) is true and (10b) is false since (to the best of my knowledge) farms raise many more chickens than cows. Thus, the cardinality of farm animals ∩ chickens is greater than farm animals ∩ non-chickens. However, if we change the count noun *farm animals* to the

---

[3] Note that comparisons of both object mass nouns and count nouns are also possible in terms of kinds:

   (i)   John is a much fussier eater than Mary. For example, she eats more fruit than he does. She eats apples and oranges and apricots, and he only eats watermelon.
   (ii) Mary likes more dogs than John. He only likes spaniels and retrievers, and she likes also Great Danes and English sheepdogs.

object mass noun *livestock*, both (10c) and (10d) may be correct, depending on whether we choose the dimension of comparison to be number/cardinality (in which case (10c) is true and (10d) is false) or volume (in which case (10d) is true and (10c) is false). (10e) is infelicitous, since count nouns cannot be compared in terms of volume.

Grimm & Levin (2012) support these generalizations experimentally, showing that judgements on *Who has more furniture/jewellery?* differ depending on context. In neutral contexts, the comparison is usually by cardinality, as Barner & Snedeker predict. However, Grimm & Levin show that, in contexts which are what they call 'functionally oriented', the judgement may depend not on cardinality, but on which set better fulfils the specified or implied function. They test this with nouns such as *furniture, jewellery, change, luggage, mail, ammunition*. Fewer items may be considered 'more' if they serve the local purpose better. Suppose Bill has six folding chairs (i.e. six pieces) while John has a bed, a sofa, a table and a chair (i.e. four pieces). In neutral contexts, where no information about the situation is presented (or in contexts in which the number of items is contextually important), informants may consider Bill to have more furniture. However, if the same data are presented to subjects together with the information that Bill and John are trying to furnish their new flats, and subjects are then asked 'Who has more furniture?', a significant number of subjects answer that John does, since his pieces of furniture, fewer in number, will result in a better-furnished flat. Gafni & Rothstein (2014) replicates these results for Hebrew. Grimm & Levin suggest that the object mass nouns they chose are all superordinate terms naming artefacts which naturally fulfil a certain function in a given situation, and thus degree of success in filling a function can be used as a dimension for comparison. But there are other ways in which context can be manipulated in order to vary the relevant standard of comparison. Suppose Mary and Jane each collect their mail from the office at work. Mary receives two heavy boxes of books, while Jane has a big but light mailing envelope, a small box of books and six letters. Compare the sentences in (11):

(11)   a Jane received more mail than Mary this morning.
         b Mary had more mail to carry home than Jane.

Informants clearly consider (11a) true. However, the same informants also consider (11b) true, because the use of the verb *carry* makes the dimension of weight/bulk more salient than number of items. Clearly, it is the object mass noun which allows this variation in choice of dimension of comparison. In the situation just described, (12) is false:

(12)   Mary had more pieces of mail to carry home than Jane.

Simple count nouns (as well as classifier constructions) behave the same as in (12). If Mary had two big, heavy parcels, and Jane had four small light parcels, then (11b) may be considered true, but (13) is false, since the count noun forces a cardinal comparison:

(13)   Mary had more parcels to carry home.

This shows that object mass nouns differ from count nouns. While count nouns force comparison in terms of cardinality, object mass nouns allow cardinal comparison, but also allow for comparison along some other contextually relevant continuous dimension.

We will now consider data from Brazilian Portuguese and Hungarian, where object mass nouns are much more widespread than in English and allow, but do not require, comparison via cardinality. Furthermore, unlike in English, the mass noun in a flexible pair behaves like any other object mass noun.

5.2.1   Brazilian Portuguese

Object mass nouns in Brazilian Portuguese generally allow comparison along the dimensions of either cardinality or volume: out of the blue, (14a) compares quantities of furniture in terms of numbers of pieces, but the context in (14b) makes it natural to compare in terms of volume, as in the English example in (7) above.

(14)   a João   tem   **mais   mobília**   que   a   Maria.
          João   has   more   furniture   than   the   Maria
          'João has more furniture than Maria.'
       b João tem **mais mobília** que a   Maria então ele vai precisar
          João has more furniture than the Maria so   he go   need

          de uma   caminhote   maior.
          of a   truck   bigger
          'João has more furniture than Maria, so he will need a larger moving truck.'

Comparison constructions using so-called 'bare singular nouns' reinforce this in interesting ways. As we saw in Chapter 4, Brazilian Portuguese has a mass/count distinction, characterized by the same kind of properties that are associated with the mass/count distinction in English. Count nouns, but not mass nouns, take indefinite

determiners (as in 15a), can be modified by numericals, and pluralize
with numericals above one (although plural morphology can easily be
dropped), as in (15b).

(15) a uma   minhoca,   #um ouro
         an/one earthworm.SG, a/one gold.SG
      b duas   minhoca(-s),   #dois ouro(-s)
         two   earthworm(-PL) two   gold(-PL)

However, Brazilian Portuguese also has a bare singular form
as in (16).

(16) Minhoca   cava   buraco.
      earthworm.SG dig.PRS.3SG hole.SG
      'Earthworms dig holes.'

Pires de Oliveira & Rothstein (2011) show that bare singulars in
Brazilian Portuguese are mass nouns. They argue first that the arguments against analysing bare singulars as mass are invalid. Schmitt &
Munn (1999) claim that bare singulars cannot be mass nouns, since
they allow distributive predicates as in (17a), and can be antecedents
of reciprocals, as in (17b). The examples in (18) show that mass nouns
do not allow this.

(17) a Criança   (nessa idade) pesa   vinte   kg.
         child.SG (at.this age) weigh.PRS.3SG twenty kg
         'Children (at this age) weigh twenty kg.'
      b Elefante   anda   um   atrás   do   outro.
         elephant.SG walk.PRS.3SG one   behind of.the other
         'Elephants walk one behind the other.'

(18) a #Ouro   pesa   duas   grama-s.
         gold.SG   weigh.PRS.3SG two   gram-PL
         Intended meaning: 'Pieces of gold weigh two grams.'
      b #Ouro   realça   um   atrás   do   outro.
         gold.SG   fall.PRS.3SG one   behind of.the other
         Intended meaning: 'Pieces of gold fall down one after the other.'

Pires de Oliveira & Rothstein show that this contrast shows up only
if bare singulars are contrasted with substance mass nouns. Object
mass nouns do allow distributive predicates and reciprocals, as (19)
shows.[4] So the data in (17) are not a good argument against categoriz-
ing bare singulars as mass.

---

[4] Schmidt & Munn (1999) also suggest that, if bare singulars were mass nouns, they
should have a 'ground' reading. However, if they are object mass nouns, there is
no reason to assume this. See Chapter 7 for further discussion.

(19) a Mobília   (nesta loja)   pesa   20 kilo-s.
         furniture (in.this store) weigh.PRS.3SG 20 kilo-PL
         'Furniture (in this store) weighs 20 kilos.'
      b Mobília   (dessa marca) encaixa uma na   outra.[5]
         furniture (of.this brand) fit.PRS.3SG one in.the other
         'Pieces of furniture (of this brand) fit into each other.'

Pires de Oliveira & Rothstein go on to show that bare singulars pattern like mass nouns in many ways. Bare singulars and mass nouns have only a generic interpretation in the subject position of stage-level predicates, while bare plurals are ambiguous between a generic and an existential interpretation (20). The same contrast shows up in the complement of *gostar* 'to like' (21):

(20) a Bombeiro-s são   disponíveis. (generic OR existential readings)
         fireman-PL be.PRS.3PL available.PL
         'Firemen in general are available.' OR 'Some firemen are available.'
      b Bombeiro   é   disponivel. (ONLY generic reading)
         fireman.SG be.PRS.3SG available
         'Firemen in general are available.'
      c Petróleo   é   disponivel. (ONLY generic reading)
         oil.SG   be.PRS.3SG available.
         'Oil is available.'

(21) a João gosta   de cachorro-s. (kind OR specimen readings)
         João like.PRS.3SG of dog-PL
         'João likes dogs in general.' OR 'João likes some individual dogs.'
      b João   gosta   de   cachorro (kind/#specimen)
         João   like.PRS.3SG of   dog.SG
         'João likes dogs in general.'
      c João   gosta   de   suco. (kind/#specimen)
         João   like.PRS.3SG of   juice.SG
         'João likes juice in general.'

Bare singulars and mass nouns have only kind interpretations with kind-level predicates as in (22a,b), while bare plurals can also denote pluralities of subkinds (22c):

(22) a Baleia   está   em   extinção.
         whale.SG be.PRS.3SG in   extinction
         'Whales (as a kind) are on the verge of extinction.'
      b Petróleo é   abundante.
         oil.SG   be.PRS.3SG abundant
         'Oil is abundant.'

---

[5] (19b) is also grammatical in European Portuguese. There is a real contrast between English and Portuguese in this respect. (i) is unequivocally ungrammatical in English:

(i)   #Furniture from Ikea fits into each other.

c Baleia-s   estão   em extinção.
   whale-PL be.PRS.3PL in   extinction
   'Whales (in general) are / the whale is on the verge of extinction.'
   OR
   'Some kinds of whales are on the verge of extinction.'

Further constructions showing that bare singulars pattern like mass
nouns are discussed in Pires de Oliveira & Rothstein (2011).

All count nouns have a bare singular counterpart in Brazilian
Portuguese. If these bare singulars are mass nouns, then all count
nouns in Brazilian Portuguese are part of a flexible pair, comparable
to *stone/stone(s)* in English, with the so-called 'bare singular' as the mass
partner. As the data in (17) show, these mass nouns must be object
mass nouns, since distributive predicates distribute to the individuals
in their denotations. This correctly predicts that comparison in terms
of cardinality is possible. As in English, though, there is a crucial
contrast between object mass nouns and count nouns. Count nouns
force a comparative evaluation in terms of cardinality, while the
mass counterpart **allows** it but does not force it. Consider the data
in (23):

(23) a João tem **mais livro-s** que a   Maria. (cardinal[ok], volume#)
         João has more book-PL than the Maria
         'João has more books than Maria.'
      b João tem **mais livro**   que a   Maria. (cardinal[ok], volume[ok])
         João has more book.SG than the Maria
         'João has more book than Maria.'

(23a) only compares cardinalities and is true only if João has
a greater number of individual books than Maria, while (23b) can
be used either to assert that João has a greater number of individual
books than Mary, or that he has a greater volume or weight of
book(s) than she has (though fewer books). Quantifiers such as
quanto/quantos 'how much / how many', *muito/muitos* 'much/many',
show the same pattern. *Quantos* and *muitos* (which have plural morphology) take count noun complements and allow quantity evaluations only in terms of cardinality, while *quanto* and *muito* take mass
noun complements and allow either a cardinal or a volume reading.
(24a) needs a cardinal number as an answer, while (24b) can be
answered either by a cardinal like *two hundred* or a measure phrase
like *two shelvesful*. Formulating the question using the mass form is
slightly more appropriate if an approximate answer is required,
a point we will return to in Section 5.4.

(24) a **Quanto-s**   **livro-s** ele comprou? (Pires deOliveira &
                                        Rothstein 2011: (52b))
       what.quantity-PL book-PL he buy. PST.PFV.3SG
       'How many books did he buy?'
  b **Quanto**   **livro**   você comprou?
       what.quantity book.SG you   buy.PST.PFV.3SG
       'What quantity of books did you buy?'

(25) a João tem   **muito-s livro(-s)**. (cardinal^{ok}, volume#)
       João have.PRES.3SG a-lot-PL book(-PL)
       'John has many books.'
  b João tem   **muito**   **livro**. (cardinal^{ok}, volume^{ok})
       João have.PRES.3SG a-lot.SG book.SG
       'João has a lot of books / a large quantity of book-stuff.'

(25a) shows that this semantic contrast holds even when plural morphology is dropped from a count noun so that the count/mass contrast is marked only on the quantifier, as happens in some dialects of Brazilian Portuguese. (26) is a nice additional example from Pires de Oliveira & Rothstein (2011).

(26) a Essa   lata tem   **mais minhoca**   do   que
       this   can have.PRS.3SG more earthworm.SG of.the than
       aquela. (Pires de Oliveira & Rothstein 2011: 62)
       that-one
       'This can contains a bigger quantity of earthworm than that one.'
  b Não esse   tem   10 e   aquele tem
       no, this   have.PRS.3SG 10 and that   have.PRS.3SG
       12 **minhoca-s**.
       12 earthworm-PL
       'No, this can has 10, and the other one has 12 earthworms.'
  c Mas   esse   pesa   mais.
       but   this   weigh.PRS.3SG more
       'But this one (i.e. this can) weighs more.'

Crucially, these pairs differ from English flexible pairs like *stone/ stone(s)*. As we saw in (5) above, and as Barner & Snedeker showed, in English the mass item in a flexible pair behaves like a substance mass noun, and is compared in terms of a continuous non-cardinal dimension. Three large stones count as 'more stone' (though fewer stones) than fifteen very small stones. It seems impossible to answer (5b) *Which garden has more stone in it?* by comparing which garden has more individual stones in it. This contrasts with (27), where the mass noun *pedra* allows either a cardinal or a non-cardinal evaluation, while the plural count noun *pedras* allows only comparison in terms of number of units.

(27) a Esse jardim tem   mais pedra/   pedra-s do
         this garden have.PRS.3SG more stone.SG/ stone-PL of.the
         que aquele.
         that that-one
         'This garden has more stone/stones than the other one.'
      b João tem   mais corda/corda-s   que Pedro.
         João have.PRS.3SG more rope.SG/rope-PL that Pedro
         'João has more rope/ropes than Pedro has.'

We will return to these data below. Summing up the data in this
section, we see that Brazilian Portuguese is a language in which all
count nouns are part of a flexible pair, since all count nouns have
mass counterparts. Object mass nouns, whether or not they are part of
a flexible pair, consistently allow both cardinal and non-cardinal
quantity evaluations, like object mass nouns in English. In contrast,
count nouns force a cardinal interpretation.

5.2.2 Hungarian

A similar pattern holds in Hungarian. Hungarian has two quantity
question words, *hány*, the equivalent of 'how many', and *mennyi*,
roughly equal to 'how much'. Hungarian nouns do not pluralize in
agreement with numericals or quantity expressions, and thus both
hány and *mennyi* are followed by singular nouns, but with a difference
in interpretation. *Mennyi* naturally appears with substance nouns and
requires a non-cardinal answer, as in (28). *Hány* requires a cardinal
answer and appears with count nouns, or imposes a packaging interpretation on mass nouns, as in (29). Crucially, in (29), when the question is asked with *hány*, the answer cannot include the measure
suffix *-nyi*, in contrast to (28.ii).

(28) Mennyi   rizs-et   vettél?
      how.much   rice-ACC   buy.PAST.2.SG
      'How much rice did you buy?

      i   Három   #(kiló-t).   ii Három   zacskó   (-nyi)-t.
          three   kilo-ACC   three   bag   (-NYI)-ACC
          'Three kilos.'   'Three bags(ful).'

(29) a Hány   könyv   van   a   táská-d-ban?
         how.many   book   is.3SG the bag-YOUR-in
         'How many books are there in your bag?'

      (i) Csak   hárrom.   (ii) #Három   kilo-t.
           only   three   three   kilo-ACC
           'Only three.'   'Three kilos.'
      b Hány   rizs-et   vettél?
         how.many   rice.ACC   buy.PAST.2.SG

    (i)   #Három kilo-t.   (ii)   Három zacskó (#-nyi)-t.
         three   kilo-ACC   three   bag   (#-NYI)-ACC
         'Three kilos.'   'Three bags.'

Mennyi as well as *hány* occurs with nouns like *könyv*, and (30) occurs alongside (29a).

(30)   Mennyi   könyv-et   tudsz   cipelni?
        how.much   book.SG-ACC able.2.SG to carry
        'What quantity of books are you able to carry?'

However, there is a difference of interpretation. While *hány* forces an answer in terms of cardinality, *mennyi* does not impose a dimension for the quantity statement, and can be answered in terms of cardinality (as in 31a) or in terms of a non-cardinal measure dimension (as in 31b).

(31)   a Hárma-t.   b   Három kilo-t.
        three-ACC   three kilo-ACC
        'Three.'   'Three kilos.'

The parallel between these data and the Brazilian Portuguese examples is striking. Again, we have one quantity evaluation operation which forces cardinal comparisons, and a quantity evaluation operation which leaves the dimension of comparison to be contextually determined. It allows, but does not force, cardinal comparison. The data suggest that *hány* takes a count predicate as complement, while *mennyi* takes a mass complement.

It has been argued in a number of places that *könyv* in (30) is a mass noun. Schvarcz & Rothstein (in press) argue that *könyv* is ambiguous between a mass and a count reading, and that count nouns in Hungarian, like those in Brazilian Portugese, are flexible. I will argue for this explicitly in Chapter 6.

Csirmaz & Dékány (2014) offer a different analysis, suggesting that *könyv* is always mass, and that in apparent count contexts it is under the scope of a null sortal classifier. For the moment, the differences between the analyses are not important. What is important is that *könyv* has a possible non-count, i.e. mass, denotation in which it denotes sets of individuable objects and allows quantity evaluations to be cardinal or continuous depending on context.

This means we can draw the following generalizations:

(i) Count nouns force quantity evaluations in terms of cardinalities.

(ii) Object mass nouns (or naturally atomic mass nouns) allow both cardinal and non-cardinal evaluations depending on context.

They must, therefore, have a different semantic interpretation from count nouns.

(iii) In Hungarian and Brazilian Portuguese, the object mass nouns allow both cardinal and non-cardinal comparisons, just like any other object mass noun.

These data are strong evidence against Bale & Barner's hypothesis that object mass nouns and count nouns have the same denotations. They further suggest that the lack of cardinal readings in examples like (5b) *Which garden has more stone in it?* is an accidental property of English. Count nouns crosslinguistically encode semantic atomicity, and systematically privilege cardinal interpretations of *Who has more N_{count}?* In contrast, *Who has more N_{mass}?* leaves the parameter of comparison to be contextually determined. When a mass noun is naturally atomic, cardinality is one of a number of possible dimensions of comparison. The data from Hungarian and Brazilian Portuguese suggest that mass and count nouns offer different perspectives on the entities they denote, rather than reflecting some ontological difference in denotation.

A possible explanation for the lack of cardinal readings in English flexible mass nouns, as in 'Who has more stone?' (see also (5b)), is pragmatically based. In Hungarian and Brazilian Portuguese, all count nouns have a mass counterpart but not all mass nouns have a count counterpart, and this means that mass nouns are the default form and are always available. Choosing to use a count form when one is available means privileging a count interpretation, while using the default mass noun means leaving all dimensions of interpretation open. In English, flexible pairs are unusual, and mass is not the default case. This means that, while the choice of the count form privileges the count interpretation, the choice of the mass form equally privileges the non-count interpretation, and strongly encourages a non-cardinal evaluation.

Arguably, even in English the mass forms allow a cardinal interpretation in a heavily weighted context. Suppose that John and Bill are clearing stone from different areas of a field. John has to shift six large pieces of stone, while Bill has to shift about fifty small pieces. In these circumstances, 'Who has more stone to move?' may well get the answer 'Bill', since he has more work to do.

5.3 MEASUREMENT, SCALES AND CARDINALITY

We have seen that, while count nouns require comparisons in terms of cardinality, object mass nouns allow comparisons in terms of cardinality but do not force it. We now need to explain how, in sentences like (32), we can compare mass objects in terms of cardinality when we cannot count them.

(32)   John has more furniture than Mary.

If Mary has more books than John it is easy to show this. *Book* is a count noun at type $<e \times k,t>$, and so the sums of books that Mary and John have can each be assigned a cardinal property, and the relation between the two cardinal numbers can be calculated. This is not an option in evaluating (32) since entities in the denotation of *furniture* do not have cardinal properties. It is always possible to **check** the truth of (32) by counting, treating *furniture* as *pieces of furniture*, but we still need some way of **representing** its truth conditions without making reference to cardinal properties that only count noun denotations can have.

An important point to remember is that counting is an enumeration operation, and inherently linguistic. Atomic entities to be counted are put in one-to-one correspondence with the natural numbers, and in the process a list of numbers is enumerated. Each atomic entity is given a temporary label, a number, indicating its place in the counting sequence.[6] Counting, in this sense, is an operation akin to naming, since objects are associated with a (temporary) label. Cardinal comparison doesn't necessarily require counting. The independence of cardinality judgements and linguistic knowledge has been shown experimentally by experiments that show that cardinality judgements are prelinguistic. Preverbal infants can compare cardinalities successfully (Feigenson, Dehaene & Spelke, 2004), and there has been considerable research on numerosity in animals (see the review in Dehaene 2010). Hyde & Spelke (2011) and Hyde (2011) show that there are two independent cognitive mechanisms for making cardinality judgements, both of which seem to be in place in pre-linguistic infants. Their findings can be summarized roughly as follows. Cardinality comparisons of small collections of objects where the individuals are salient involves parallel individuation, or one-to-one mapping between the objects in the groups. It exploits the subitizing mechanism first described in Kaufman *et al.* (1949). (This is the

---

[6] As we will see below, we can of course give cardinal values to sums without counting, i.e. without going through the enumeration process. But the actual operation of counting is the operation of enumerating numbers and matching them with objects.

mechanism which allows humans (and many animals) to make exact, immediate and confident cardinality judgements about pluralities with a low cardinality.) Cardinal evaluation for larger groups of objects, or groups where the individuals are not salient, involves mechanisms of approximation. Neither system involves the linguistic operation of counting or explicit enumeration. So cardinality judgements must be separated from counting, and the question is: how do we make cardinality judgements and how can we represent them semantically? The first question is a psychological question that I do not discuss, but I shall offer an explicit answer to the second question, i.e. how can we represent the truth conditions for a cardinal interpretation of *A has more furniture than B*?

We have already seen in Chapter 3 that counting and measuring differ in that counting requires access to the atomic parts of a sum, while measuring gives an overall value to a sum on a dimensional scale without reference to its atomic structure. Counting a sum keeps track of how many atoms there are, but measuring a quantity does not require knowing how to count, and does not keep track of atomic parts. It only requires knowing how to match a sum with a single value on a scale.[7,8] I suggest that cardinality judgements without counting involve what is essentially a measure operation. We will now formulate a theory of scales which allows us to be precise about how measuring works, and then show how cardinal comparisons can be represented using the same mechanisms.

Precise measurement involves assigning to a sum an overall value on a dimensional scale calibrated in dimension-appropriate units. We define a scale in the following way:

[7] In principle, one can weigh sums, and write down the measure values of each sum without being able to count. If the scale is an analogue, then one can compare values in terms of their position on the scale without reference to numbers at all. For example, with a mercury thermometer on which normal body temperature is marked, it is possible to evaluate roughly how high someone's fever is by gauging the gap between the height of the mercury and the mark indicating body temperature.

[8] Historically, measuring probably developed as an indirect form of counting. Two stone of flour was measured by placing two standard stones in one pan of a balance and enough flour in the other pan to reach an equilibrium. So giving the weight of the flour involved counting the stones. But, as soon as measuring moved beyond counting individual weights of a uniform size, it had moved beyond indirect counting.

(33) A **scale** $S_{M,U}$ is a partial order $S_{M,U} = <\mathbf{N}. \geq_{M,U} \text{MEASURE}_{M,U} >$
where:
M is a dimension (e.g. volume, weight).
U is the unit of measurement in the relevant dimension, in terms
of which the scale is calibrated (e.g. *litre, kilo*).
N is the set of real numbers, or the positive real numbers, or
a subset of the real numbers, depending on the nature of the
measure and the fine-grainedness of the measurements.

Scales can be open at both ends, one end or neither end.[9]
$\text{MEASURE}_{M,U}$ is a function from objects and world-time indices to
values in **N**.

(34) A **measure predicate** at type <e,t> is a predicate of the form
$\lambda x.\alpha(\text{MEASURE}_{M,U,w,t}(x))$, with α a predicate of numbers,
like $\lambda n.n = 2$
$\lambda n.2 \leq_{M,U} n \leq_{M,U} 4$, etc.
giving measure predicates:
$\lambda x.\text{MEASURE}_{\text{VOLUME,LITRE},w,t}(x) = 2$
$\lambda x.2 \leq_{\text{VOLUME,LITRE}} \text{MEASURE}_{\text{VOLUME,LITRE},w,t} \leq_{\text{VOLUME,LITRE}} 4$, etc.

As an example, assume the scale $S_{\text{VOLUME,LITRE}}$, where N is the set of
positive real numbers. The measure head *litre* (in 35a) denotes
a function that maps a number *n* onto the set of entities (singular or
plural) whose volume measure value in litres (in w,t) is *n*. Applied to
the number 3, it gives the measure predicate (35b), denoting the set of
entities having the volume in litres measure 3. Like any other predicate, it can modify a noun at type <e,t>. Applied to WINE, it gives
(35c), denoting sums of wine which measure three litres, as we saw in
chapter 3.[10]

(35) a ⟦*litre*⟧ = $\lambda n \lambda x.\text{MEASURE}_{\text{VOLUME,LITRE},w,t}(x) = n$
      b ⟦3 *litres*⟧ = $\lambda x.\text{MEASURE}_{\text{VOLUME,LITRE},w,t}(x) = 3$
      c ⟦3 *litres wine*⟧ = $\lambda x.\text{WINE}(x) \wedge \text{MEASURE}_{\text{VOLUME,LITRE},w,t}(x) = 3$

The measure property is a property of sum, but tells us nothing
about its internal or atomic structure. Measurements on some dimensions are monotonic or extensive (Krifka 1989). If a measure function
is extensive, then the measure value of a sum is the arithmetic sum of
the measure values of its non-overlapping parts. Measurement on the
dimension of volume is monotonic since (36) holds, but this holds for
any way in which a quantity is split into two parts, and does not
presuppose any atomic structure.

---

[9] See Kennedy & McNally (1999), Rotstein & Winter (2004).
[10] I assume contextual approximation. See Lasersohn (1999), Krifka (2009).

(36)   If a = b⊔c then: $\text{MEASURE}_{\text{VOLUME,LITRE},w,t}(a) =$
$\text{MEASURE}_{\text{VOLUME,LITRE},w,t}(b\text{-}c) + \text{MEASURE}_{\text{VOLUME,LITRE},w,t}(c\text{-}b) +$
$\text{MEASURE}_{\text{VOLUME,LITRE},w,t}(b\sqcap c)$.

Hence, if a = b⊔c and $\text{MEASURE}_{\text{VOLUME,LITRE},w,t}(a) = 3$, then
$\text{MEASURE}_{\text{VOLUME,LITRE},w,t}(b) = 3 - \text{MEASURE}_{\text{VOLUME,LITRE},w,t}(c\text{-}b)$.

Different unit-types determine different dimensional scales. Scales of volume are calibrated in terms of litres or gallons and so on, while scales of weight are calibrated in terms of units such as kilo and pound. Comparisons of measures compare which quantity is assigned a higher value on the appropriate scale. *John drank more wine than Mary* compares the measure values assigned to the quantities of wine that Mary and John each drank and checks which is higher on the volume scale. In general (37) holds:

(37)   x is more than y (in w,t) if $\text{MEASURE}_{M,U,w,t}(x) >_{M,U} \text{MEASURE}_{M,U,w,t}(y)$

As we saw in Chapter 3, the unit of measure can also be derived contextually from sortal nouns. In *three glasses of wine*, the unit of measure is volume of either a standard or a contextually available glass.[11]

Note that we can make these kinds of comparisons without having precise commensurate measure values for the two quantities by evaluating their relative positions on the scale. If Mary drank a large goblet of wine, and John drank a small shot glass of wine, then we can know that, however the scale is calibrated, the quantity that Mary drank is bigger.

We can now extend the definition of 'scale' to *cardinality scales*. (The semantics of cardinality scales is worked out in detail in Rothstein 2016b.)

(38)   A cardinality scale is an order $S_{CARD,AT} = <\mathbf{N}, \geq_N. \mid \mid_{AT}>$ where CARD stands for cardinality, AT is the context that determines the set of atoms, and $\mid \mid_{AT}$ is the function that maps x onto the cardinality of the set of atomic parts of x that are in AT.

Given context AT, the cardinality measure is constant across world-time indices (excluding science-fiction contexts where sums vary their cardinality across worlds).

We chose the natural numbers here as the value domain, but the scale really represents the progression of the natural numbers. As Wiese (2003) shows, any sequence can be used to model this.

---

[11] 'Add the olive oil (about a coffee-cupful, after-dinner size)' (David 1999: 142).

The calibration is in terms of contextually determined atoms according to AT. The default choice for AT is context k, which selects the domain of semantic atoms. But another natural choice for AT is ATOM, the set of natural atoms. In other circumstances, groups or pairs may be the relevant units chosen by AT instead.

Cardinality scales are used to compare which of two sums has more atomic parts, where the atoms can be natural or semantic. If **x** is more than **y** with respect to the number of its atomic parts, then the value $|\mathbf{x}|_{AT}$ on the cardinality scale is higher than the value of $|\mathbf{y}|_{AT}$ on the same scale.

We don't need to use these scales to compare cardinalities, and in fact counting is a way of not doing so. If we compare how many cats Mary and John each have by counting, and we count to ten in the first case and seven in the second case, then we know that Mary has more cats than John because we know that ten is more than seven. However, cardinal values may be assigned in different ways, and these may use the cardinality scale. Comparisons of object mass nouns provoked by questions such as *Who has more furniture?* encourage cardinal evaluations without counting. There are several ways in which such comparisons can be carried out. With small enough quantities, cardinal comparisons can be made via parallel individuation (Hyde 2011).[12] Indirect calculation of cardinality is possible. When objects are uniform in weight, then a cardinality value for a sum can be obtained by weighing. Banks give cardinality values to sums of coins by weighing them in this way. Indirect calculation is also possible, as in 'There are twenty rows of chairs with fifteen chairs in each row, and the room is full, so there must be about 300 people here tonight.' Covert counting is one method of making these cardinal judgements. There is nothing to stop us evaluating (32) by counting the number of pieces of furniture in the sum that John and Mary each have, mapping the resulting numbers onto a value on the cardinality scale, and comparing these values.

Another natural way of assigning cardinality values is via estimation. Estimation is 'intelligent approximation' or making an 'informed guess'. Estimation can be used with any dimensional scale, but it is particularly useful when dealing with cardinal evaluations of object mass noun denotations which cannot be counted. Estimation of cardinalities is a form of measuring, since a value n is assigned to a sum on a scale $S_{CARD,AT}$ by estimating the

[12] This was presumably the case in the Barner & Snedeker experiments, since their stimuli were well within the subitizing range.

number of its atomic parts, but without counting or enumerating them. Estimated values can be mapped onto values, or onto intervals surrounding a value on a scale, and compared, without precise or explicit numerical values being available. So, *Who has more furniture?* and examples like (32) can be evaluated by assigning approximate positions on a cardinal scale to two quantities of furniture and comparing them, without ever counting the individual pieces of furniture.[13]

Since cardinal comparisons can compare positions on the cardinal scale and need not involve counting, cardinality can be a possible dimension of comparison also with mass nouns. For object mass nouns, which denote sets of individuable entities, the cardinal scale is particularly salient, but it is only one among a number of dimensional options.

The proposal that estimation is connected to cardinal evaluations of mass nouns is supported by some empirical observations. Pires de Oliveira (p.c.) and Schvarcz (p.c.) each point out for Brazilian Portuguese and Hungarian (respectively) that there is a tendency to phrase a question using a count noun if a precise answer is required, while the bare singular mass noun is more appropriate when an approximate answer is suitable. Use of the count noun would make the counting operation salient, while use of the mass noun would make salient evaluation of cardinalities via an alternative operation such as estimation. So, if a question is asked in Hungarian using *hány*, an exact answer is more appropriate than an approximative answer (as in 39a), and if the question is asked using *mennyi*, the converse is the case (as in 39b). Intuitions about the similar examples in Brazilian Portuguese are the same.

(39)   a Hány   könyv   van   a   könyvtárad-ban?
          how.many   book.SG   is   the   library.POSS.2.SG-in
          'How many books are there in your library?'
          Pontosan 5,723 /   ??? körülbelül öt ezer
          'exactly 5,723' /   'approximately 5,000'
       b Mennyi   könyv   van   a   könyvtárad-ban?
          how.much   book   is   the   library.POSS.2.SG-in
          'How much book is there in your library?'
          ???Pontosan 5,723 /   körülbelül öt ezer
          'exactly 5,723' /   'approximately 5,000'

---

[13] As Dan Hyde pointed out to me, cardinal scales are reminiscent of the 'number line' discussed in Dehaene (2010), a spatial representation of the numbers on which we plot relative numerical values. There are obvious differences, in particular Dehaene show that there is evidence that numbers on the number line are not equidistant: distances between numbers decrease as the values get higher. However, both the number line and cardinal scales allow comparisons of values in terms of relative position in a (partial) order.

That estimation can be considered a grammatical measure operation is also supported by some crosslinguistic case studies. We saw in Chapter 3 that measuring and counting may be associated with different grammatical properties. Estimation constructions in Mandarin and Russian both show the grammatical properties displayed by measure constructions in those languages. Large-number estimation is analysed in Li & Rothstein (2012). As we saw in Chapter 3, counting and measuring in Mandarin necessarily involves classifiers.

(40) a sān   gè   xuéshēng
         three $Cl_{general}$ student
         'three students'
      b sān   bang   ròu
         three Cl_{pound} meat
         'three pounds of meat'

Inserting *de* after the classifier forces a measure interpretation, and is not possible with count classifiers (Cheng & Sybesma 1998).

(41) a sān   bàng   de   ròu
         three Cl_{pound} DE   meat
         'three pounds of meat'
      b sān   gè   (#de) xuéshēng
         three $Cl_{general}$ (#DE) student
         'three students'

However, *de* phrases are possible with count classifiers with high round numbers (Tang 2005; Hsieh 2008) and with approximative interpretations. The examples in (42) are from the PKU Corpus, cited in Hsieh (2008):

(42) a míngtiān de   huódòng xūyào yì   bǎi   zhāng
         tomorrow MOD   activity need   one hundred Cl_{piece}
         de   fànzuōzi.
         DE   square table
         'Tomorrow's activity needs one hundred square tables.'
      b nàbiān   zhòng le qī bā kē,   shí lái   kē
         there.then plant PFV seven eight Cl_{plant}, ten around Cl_{plant}
         de   júzi   shù.
         DE   mandarin tree
         'On that side were planted seven or eight, or around ten mandarin trees.'

Li & Rothstein (2012) argue that these constructions are estimations. If estimation is a form of measuring, then the felicity of *de* is explained. *De* is infelicitous with exact figures, which can be acquired only by counting and not by estimation.

(43) a #wǒmen xūyào yì bǎi-   líng bā   zhāng de fànzuōzi.
         we   need one hundred zero eight Cl$_{piece}$ DE square-table
         Intended reading: 'We need one hundred and eight square tables.'
      b #yì-nián zhòngzhí le   yì   bǎi   sān-shí qī
         one-year plant   PFV   one hundred thirty   seven
         kē   de   shùmù.
         Cl$_{plant}$ DE   tree
         Intendend reading: 'They planted one hundred and thirty-seven trees a year.'

Russian Approximate Inversion constructions are a second estimation construction displaying the grammatical properties of measuring. A number of linguists (Mel'čuk 1985; Franks 1995; and others) have shown that inverting a numeral and a noun in Russian has an approximative effect:

(44) a Ivan   pročital dvadcat' knig.
         Ivan   read   twenty   books
         'Ivan read twenty books.'
      b Ivan   pročital knig   dvadcat'.
         Ivan   read   books   twenty
         'Ivan read about/approximately twenty books.'

Khrizman & Rothstein (2015) show that the properties ascribed to these approximative constructions are all properties associated with measure constructions. Approximate Inversion phrases take singular agreement (Franks 1995):

(45) rabotalo/?# rabotali v etom magazine čelovek pjat'.
      work.SG/work.PL   in this store   people five
      'About five people worked in this store.'

They cannot be modified by individuating 'which' relative clauses, but only by 'that' clauses (Yadroff & Billings 1998), naturally associated with non-individuating amount relatives (Carlson 1977):

(46) knig   pjat',   *čto/#kotorye*   my kupili   včera
      book.PL   five   that/#which.PL   we bought   yesterday
      'approximately five books *that/#which* we bought yesterday'

They are also degraded in contexts which require individuation, for example they do not provide antecedents for distributive adverbials (Franks 1995):

(47)   studentov pjat' #pomogalo drug drugu / #pomogali drug drugu.
       students five helped.SG each other / helped.PL each other
       Intended reading: 'About five students helped each other.'

Khrizman & Rothstein (2015) argue on the basis of this and additional data that the approximation is a form of measurement, and they provide an appropriate compositional semantic analysis.

Approximation is a very wide phenomenon, and is not restricted to the mass domain, nor is it necessarily a measure operation. Approximative count values are expressed using *approximately n, about n*, and they may also be expressed modally as in *There must be three hundred people here*. These values may be assigned in different ways, including modal approximation (Zaroukian 2011), mistaken counting ('I counted, but I lost count / may have counted some people twice'), indirect calculation. There are also explicit approximative classifiers like *hundreds of cats*, discussed in Chapter 2, which give very approximate values by specifying a wide range within which the cardinal value will fall. So I am not suggesting that all approximation is measuring, and indeed each approximation method needs to be analysed independently, to see what it actually consists of. But there is reason to believe that some methods of approximating cardinalities involve what are technically measure operations, and not counting.

5.4   COUNT VS MASS / COUNTING VS MEASURING

Let us sum up where we are. Counting and measuring are two different operations. Measuring is assigning a quantity a value on a dimensional scale, where the choice of dimensional scale is determined by context. Counting is putting the atomic parts of a plural entity into one-to-one correspondence with the natural numbers. It is essentially a linguistic operation since it involves enumerating numericals. Cardinal predicates express counting values, properties of pluralities with a particular number of atomic parts. They can only be predicated of count nouns. However, a cardinal scale with dimension AT allows us to measure and compare in cardinalities, without necessarily counting them.

Comparisons of quantities are always dependent on choice of parameter of evaluation. Cardinality is one possible choice.

In the count domain, quantity comparisons are always in terms of cardinality, since the semantically encoded atomic structure of the predicate makes this the only parameter of evaluation available. Comparisons may be direct. If Mary has six books and John has four books, then Mary has (two) more because six is greater than four, and no other argumentation is necessary. But *Who has more books?* may still be answered without arithmetical calculation, by plotting relative values on the cardinality scale.

In the mass domain, things are more complicated. Choice of dimension for measurement and comparison is context-dependent, for example flour can measured in terms of weight (grams, kilos) or volume (cups). For object mass nouns, atomicity is one of a number of possible dimensions. It may be the most salient dimension in neutral contexts, but contexts can be manipulated. Since object mass noun denotations cannot have cardinal properties, counting is impossible and measure values must be mapped onto a cardinality scale, and compared in terms of their position on the scale. This difference explains the data in (48).

(48)   a John has more tables than Bill has books.
       b ??John has more tables than Bill has furniture.
       c Bill has more books than John has furniture.

Two sums in the count domain are compared directly in terms of their cardinalities. (48a) is true if John has ten tables and Bill has nine books. (48b) is much less felicitous, even though the predicates being compared are more naturally comparable, since *furniture* is not a count noun. Counting furniture is not possible, so in order to compare them, both the mass noun denotation and the count noun denotation need to be mapped onto some relevant scale so that their scalar values can be compared. It could be a cardinality scale, but we could also use (48b) to assert that John's tables take up more space than Bill's furniture, in which case the scale is one of volume. (48c) raises the same problem and is more naturally evaluated on a scale of volume for pragmatic reasons. This implies that the count noun in (48b,c) is being treated as a mass noun, an issue we will now address directly.

We can also draw some conclusions about the count/mass distinction. We have seen that counting is an operation associated with count nouns, and measuring is associated with mass nouns. Even when cardinality judgements are made about object mass noun denotations, counting is not involved, and scalar mechanisms familiar from measuring contexts are used.

We can formulate the following generalization:

(49)   a Counting is an operation on count noun denotations.
       b Measuring is an operation on mass noun denotations.

As we have seen, mass nouns cannot be counted, but only measured. But can count denotations be measured? The weak version of the generalization in (49) would allow that only count nouns are countable, but that all nouns are measurable. The strong version of (49) is that only count nouns are countable and only mass nouns are measurable. The contrast between object mass nouns and count nouns with respect to cardinality judgments supports the weak version, but does not say anything about the strong version.

The evidence for or against the strong version of (49) depends on the account one gives of examples such as (50), where plural count nouns appear with measure predicates. (50) provides *prima facie* evidence that count noun denotations can be measured.

(50) a five kilos of books
      b three hundred grams of lentils

However, Rothstein (2011) argues that there is good reason to accept the strong version of (49), which would mean that *books* and *lentils* in (50) are being interpreted as mass nouns. There is some evidence to support the claim. Note first that only bare NPs can be modified by measure predicates, as (51) shows:

(51) #five kilos of three books

While (50a) denotes sums of books that weigh five kilos, (51) cannot be used to denote sums of three books which weigh five kilos, although there is nothing in principle to block a plurality being in the intersection of the denotation of *three, five kilos* and *books*. But if *three books* is a count noun phrase and *five kilos* requires a mass complement, then the infelicity of (51) is explained.

Second, Rothstein (2011) notes that plural count nouns lose their 'count' properties when modified by measure predicates. (52a) shows that *books*, under the scope of a measure predicate, cannot be the antecedent for the reciprocal. (52b,c) show that bare plurals modified by measure phrases take mass quantifiers *much* and *little* instead of count quantifiers.

(52) a #Twenty kilos of books are lying on top of each other on the floor.
                                  (Rothstein 2011: (45))

      b I haven't read much/#many of the twenty kilos of books that we sent.
                                  (Rothstein 2011: (41))

      c A little of the twenty kilos of oranges that we picked satisfied our appetite.

These data suggest that a bare plural under the scope of a measure predicate is an object mass noun.

Rothstein (2011) shows that the operation of shifting a bare plural count noun N_k back to a mass reading is very simple. The set $\langle e \times k, t \rangle$ needs to drop its k index and return to type $\langle e,t \rangle$. The operation which does this is (53):

(53) $\text{SHIFT}(N_k) = \pi_1(N_k) = \{x: x \in \pi_1(N_{\langle e \times k,\ t \rangle})\}$

The plural count noun *books* at type $\langle e \times k, t \rangle$ denotes a set of ordered pairs, whose first element is a plurality of books, and whose second element is the contextual index k. SHIFT takes this back into an object mass noun at type $\langle e,t \rangle$ by collecting all the pluralities from the ordered pairs, i.e. $\pi_1(\text{BOOKS}_k)$, and forming them into a set. The resulting predicate is of the same type as $\text{BOOK}_{\text{root}}$, but not necessarily identical to it,[14] since it is derived from the count noun BOOK_k, itself a subset of $\text{BOOK}_{\text{root}}$. This is shown clearly in (54). *Fifty kilos of carpets* denotes a set of sums of carpets that are in the intersection of $\text{CARPET}_{\text{root}} \cap k$ closed under sum, and FIFTY KILOS.

(54)   *fifty kilos of carpets*:
        $\lambda x.x \in \pi_1(^*\text{CARPET}_{\langle e \times k,\ t \rangle}) \wedge \text{MEASURE}_{\text{WEIGHT, KILO, w,t}}(x) = 50$

In (54), by hypothesis, the bare plural *carpets* is a mass N at type $\langle e,t \rangle$, derived from the count noun by the operation in (53). Since it is derived from $^*\text{CARPET}_k$, it will include in its denotation only pluralities of entities that originally made it into the denotation of the singular count noun CARPET_k, i.e. CARPET $\cap$ k. It will not necessarily be identical to the root noun $\text{CARPET}_{\text{root}}$ whose denotation is presumably identical to the mass nouns *carpeting*.

There is thus good reason to assume the strong version of (49), at least tentatively.

To sum up, we have come to the following conclusions. No matter what your theory of count and mass nouns is, it must be able to capture the generalization that count nouns have denotations which can be counted (but quite possibly not measured), and mass nouns have denotations which can be measured but not counted. Object mass nouns are distinct from count nouns, and must be given different kinds of interpretations. Not all cardinality judgements involve counting, and dimensional scales must include cardinality scales.

---

[14] In fact it is identical to the set of instantiations of the plural kind $^{\cup\cap}\lambda x.\text{BOOKS}(x)$ in Chierchia (1998a).

5.5 QUESTIONS FOR FURTHER DISCUSSION AND INVESTIGATION

1 As usual, investigate quantity comparisons in whatever language you have access to. Explore what dimensions are relevant for comparing quantities, and what contextual factors play a role in determining parameters of evaluation. How are object mass nouns compared?

2 What different ways of expressing approximation are there?

3 Flexible nouns seem to vary between truly flexible nouns like *stone/ stone(s)*, where the mass and count nouns present the same entities from different perspectives, to pairs like *brick/brick(s)* where the count noun includes in its denotation only very specific units of N_{mass} – in this case, units of brick which have a uniform shape and conform to standard specifications. Consider what nouns are truly flexible, and which are not. What principles of individuation are used in the second case? What role does: (i) natural atomicity, and (ii) the concept of artefact, play in this?

4 How might semantic atoms be individuated for abstract nouns? For example, *advice* and *information* are mass in English but count in Modern Hebrew.

5 There is almost no discussion in the literature on abstract count nouns (an exception is Grimm 2014, 2015). What might they denote? How are abstract nouns compared in terms of quantity?

6 A Crosslinguistic Perspective

'There are more things in heaven and earth, Horatio / Than are dreamt of in your philosophy.'

William Shakespeare, *Hamlet* 1.5

6.1 INTRODUCTION

The theme throughout this book has been that differences between counting and measuring are expressed in many aspects of grammar: in the interpretation of numericals, in the syntax of classifiers, in the nominal system and in comparatives. At the end of the last chapter, I suggested that there is a close connection between the count/mass distinction on the one hand and the counting/measuring distinction on the other. Count noun denotations are countable, while mass noun denotations are not countable but are measurable. What I will do in this chapter is consider how counting and measuring are expressed in a number of languages in which the mass/count distinction is either not realized, or realized very differently from in English. I want to show two things: first, there is a great deal of variation in the ways in which mass and count are expressed crosslinguistically, and second, there is a startling similarity among the languages we will discuss in the grammatical properties characterizing counting and measuring expressions (as was already suggested at the end of Chapter 3). In particular, measure heads (i.e. measure classifiers) are of type <n,<e,t>> and combine with a numerical at type n to form a measure predicate. In contrast, individuating classifiers, as well as other classifiers which allow counting, combine with N to form a predicate expression.

I will begin by reviewing some of the literature on crosslinguistic variation, and then present case studies of three different languages, Mandarin, Hungarian and Yudja.

There is considerable literature discussing potential universal generalizations about counting. Implicational relations were proposed by Greenberg (1974), who suggested a universal implicational relation between numeral classifiers and the lack of obligatory plural marking. Recently, the tendency has been to propose universal parameters rather than universal patterns. Two different influential proposals were made by Chierchia (1998b) and Chierchia (2010), each of which suggests a different way in which languages can be grouped typologically with respect to their strategies for expressing counting. Both proposals group languages into three different types.

Chierchia (1998b) proposed a parametric account of variation in the mass/count distinction, based on Carlson's (1977) proposal that nouns can be predicates at type <e,t>, denoting a set of entities, or arguments at type e denoting kinds. If N is an argument, then it can fill an argument position, while if it is a predicate, it must combine with a determiner to reach the type of arguments. Chierchia suggests that languages differ as to whether nouns are predicates or arguments. The two features [±predicate] and [±argument] predict three different language types: [+predicate, +argument], [–predicate,+argument], and [+predicate,–argument]. (The [-, -] assignment is impossible since languages must have nouns which appear in at least one way.) English is a [+predicate, +argument] language, Mandarin is [–predicate,+argument], while French is [+predicate,–argument]. Chierchia (1998b) hypothesizes that all languages fall into one of these patterns. He argues that a particular feature assignment necessarily entails a family of morphosyntactic properties.

English is a [+predicate,+argument] language. Nouns are either [+predicate] or [+argument]. Count nouns are predicates, and must combine with determiners to fill an argument position, thus bare singular count nouns are predicted to be ungrammatical (as in 1a). Mass nouns are arguments and can be used as bare singular terms in argument position (as in 1b). Shift operations between argument and predicate are allowed under appropriate conditions to cover the range of empirical facts.

(1)   a   I saw #(a) dog.
        b   I bought wine.

Classifier languages, such as Mandarin, are [–predicate,+argument] languages, since all bare singular nouns can occur as arguments (as in 2).

(2)   a wǒ   kànjiàn   gǒu   le.
         I   see   dog   PART
         'I saw a dog/dogs, the dog(s).'
      b wǒ   mǎi   le   jiǔ.
         I   buy   PFV wine
         'I bought wine.'

Along with allowing all nouns as bare singulars, Mandarin will not
allow cardinal predicates to modify nouns directly, and numericals
will take classifier+N sequences instead of bare nouns as
complements.

(3)   a sān   #(zhī)   gǒu
         three Cl$_{small\ animal}$ dog
         'three dogs'
      b liǎng #(kē)   shù
         two   Cl$_{plant}$ tree
         'two trees'

These languages will also lack nominal pluralization,[1] since the
plural operator does not apply to mass or kind terms. The bare noun
will have a general number interpretation which includes the plural
as in (2a). In a classifier language, there is no obvious way to distinguish count nouns and mass nouns grammatically, since all nouns
have the same properties.

Chierchia's hypothesis that bare nouns in Mandarin denote kinds is
supported by arguments in R. Yang (2001), X. P. Li (2011, 2013) and He
& Jiang (2011), who show that bare nouns in Mandarin have the
properties that Carlson (1977) claimed were characteristic of kind-
denoting terms, including the fact that they induce narrow scope
existential readings.

French, as a [+predicative,−argument] language, has complementary properties. There will be a count/mass distinction, count nouns
will be marked for singular and plural, and all nouns, count and mass,
will occur with determiners, as shown in (4).

(4)   a J'ai   vu   #(un) chien.
         I AUX saw   a   dog
         'I saw a dog.'
      b J'ai   acheté #(du) vin.
         I AUX bought some wine
         'I bought (some) wine.'

---

[1] There is a suffix -men which applies only to pronouns and [+animate] nouns, and
which has a much more restricted semantic interpretation that the general plural
operation.

Since English is [+predicate,+argument], count nouns will behave roughly like nouns in French, while mass nouns will have some properties in common with Mandarin nouns, as illustrated in (1) above.

Chierchia hypothesizes that, despite much surface variation, languages should fit into one of these three patterns.

However, research has shown that crosslinguistic variation is very wide. Wilhelm (2008) shows that Dëne Sųłiné, a North Athabaskan language spoken in Northwest Canada by the Chipewyan people, has a mass/count distinction, since some, but not all, nouns can be directly modified by a numeral, as in (5):

(5)   a sôlághe dzóa
          five   ball
          'five balls'
     b #sôlághe thay
          five   sand

However, Dëne Sųłiné has no other property associated with the mass/count distinction. It allows bare nouns, and does not mark pluralization in any way. Müller, Storto & Tiago (2006) and Doron & Müller (2013) have shown the same for Karitiana. Schmitt & Munn (2002) show that Brazilian Portuguese allows bare singular count nouns, and Pires de Oliveira & Rothstein (2011) that these bare singulars are really mass nouns (see Chapter 5), showing that some individual nouns can be both predicates and arguments, which Chierchia's system predicts to be impossible.

Furthermore, systems of pluralization show a great deal of variation. A number of languages, including Turkish, Armenian and Hungarian, have a mass/count distinction and morphological singular/plural distinction, but do not mark nouns modified by cardinals as plural. (6) is an example from Turkish:

(6)   a çocuk b çocuk-lar c iki çocuk
          boy   boy–PL   two boy
          'boy'   'boys'   'two boys'

Furthermore, in Turkish, as in many other languages, plural morphology appears on mass nouns, with a variety of interpretations, including the so-called 'plural of abundance'. Other languages which allow plural marking on mass nouns include Greek (Tsoulas 2006; Alexiadou 2011), Persian (Ghaniabadi 2012), Modern Hebrew (Epstein-Naveh 2015).

Other variations on the system of pluralization can be found in indigenous languages of Canada, including, for example,

Halkomelem Salish (Mithun 1988; Wiltschko 2008) and Ojibwe (Mathieu 2012).

Chierchia (2010), which we discussed in Chapter 4, rejects the feature-based account from his (1998b) paper and proposes a different categorization of languages. Starting from the assumption that the mass/count distinction is cognitively based, he assumes that it must be expressed in all languages. He proposes three general language groups: classifier languages such as Mandarin, where the mass/count distinction shows up at the classifier level; number marking languages such as English, where it shows up at the nominal level and is marked through morphology, in particular pluralization; and languages such as *Dëne Sųłiné*, where there is a mass/count contrast at the nominal level, but where all nouns are bare.

This categorization of language types is much more general, and allows for more variation. Nonetheless, it still implies a level of generalization which misses a lot of variation. For example, Western Armenian and Hungarian allow both number marking and classifiers, although not in the same nominal phrase. The examples in (7) (from Bale & Khanjian 2008) show the data from Western Armenian. The Hungarian data will be discussed in Section 6.3.

(7)   a shenk-me   desa-r
          building-INDEF.SG   saw-2.SG
          'You saw a building.'
    b shenk-er   desa-r
          building-PL   saw-2.SG
          'You saw some buildings.'
    c yergu had shenk
          two   Cl   building
          'two buildings'
    d #yergu had shenk-er
          two   Cl   building-PL

Lima (2010, 2012, 2014) has shown that Yudja has apparently no mass/count distinction at all, and that all mass nouns can be modified by cardinal numbers. As we will see later in the chapter, *txabïu y'a* 'three water' refers to three individuable portions of water, with the criterion of individuation clearly context-dependent.

Further examples of crosslinguistic variation are to be found in Doetjes (2012), Corbett (2000), Aikhenvald (2003), Bisang (2012) and many others. Aikhenvald (2003) shows that there are classifier languages in which obligatory number marking exists, including some South Dravidian languages and some Algonquin languages. Bisang

(2012) discusses Ejagham, described in Watters (1981), which has both numeral classifiers and obligatory singular/plural marking.

My goal in giving this very brief and partial overview was to show how wide the variation in the expression of counting and measuring actually is, and how difficult any attempt to parameterize will be. What I propose to do in the rest of this chapter is to approach the issue of variation from a different direction, and discuss in some depth the ways in which three typologically unrelated languages express counting and measuring, and see how they fit into the picture that we have built up in the previous five chapters. I hope that focusing on the count/measure contrast will help some order emerge from the data that we will consider. We will look in turn at Mandarin, Hungarian and Yudja.

6.2 MANDARIN – A CLASSIFIER LANGUAGE

In Mandarin, no N can be directly modified by a numeral, and in that sense Mandarin clearly has no count/mass distinction. Instead, a numeral classifier must come between the numeral and the N (8a–c). Container classifiers (8d) and measure heads (8e) occur in the same position.

(8) a sān   #(zhī)   gǒu   (= (3a))
        three   Cl$_{\text{small animal}}$ dog
        'three dogs'
     b liǎng   #(kē)   shù   (=(3b))
        two   Cl$_{\text{plant}}$ tree
        'two trees'
     c sān   #(gè)   rén
        three   Cl$_{\text{general}}$ rén
        'three people'
     d sān   #(píng)   jiǔ
        three   Cl$_{\text{bottle}}$ wine
        'three bottles of wine'
     e sān   #(jīn)   mǐ
        three   Cl$_{\text{pound}}$ rice
        'three pounds of rice'

Numeral classifiers name or identify the unit in which instances of N appear. Lyons (1977) writes that this type of classifier 'individuates whatever it refers to in terms of the kind of entity that it is' (p. 463). Lyons calls these 'sortal' classifiers; we will call them either sortals or individuating classifiers. Among the many sortal classifiers available, *zhī* is the classifier used with small animals, *kē* is used with plants.

The general default classifier is *gè*, which is used with naturally atomic predicates if no more specialized classifier is lexically specified.

These classifiers contrast with container classifiers such as *píng* in (8d), which imposes a unit structure on a substance, and measure classifiers such as *jīn* in (8e), which denote a measure unit.

Some, but not all, classifiers may be derived from nouns. For example, *píng* as a noun means 'bottle' and *kuāng* as a noun means 'basket'. However, the classifier and the noun uses are distinct. When used as nouns, these items need to be preceded by a different classifier in order to be counted (examples from Li 2013).

(9) a yì   píng   shuǐ   a′ yí   gè   píng[2]
        one   Cl_bottle   water   one   Cl_general   bottle
        'one bottle of water'   'one bottle'
     b yì   kuāng   píngguǒ   b′ yí   gè   kuāng
        one   Cl_basket   apple   one   Cl_general   basket
        'one basket of apples'   'one basket'

Nouns do not always occur with classifiers. As shown in (2), bare nouns can occur freely, they can denote single entities or pluralities of entities, depending on context and position in the sentence, and they can be interpreted as definite or indefinite (Li & Bisang 2012).

Yang (2001) and Li (2013) both argue that bare nouns in Mandarin denote kinds, which, in the appropriate context, can shift to a predicate interpretation denoting the set of instantiations of the kind. These data lead to the apparent conclusion that there is no mass/count distinction in Mandarin.

However, many linguists have suggested that, despite surface appearances, the mass/count distinction is present in Mandarin. Chierchia (2010) argues that, since the mass/count distinction is an expression of our perceptual relation to the world, it should be expressed crosslinguistically, and the apparent parallels between classifier phrases headed by sortal classifiers on the one hand and count nouns on the other gives grammatical support to the claim.

The most detailed syntactic account of this approach is in Cheng & Sybesma (1998, 1999, 2012) and Cheng (2012). These papers follow Tai & Wang (1990) and Croft (1994), and argue that Mandarin classifiers (in fact, Chinese classifiers in general) can be divided into two groups, classifiers and massifiers, roughly following Lyons' (1977) division of classifiers into sortal and mensural.

---

[2] In some dialects, in particular the Beijing dialect of Mandarin, *píng* can only be used as a noun when the nominalizer *-zi* is affixed to it.

A classifier, or count-classifier, names the unit structure of individuals, while a massifier imposes a structure on the denotation of a noun. Cheng & Sybsema (1998) write: 'massifiers create a measure for counting, count-classifiers simply name the unit in which the entity denoted by the noun it precedes naturally presents itself'(p. 4).

The classifiers in (8a–c) are count-classifiers, indicating respectively units of small animals and plants, and a general unspecified 'natural object'. Other classifiers make reference to the shape of the individuated entity, like *tiáo*, the word for 'tail', which is used as a classifier for long, thin objects. Massifiers, in constrast, package or create units, bottle-units in (8d) and pound-units in (8e).

Cheng & Sybesma argue that the two kinds of classifier heads have different syntactic properties: in particular, massifiers, but not classifiers, can be followed by *de*, which imposes a measure interpretation on the classifier. This is illustrated in (10). *sān wǎn de tāng* 'three bowls **de** soup' naturally denotes a quantity of soup, so (10a) could naturally be used to talk about spilt soup. For (10b), Cheng & Sybesma claim: 'the default interpretation of [(10b)] on the other hand is that there are three bowls, filled with soup, standing on the table' (Cheng & Sybesma 1998: 6).

(10) a zhuōzi-shàng   yǒu   sān   wǎn   de   tang.
         table-top   there-is   three   Cl$_{bowl}$ DE   soup
         'There is enough soup on the table to fill three bowls.'
      b zhuōzi-shàng   yǒu   sān   wǎn   tang.
         table-top   there-is   three   Cl$_{bowl}$ soup
         'There are three bowls of soup on the table.'

Cheng & Sybesma (1999) argue that classifiers and massifiers select for count nouns and mass nouns respectively, that they occur in different positions in the tree and lead to different tree structures. We can distinguish two separate questions. One is whether there is a distinction between count and mass nouns encoded in the lexicon to which classifiers, and possibly other grammatical phenomena, are sensitive. The second is whether there is a contrast between phrases headed by mass and count classifiers which is comparable to the contrast between mass and count nouns.

The first question can be treated as definitional. If we define count nouns as nouns which can be directly modified by cardinals, then there are no count nouns in Mandarin. But the question can also be interpreted more subtly. As in English, we can distinguish in Mandarin between naturally atomic predicates, like *gǒu* 'dog', and substance predicates, such as *jiǔ* 'wine'. Cheng & Sybesma suggest that classifier selection is sensitive to this distinction. The general sortal classifier, *gè*, as well as other sortal classifiers, take naturally atomic nouns as complements, and can therefore be analysed as selecting for count nouns.

Sensitivity to natural atomicity, however, is not the same as selection for count nouns, as we have seen in Chapters 4 and 5. In English, adjectives like *big* modify both mass and count predicates, as long as they are naturally atomic, as in *big dogs, big furniture,* #*big water*. In both European and Brazilian Portuguese (but not English), reciprocals can take both count nouns and naturally atomic mass nouns as antecedents, but not substance mass nouns (Chapter 5, example (19b)). This shows that natural atomicity is independent of the property of being grammatically count. The fact that sortal classifiers apply to nouns like *gǒu* 'dog' does not mean that *gǒu* is count. Plausibly, sortals presuppose that their complements are naturally atomic. This seems all the more likely since they are in general presuppositional. For example, *tiáo* 'tail' presupposes that its complement is long and thin as in *yì tiáo yú*, literally 'one tail of fish', and the incorrect choice of classifier will result in infelicity and not falsity or ungrammaticality. The general classifier, *gè*, will presuppose only natural atomicity.[3]

Bare nouns like *gǒu*, which denote sets of naturally atomic entities, have all the properties of mass nouns listed above – in particular, they can denote kinds, single entities or pluralities of entities. Rather than being count nouns, they may well be naturally atomic object mass nouns, parallel to *furniture* in English, and bare singulars in Brazilian Portuguese. A classifier+N phrase like *zhī gǒu* is then semantically parallel to a count noun in English, or, more precisely, to a count noun phrase such as *piece of furniture*,[4] while bare nouns will be analogous to English mass nouns.

This parallelism is only partial. Cl+N phrases headed by individual classifiers are not marked for singular/plural (unlike count nouns). Mandarin bare nouns seem to be kind-denoting terms (Yang 2001; Li

[3] Erbaugh (2002) shows that *gè* does occur as a default classifier. However, *gè* N is considered substandard when there is a lexically selected classifier. *yí gè yú* 'one GE fish' is dispreferred, since the 'correct' classifier to use is *wěi* or *tiáo* 'tail', as in *yì wěi yú* and *yì tiáo yú*, literally 'one tail of fish'. *yí gè jiājù* 'one GE furniture' is strongly dispreferred, since the appropriate classifier is *jiàn* 'item' as in *yí jiàn jiājù*, 'one item of furniture'.
[4] Classifier languages differ as to whether they allow bare classifier+N phrases, and if so, under what conditions. Discussion of this is far beyond the scope of this book. See Cheng & Sybesma (2005), Sybesma (2007), Li & Bisang (2012) and others.

2011, 2013), while English mass nouns may start at the predicate type. However, tentatively, we can suggest that the mass/count distinction is paralleled in Mandarin by a contrast between bare nouns (= mass nouns) and classifier phrases headed by a sortal classifier (= count nouns). In the course of this section, we will see that there is evidence in support of this analysis.

I have just essentially proposed that the mass/count contrast shows up in Mandarin as a contrast not between nouns, nor between classifier phrases, but as a contrast between bare (mass) nouns and classifier+N phrases headed by a sortal classifier. It leaves open a second question: is there a contrast between types of classifiers which parallels the mass/count distinction (as Cheng & Sybesma suggest)? I shall argue in the rest of this section that the answer is no, and that the most insightful way to classify classifiers is in terms of their semantic contributions to counting and measuring interpretations.

Clearly, there are semantic distinctions between classifiers. For example, Yip (2008) shows that true measure classifiers like *jīn* 'pound' contrast with sortal classifiers such as *kē, zhī* and *gè*. Li (2011, 2013) argues classifier heads must be categorized in terms of the semantic functions that they can have. He argues that there is a three-way division between:

(i) classifiers which can only have an individuating function. These include the pure sortals, such as *kē, zhī* and *gè*, which apply to naturally atomic predicates as in (8a–c), which he characterizes as [+C, –M];

(ii) measure classifiers such as *jīn* 'pound' and *gōngjīn* 'kilo', which are pure measure heads and which are [–C, +M];

(iii) classifiers which are ambiguous between two uses such as *píng* 'bottle' and *xiāng* 'box', which are [+C, +M]. These are classed by Cheng & Sybesma as massifiers, since they do not apply to naturally atomic predicates. However, they can be used both as individuators which identify countable units, and as measure heads, as Li (2011, 2013) shows. In (11a) *sān píng jiǔ* is used to individuate three bottles of wine, while in (11b) it is a measure expression, measuring a quantity:

(11) a wǒ kāi le sān píng jiǔ. (Li 2011: ch. 3 (62))
I open PFV three Cl$_{bottle}$ wine
'I opened three bottles of wine.'

b wǒ-de wèi néng zhuāngxià sān píng jiǔ.
my DE stomach can hold three Cl$_{bottle}$ wine
'My stomach can hold three bottles of wine.'

As Cheng & Sybesma (1998) show, *de* forces a measure reading, and is infelicitous in a context which requires the individuating interpretation.

(12) a #wǒ kāi   le   sān   píng   de   jiǔ.   (Li 2011: ch. 3 (63))
         I   open PFV three Cl$_{bottle}$ DE wine
         Intended: 'I opened three bottles of wine.'
      b wǒ de   wèi   néng zhuāngxià sān   píng   de jiǔ.
         my DE stomach can hold   three Cl$_{bottle}$ DE wine
         'My stomach can hold three bottles of wine.'

These [+C, +M] classifiers are clearly different from sortal [+C, −M] classifiers. Sortals name naturally atomic units. [+C,+M] classifiers on their individuating [+C] use impose an individuating structure on non-atomic substances, such as *jiǔ* 'wine' in (12a), or pluralities such as books, as in *sān xiāng shū* 'three boxes of books'. However, like sortals, [+C,+M] classifiers on their [+C] use individuate units which can be counted. Li & Rothstein (2012) give several pieces of evidence that sortals and [+C,+M] classifiers pattern together grammatically when the [+C,+M] has its individuating meaning. We give two of the arguments here.

First, the numerical can be dropped before a sortal classifer (as in 13a), but not preceding a measure head (as in 13b). *píng* in the individuating context in (14a) behaves like the sortal and can occur without a numerical, while in a measure context, the number is obligatory (15b). (See also examples in Li & Bisang 2012.)

(13) a wǒ   mǎi   le   (yì)   běn   shū.
         I   buy PFV one Cl$_{volume}$ book
         'I bought a book.'
      b tā   hē   le   #(yì) shēng shuǐ.
         he   drink PFV one Cl$_{litre}$ water
         'He drank a litre of water.'

(14) a tā zuǒ-shǒu ná   le   (yì) píng   hóng-jiǔ.
         he left-hand take PFV one Cl$_{bottle}$ red-wine
         'He is carrying a bottle of red wine in his left hand.'
      b tā-de jiǔliàng   shì #(yì) píng   hóng-jiǔ.
         His drinking-ability be one Cl$_{bottle}$ red-wine
         'His drinking ability is one bottle of red wine.'

Second, individuating and measure classifiers interact differently with the modifier *duō* 'more'. Lǚ (1980/1999) observes that *duō* can follow either the numeral or the classifier.

(15) a èr-shí   duō   gōngjīn   píngguǒ
         twenty more   Cl$_{kilo}$ apple
         'more than twenty kilos of apples'

b sān   gōngjīn   duō   píngguǒ
  three   Cl$_{kilo}$ more   apple
  'more than three kilos of apples'

In (15a) *duō* modifies the numeral, while in (15b), it apparently modifies the numerical +classifier expression.[5]

However, as (16) shows, *duō* can only precede a sortal classifier.

(16) a shí   duō   gè   píngguǒ
         ten   more   Cl$_{general}$ apple
         'more than ten apples'   (10 apples < value <20 apples)
      b #liù   gè   duō   píngguǒ
         six   Cl$_{general}$ more   apple

With [+C,+M] classifiers, the position of *duō* affects the interpretation. When *duō* precedes the classifier *píng*, either the measure or the individuating reading is possible, but when it follows the classifier, only the measure reading is possible:

(17) a tā   ná   le   shí   (duō)   píng   (#duō)   jiǔ
         he   take   PVF   ten   more   Cl$_{bottle}$ more   wine
         'He carried more than ten bottles of wine.'
      b tā   hē   le   shí   (duō)   píng   (duō)   jiǔ
         he   drink   PVF   ten   more   Cl$_{bottle}$ more   wine
         'He drank more than ten bottles of wine.'

(17a) is only felicitous with *duō* follows *píng* in a context in which *shí píng* can be treated as a measure expression – for example, if all the wine is carried in a single giant jug or container.

These data show that a two-way division of classifier heads into classifiers and massifiers (or count heads and mass heads) is missing an important generalization. There are sortal classifiers which have individuating interpretations and measure classifier-heads which express measure units, and there are also classifiers which can be used in both ways. Expressions like *píng* can have both an individuation and a measure function, just like container classifiers in English.

So, measure classifiers split into two groups, inherent measure functions, like *jīn* 'pound', which name units on a scale of measurement and are [–C,+M], and *ad hoc* measures derived from containers and similar entities which can have two uses, as expressed by the features [+C,+M].

---

[5] Li & Rothstein (2012) point out a difference in meaning. In (15a), the number of kilos is above twenty, while in (15b) the number of kilos is above three but probably less than four. They discuss possible pragmatic explanations.

Individuating classifiers also divide into two groups. One group is the [+C,+M] classifiers, which on their individuating use 'package' either substances or pluralities into individuable, and thus countable, units. The other group consists of the 'pure' individuators which are [+C,–M]. These include sortals, which name naturally occurring atomic units. Crucially, the group also includes non-sortal individuating classifiers, for example apportioning or partition classifiers such as *piàn* 'piece', and group classifiers such as *qún* 'group'. As Li (2013) shows, these pattern like sortals with respect to the tests listed above.

This means that classifiers as a class cannot be lexically specified as either classifiers or massifiers. Instead, we need to ask: what is the range of uses to which they can be put, and the interpretation which they have in a particular context? Grammatical tests such as the position of *duō*, use of *de*, and optionality of the numerical distinguish only between individuating and measure interpretations and not between the lexical properties or specifications of the classifiers as [±C,±M]. So, at the classifier level, it is the contrast between measure and individuating interpretations which is binary, and not the lexical distinction between classifiers.

The distinction between counting and measuring that these data show reminds us directly of the contrasts between counting and measuring discussed in Chapter 3. There we argued that counting and measuring were associated with different syntactic structures in English, Hebrew and Hungarian, and have different compositional interpretations. *Three glasses of wine* and *šloša bakbukey yayin* and *három pohár bor* on the counting reading have the right-branching structure in (18a), while the measure interpretation has the structure in (18b), with the numerical combining with the measure classifier to form a predicate phrase.

(18) a [three [glasses [(of) wine_NP]_NP]_NP] (= Chapter 3 (1b))
      b [[three glasses]_MeasP (of) [wine_N]] (= Chapter 3 (1d))

Mandarin is different from both English and Hebrew in a very obvious sense: *glasses* in (18) and the analogous expression in Hebrew are, by hypothesis, nouns, whereas in Mandarin they are grammatically classifiers. (We return to this point in Chapter 8.)

Given that *sān píng jiǔ* is ambiguous in exactly the same way that *three glasses/bottles of wine* is ambiguous, it is an obvious question whether in Mandarin the semantic ambiguity is associated with a structural ambiguity. Li (2011, 2013) argues that, indeed, in Mandarin numerical+classifier+noun strings are ambiguous.

In individuating phrases, the classifier combines with the noun to form a predicate (19a), while in measure phrases, the numerical and the classifier combine to form a phrase which is predicated of the noun as in (19b):

(19)   a individuating reading: [sān   [píng$_{Cl}$ [jiǔ]$_N$]$_{Cl'}$]$_{ClP}$
                                            three   Cl$_{bottle}$ wine
         b measure reading: [[sān   píng$_{Cl}$]$_{MeasP}$ [jiǔ]$_N$]$_{ClP}$
                                            three   Cl$_{bottle}$ wine

The data already presented in this section (and discussed briefly at the end of Chapter 3) support the claim that measure readings have the structure in (19b), with the classifier measure head applying to the numerical to form a measure predicate.

First, as we saw in (13)–(14), measure classifiers must be preceded by numericals, while individuating classifiers can occur in bare Cl+N phrases. This is predicted if the measure classifier combines with the numerical to form a predicate as in (19b). Second, the modifier *duō* can follow a classifier in a measure reading, but not in an individuating reading. Since *duō* modifies an expression of quantity, this supports the claim that *sān píng* is a measure predicate expressing a quantity property in (19b), but not in (19a). Third, as we saw in (10), the particle *de* can follow a classifier with a measure interpretation, although, as Li (2011, 2013) shows, without *de* the classifier phrase is ambiguous. Since *de* is generally assumed to attach at the right edge of a predicate constituent, this is direct support for the claim that *sān* and *píng* form a predicate phrase in (19b).

The data similarly support the structure in (19a) for individuating classifier phrases, with the classifier taking an NP complement to make a classifier phrase, which is then optionally modified by a numerical. The numerical is optional since it is a non-selected modifier in specifier position. *duō* cannot follow the classifier since in that position it would come between the classifier and its NP complement, and would not follow an expression of quantity, and *de* cannot follow the classifier head since it is not at the right edge of a predicate.

These data mean that there is good evidence that the same geometric contrast between counting and measuring classifier phrases is found in English, Hebrew and Mandarin, despite the very different typological properties of the languages, including the fact that classifiers are functional heads in Mandarin and nouns in English and Hebrew. In all three languages, measure heads combine with a numerical to form a measure predicate, while individuating classifiers combine with an NP to form a classifier phrase which can be modified by a numerical. The semantic interpretation is essentially the same as in English. A measure classifier like *jīn* 'pound', or *píng* 'bottle', on its measure interpretation is type $<n, <e,t>>$ (20a). It combines with the numerical *sān* 'three' at type n as in (20b). It shifts to the modificational type at $<<e,t>,<et>>$ as in (20c):

(20)   a   *jīn:* $\lambda n\lambda x.\text{MEASURE}_{\text{WEIGHT,POUND}}(x) = n$[6]
     b   *sān jīn:* $\lambda x.\text{MEASURE}_{\text{WEIGHT,POUND}}(x) = 3$
     c   *sān jīn mǐ:* $\lambda P\lambda x.\text{MEASURE}_{\text{WEIGHT,POUND}}(x) = 3 \wedge P(x)$

NPs denotes kinds at type Σ, and, as Carlson (1977) and Chierchia (1998a) show, there is a natural shift from the kind to the set of entities instantiating the kind via the operator '$^{\cup}$'. *sān jīn mǐ* 'three pounds of rice' will have the interpretation in (21). *mǐ* denotes RICE_Σ, the rice-kind, and *sān jīn* applies to the set of quantities of rice denoted by $^{\cup}\text{RICE}_\Sigma$. *sān píng jiǔ* works the same way.

(21)   *sān jīn mǐ:* $\lambda P\lambda x.\text{MEASURE}_{\text{WEIGHT,POUND}}(x) = 3 \wedge P(x) \ (^{\cup}\text{RICE}_\Sigma)$
                       $= \lambda x.\text{MEASURE}_{\text{WEIGHT,POUND}}(x) = 3 \wedge {^{\cup}}\text{RICE}_\Sigma(x)$

(22)   *sān píng jiǔ:* $\lambda P\lambda x.\text{MEASURE}_{\text{VOLUME,BOTTLE}}(x) = 3 \wedge P(x) \ (^{\cup}\text{WINE}_\Sigma)$
                       $= \lambda x.\text{MEASURE}_{\text{VOLUME,BOTTLE}}(x) = 3 \wedge {^{\cup}}\text{WINE}_\Sigma(x)$

It is a bit more complex to give an interpretation for individuating classifiers. Sortal classifiers express at the syntactic level the operation that maps bare nouns onto countable predicates. In the framework of Rothstein (2010) discussed in Chapter 4, Mandarin sortal classifiers are of type $< \Sigma,<e\times k,t>>$, mapping kinds onto k-indexed predicates. They apply to the kind NP at type Σ and pick out the instantiations which count as atoms in a given context k. This is shown in (23): the general sortal classifier *gè* denotes the expression in (23a). It applies to *rén* 'people' to give (23b), the set of instantiations of the kind PEOPLE_k which count as countable atoms in context k. This set is then pluralized and modified by *sān* (23c):

(23)   Let a, x be variables of type $e\times k$, k a context.
     We define: $\mathbf{a} \sqsubseteq_k \mathbf{x}$ iff $\pi_1(\mathbf{a}) \in k$ and $\pi_1(\mathbf{a}) \sqsubseteq \pi_1(\mathbf{x})$ and $\pi_2(\mathbf{a}) = \pi_2(\mathbf{x}) = k$

     a   *gè:* $\lambda\Sigma\lambda\mathbf{x}.\pi_1(\mathbf{x}) \in {^{\cup}}\Sigma \cap k \wedge \pi_2(\mathbf{x}) = k$
     b   *gè rén:* $\lambda\mathbf{x}.\pi_1(\mathbf{x}) \in {^{\cup}}\text{PEOPLE}_\Sigma \cap k \wedge \pi_2(\mathbf{x}) = k$
     c   *sān gè rén:* $\lambda\mathbf{x}.\forall\mathbf{a} \ [\mathbf{a} \sqsubseteq_k \mathbf{x} \to \pi_1(\mathbf{a}) \in {^{\cup}}\text{PEOPLE}_\Sigma \cap k] \wedge \pi_1(\mathbf{x})_k = 3$

---

[6] In the interests of readability, I will from now on omit the world and time indices on these functions.

Other sortals have the same basic semantic content but are associated with presuppositions indicating what N denotations they can apply to. *zhī*, the sortal for small animals, has the denotation in (24a). It applies to *gŏu* and gives the set of instantiations of the kind DOG_k which count as atoms in context k, and presupposes that all instantiations of DOG_k are small animals. So *zhī gŏu* denotes a set of k-indexed dogs. *sān zhī gŏu* 'three small dogs' has the interpretation in (24c). Note that if the presupposition is violated and *zhī* takes as a complement an NP which does not denote a kind of small animal, the resulting sentence is infelicitous but not false.

(24)   Let a, x be variables of type e×k, k a context.

   a   *zhī*: $\lambda\Sigma\lambda\mathbf{x}.\pi_1(\mathbf{x}) \in {}^{\cup}\Sigma \cap k \wedge \pi_2(\mathbf{x}) = k$
           Presupposition: ${}^{\cup}\Sigma \subseteq$ SMALL ANIMAL
   b   *zhī gŏu*: $\lambda\mathbf{x}.\pi_1(\mathbf{x}) \in {}^{\cup}DOG_\Sigma \cap k \wedge \pi_2(\mathbf{x}) = k$
           Presupposition: ${}^{\cup}DOG_\Sigma \subseteq$ SMALL ANIMAL
   c   *sān zhī gŏu*: $\lambda\mathbf{x}.\forall\mathbf{a}[\mathbf{a}\sqsubseteq_k \mathbf{x} \rightarrow \pi_1(\mathbf{a}) \in {}^{\cup}DOG_\Sigma \cap k] \wedge \mid \pi_1(\mathbf{x}) \mid_k = 3$

Individuating classifiers which are not sortal, like *píng* on its individuating reading, are also expressions of type <Σ,<e×k,t>>, and map kinds onto contextually determined atomic instantiations of the kind. However, sortals map a kind X onto an indexed subset of instantiations of the kind X, and in *sān zhī gŏu* the indexed instantiations of the dog kind are directly counted. With container classifiers like *píng*, it is the containers (in this case the bottles) which are being counted and not the stuff contained in the containers. This means that the classifier has the k-index and not the complement, and *sān píng jiŭ* is counting bottles of wine, and not the wine itself. *píng* as an individuating container classifier must denote a function from a kind to a set of k-indexed bottles containing instantiations of the kind, as in (25a). *píng jiŭ* denotes a set of k-indexed bottles containing instantiations of $WINE_k$ as in (25b) and the full numerical phrase has the interpretation in (25c).

(25)   Let a, x be variables of type e×k, k a context.

   a   *píng*: $\lambda\Sigma\lambda\mathbf{x}.\pi_1(\mathbf{x}) \in$ BOTTLE $\cap k \wedge \pi_2(\mathbf{x}) = k \wedge$
           $\exists y[y \in {}^{\cup}\Sigma \wedge$ CONTAIN$(\pi_1(\mathbf{x}), y)]$
   b   *píng jiŭ*: $\lambda\mathbf{x}.\pi_1(\mathbf{x}) \in$ BOTTLE $\cap k \wedge \pi_2(\mathbf{x}) = k \wedge$
           $\exists y[y \in {}^{\cup}WINE_\Sigma \wedge$ CONTAIN$(\pi_1(\mathbf{x}), y)]$
   c   *sān píng jiŭ*: $\lambda\mathbf{x}.\forall\mathbf{a}[\mathbf{a}\sqsubseteq_k \mathbf{x} \rightarrow \pi_1(\mathbf{a}) \in$ BOTTLE $\cap k] \wedge$
           $\exists y[y \in {}^{\cup}WINE_\Sigma \wedge$ CONTAIN$(\pi_1(\mathbf{a}), y)] \wedge \mid \pi_1(\mathbf{x}) \mid_k = 3$

This correctly predicts that semantic content of the classifier, namely containment in a bottle, is part of the truth conditions of a sentence containing (25c), unlike the lexical selection properties of *zhī* which are presuppositional.

We now compare the Mandarin system for expressing countability with the English system. We saw that we could not argue for a lexical distinction between count and mass nouns in Mandarin. All bare nouns, whatever their content, are kind-denoting, and none can be directly modified by numericals. The countable equivalent of the English count noun *dog* is the classifier expression *zhī gǒu* at type $<e \times k, t>$. However, there is no identifiable grammatical class of count nouns, since expressions like *zhī gǒu* are categorically indistinguishable from other individuating classifiers at type $<e \times k, t>$, including phrases headed by container classifiers. These are not comparable to count nouns but to complex expressions equivalent to English *bottle of wine*. One might try to argue that sortal+NP phrases are lexically distinguishable from container+NP phrases, since sortals map kind-denoting noun phrases NP_Σ onto a subset of $^\cup NP_\Sigma$, while containers map NP_Σ onto a set of entities containing $^\cup NP_\Sigma$. However, this doesn't work either. Partition classifiers such as *kuài* and *piàn* are not sortal, since they impose a division on the substance, but they still map a kind NP_Σ onto a subset of $^\cup NP_\Sigma$. Although not sortal, they cannot be followed by either *duō* or *de*:

(26) a yí   kuài   (#de)   xīgua
         one   Cl$_{piece}$ DE   watermelon
         'one piece of watermelon'
      b #yí   kuài   duō   xīgua
         one   Cl$_{piece}$ more   watermelon
      c yí   piàn   (#de)   bùliào
         one   Cl$_{piece}$ DE   fabric
         'one piece of fabric'
      d #yí   piàn   duō   bùliào
         one   Cl$_{piece}$ more   fabric

Group classifiers, such as *qún*, also show the same grammatical properties as sortals, and partition classifiers, although they map quantities of atomic entities onto singular groups (Li 2011).

(27) a yì   qún   (#de)   háizi
         one   Cl$_{group}$ DE   children
         'one group of children'
      b #yì   qún   duō   háizi
         one   Cl$_{group}$ more   children

It seems clear that neither naturally atomic nouns nor phrases consisting of a sortal classifiers and an NP form an identifiable grammatical class in Mandarin. Instead, the grammatical distinction is between expressions which are countable, and those which are not. Countable expressions are Classifier+NP phrases at type <e×k,t>. They are headed by classifiers which are individuators, and which mark entities as contextually determined atomic countable units, semantic atoms. These semantic atoms may be coextensive with natural atoms (when the classifier is a sortal), they may be carved out of substances or pluralities (when the classifier is a partition classifier or a container classifier) or they may be groups (when the classifier is a group classifier.) All these classifier+NP expressions are countable.

Non-countable expressions are bare NPs, and phrases of the form Numerical+Classifier+NP, where the classifier is a measure head.

Strikingly, numerical phrases involving counting have the same geometric structure as English, Hebrew and Hungarian counting classifier constructions, while numerical measure phrases are geometrically analogous to measure phrases in these languages, as shown in (19).

We conclude this section by returning to the assertion we made earlier that bare nouns such as *gǒu* 'dog' and *shū* 'book' are object mass nouns parallel to *furniture* in English and the bare singular *livro* and *könyv* 'book' in Brazilian Portuguese and Hungarian.

We saw in Chapter 5 that, while count nouns are always compared with respect to cardinalities, object mass nouns can be compared along any contextually relevant dimension. If naturally atomic bare nouns in Mandarin are object mass nouns and classifier+NP phrases denote pluralities which can be counted, then we expect a similar contrast in quantity judgements. Preliminary inquiries about this question support this prediction.[7] The crucial example is (28), where Mandarin *hěn duō* 'much/many' and *tài duō* 'too much/many' can occur both with and without a classifier. A natural translation into English would be 'You have taken too many books, your baggage will be overweight.'

(28) nǐ   dài tài duō   (běn) shū le, xínglǐ huì
      you take too much/many Cl_volume book PART baggage will
      chāozhòng de.
      overweight DE

Predictably, both *tài duō běn shū* (with the classifier *běn*) and *tài duō shū* (without the classifier, and with a bare NP *shū*) allow for a cardinal evaluation. Both can be used if I have ten books in my bag and I want to assert that these are too many individual books to put in my baggage.

However, imagine a situation in which the bag contains the two volumes of the Compact Edition of the *Oxford English Dictionary* (which weighs in at almost seven kilos). In this case, it is only appropriate to use (28) without the classifier, since only the object mass noun (but not the classifier construction) allows comparison on a non-cardinal dimension. The contrast between *shū* and *bĕn shū* is the same as the contrast between *furniture* and *pieces of furniture* in English and *livro/livros* in Brazilian Portuguese, and supports the claim that naturally atomic bare nouns in Mandarin are object mass nouns and not count.

6.3   HUNGARIAN – A MIXED LANGUAGE

Hungarian poses a problem for any standard typology of mass/count since it has both an apparent distinction between mass and count nouns and a system of sortal individuating classifiers. Csirmaz & Dékány (2014) show that numbers can be followed either by a classifier+N or by a bare, naturally atomic noun. In all the examples in (29) the classifier is optional. *Darab* is the general classifier, which they suggest is roughly equivalent to the Mandarin *gè*. However, not all bare nouns can be modified by numerals, as in (30), giving the impression that there is a mass/count distinction:

(29)   a   két   (fej)   hagyma
             two   (Cl$_{head}$)   onion.SG
             'two onions'
         b   három (szál)   rózsa
             three   (Cl$_{thread}$) rose.SG
             'three roses'
         c   három (darab)   könyv[8]
             three   (Cl$_{general}$) book.SG
             'three books'

(30)   a   #három sár / #három   kosz
             three   mud / three   dirt
         b   három   darab   szemét
             three   Cl$_{general}$ dirt
             'three pieces of dirt'

---

[8] Some speakers do not accept *darab* here, and only allow the bare version.

In addition to the contrast between (29) and (30), Hungarian has a morphological singular/plural distinction, as shown in (31a,b) and as expected in so-called 'mass/count languages'. However, in numerical constructions, the noun is always singular as in (31c):

(31) a könyv/könyv-ek[9]
    book.SG/book-PL
    'book/books'
   b könyv-ek-et   vettem,   kett-őt.
    book-PL-ACC bought.I   two-ACC
    'I bought books, two of them.'
    c #három   könyv-ek
    three   book-PL
    Intended meaning: 'three books'

Csirmaz & Dékány suggest that Hungarian is a classifier language like Mandarin. Nouns have mass denotations, denoting unindividuated 'stuff'. Mass usage of bare nouns shows up in contexts like (32), where the bare noun *szendvics* is preverbal and has a number-neutral interpretation. (32) is true in a situation in which Feri eats a whole sandwich, more than one sandwich, or parts of one or more sandwiches. Farkas & de Swart (2003) analyse this use of bare N as bare noun incorporation.

(32) Feri   szendvics-et   eszik.(Csirmaz & Dékány 2014: (6))
    Feri.NOM sandwich-ACC eats
    'Feri eats (a) sandwich.'

Direct modification of bare nouns by a numerical is possible because there is a null sortal classifier, equivalent to Mandarin *gè*, as in (32):

(33) három ⊘   könyv
    three   Cl$_{general}$ book.SG

Since the null classifier, like *gè*, can only apply to naturally atomic mass nouns, the infelicity of (30a) and the obligatoriness of the classifier in (30b) are explained.

However, the plural data in (31a,b) are surprising. According to the received wisdom, we do not expect a classifier language to have a distinction between singular and plural nouns. Dékány (2011), discussing this problem, suggests that plurality in Hungarian is a plural individuating classifier which bridges both number and classifier positions. However, Schvarcz & Rothstein (in press) give a number of arguments for why this is not plausible. These include the following.

[9] -*k* is the plural suffix. -*e*- is a link vowel. We will not always mark these.

First, bare NP complements like those in (32) can be plural as well as singular:

(34)   János és   Béla rózs-ák-at / rózs-át   keresnek
        János and Béla rose-PL-ACC rose.SG-ACC looking.for.they
        a   piacon.
        the   market
        'János and Béla are looking for roses on the market.'

If plural bare nouns are classifier structures, this is unexpected, given that these complements are supposed to be incorporated bare NPs. Furthermore, the bare plural in (34) can have a kind interpretation, which should not be possible if plurality is an (individuating) classifier.

Second, classifiers can be suffixed onto nouns, and the resulting N can be pluralized, although the mass noun itself cannot be marked plural, as in (35). This is again surprising if the plural is itself a classifier. Other arguments are presented in Schvarcz & Rothstein (in press) and will not be repeated here.

(35)   a szemét-darab-ok
           dirt-Cl$_{darab}$-PL
           'pieces of dirt'
        b #szemet-ek
           dirt-PL

Schvarcz & Rothstein show that plurality in Hungarian has many of the properties that we expect in mass/count languages. Pluralization of substance nouns in the appropriate context may have the same pluralities-of-kinds readings that we find in English (36):

(36)   a Cukr-ok-at   vettem   az ínyencbolt-ban: feldolgozatlan
           sugar-PL-ACC   bought.I the gourmet.shop-in unprocessed
           nádcukr-ot   befőzőcukr-ot   és   barna
           cane.sugar-ACC canning.sugar-ACC   and   brown
           mokkacukr-ot.
           sugar.cube-ACC
           'I bought (different kinds of) sugars at the gourmet shop:
           unprocessed cane sugar, sugar used for canning, and brown
           sugar cubes.'
        b Újrahasznosítás-kor kérjuk szétválasztani a   különféle
           recycling-upon   please separate   the   various
           szemet-ek-et.
           trash-PL-ACC
           'When recycling, please separate the various kinds of trash.'

Abundance plurals are also available for substance mass nouns in high register:

(37) A   múlt szemete-i   marjá-k   a   lelkem   mind a   mai
      the past trash-PL.POSS burn-3.PL the soul.my till   the very
      napig.
      today
      'The trash of the past is burning my soul till this very day.'

Schvarcz & Rothstein (in press) argue that nouns like *könyv* are ambiguous between a count and a mass reading – in other words, they are flexible nouns, just like *stone* in English, and *livro* in Brazilian Portuguese. We already saw that quantity readings support this analysis, since nouns like *könyv* oscillate between an object mass noun interpretation and a count noun interpretation, depending on the context in which they appear. Following the question word *hány* 'what quantity', which is ungrammatical with mass nouns like *szemét* 'trash', *könyv* can have only a cardinal interpretation. Following *mennyi*, which is normally used as a question word with nouns like *szemét*, *könyv* has an object mass noun interpretation.

(38) a Hány   könyv van   a   táskád-ban?
         what.quantity book   is.there the bag.your-in
         'How many books are there in your bag?'

      b Csak három.   c #Három kiló-t.
         only three   three   kilo-ACC
         'Only three.'   'Three kilos.'

(39) a Mennyi   könyv-et   tudsz   cipelni?
         what.quantity book-ACC   able.you carry
         'What quantity of book can you carry?'

      b Három   kiló-t.   c Hármat.
         three   kilo-ACC   three-ACC
         'Three kilos.'   'Three.'

Schvarcz (2014) brings another argument which distinguishes between mass nouns and flexible nouns, and which shows that flexible nouns have different interpretations in mass and count contexts. The quantity expression *mennyiség* follows substance nouns like *szemét* 'trash/dirt' and *cukor* 'sugar'.

(40) a ez   a   cukor/szemét mennyiség
         this the sugar/trash   quantity
         'this quantity of sugar'
      b #ez a   mennyiség   cukor/szemét
         this the quantity   sugar/trash
         Intended: 'this quantity of sugar/trash'

However, with flexible nouns like *könyv*, both orders are possible, but there is an accompanying difference in interpretation. When *mennyiség* precedes *könyv*, the quantity is assumed to be specified in terms of cardinality (41a). When *mennyiség* follows the noun, as in the felicitous examples in (40a), a non-cardinal evaluation is normal. (41b) naturally makes reference to the overall quantity of reading matter, including the length of the book, and not just the cardinality.

(41)   a Ezt a   mennyiség könyv-et   nem tudom belenyomni
          this the quantity book-ACC not can   push
          a   táskámba, öt   már   túl sok.
          the bag.my,   5   already too much
          'I cannot fit this quantity of books into my bag, five is already too much.'
      b Egy életbe telne   hogy elolvassam az könyv
          a   life   would.take that read.I   the book.SG
          mennyiség-et.
          quantity-ACC
          'It would take a lifetime to read that quantity of books!'

These data are explained if we assume that Hungarian has a mass/count distinction, but that many nouns are flexible between a count and an object mass noun interpretation. In this respect, Hungarian is similar to Brazilian Portuguese which also has a mass/count contrast, and flexible nouns. In both languages, the norm is for count nouns to be part of a flexible pair, although, in Hungarian, a small group of nouns are more resistant to being used in mass contexts and prefer count interpretations.

However, there are three crucial properties which distinguish Hungarian from Brazilian Portuguese and other mass/count languages. First, Brazilian Portuguese mass nouns seem to have a kind interpretation (Pires de Oliveira & Rothstein 2011). As Schvarcz & Rothstein (in press) point out, kind interpretations of Hungarian mass and flexible nouns seem to be restricted to the preverbal incorporated position.

Second, pluralization is governed by very different principles, too complicated to discuss here. Crucially, while the language has a plural marker, nouns modified by numericals are never marked plural, as examples like *három könyv* 'three book' show.

However, generalizations about plural agreement of count nouns with numericals vary from language to language. Some languages with a mass/count contrast do not have plural agreement at all. (5) illustrated this for *Dëne Sųłiné*. Other languages which do have mass/count contrast and plural agreement may follow very different rules

from English. An example is Standard Arabic. Count nouns in
Standard Arabic are marked genitive plural when they follow the
numericals three to ten, but from eleven upwards, the noun is singular accusative:

(42)   a **kita:b**   wa:ðid
          book.SG one
          'one book'
       b Θala:Θ   **kutub**-in
          three   book.PL-GEN
          'three books'
       c Θala:Θata ?aSara   **kita:b**-an
          three   ten   book.SG-ACC
          'thirteen books'

Russian has yet another system of noun agreement with numericals.
Numericals from two to four induce so-called 'paucal case marking'
on the noun which follows, where paucal case is almost always identical with the genitive singular. Numericals from five upwards assign
genitive plural. So the absence of plural marking on count nouns
modified by numericals in Hungarian is another pattern among the
variety available crosslinguistically.[10]

   The third property which distinguishes Hungarian from Brazilian
Portuguese and English is that Hungarian appears to have both
a count/mass distinction and a system of sortal individuating classifiers. Under the widely accepted assumption that sortal classifiers and
count nouns belong to two complementary systems, this is not
expected. This, together with noun flexibility and the absence of
plural agreement, means that 'three roses' can be expressed in one
of two ways, as shown in (29b), repeated here as (43):

(43)   a három   szál   rózsa   b három   rózsa
          three   Cl_thread   rose.SG   three   rose.SG
          Both: 'three roses'

In (43a), the mass noun *rózsa* is used in a classifier construction, while
in (43b), the count noun *rózsa* is directly modified by the numerical
három. But this is only surprising if we assume that sortal classifiers
and a lexical mass/count contrast must be complementary systems.

[10] Since, in many dialects of Brazilian Portuguese, plural morphology on the noun
    is often omitted, examples like (i), looking very like the Hungarian examples,
    may occur.

    (i)   dois/muito-s   livro
          two many-PL   book.SG
          'two/many books'

In fact, there is no *prima facie* reason why this should be the case. If count nouns and sortal classifiers are two ways of marking nouns as grammatically countable, there is no reason why they should be mutually exclusive. The evidence from both Hungarian and Western Armenian (cited in example (7)), as well as Turkish, suggests that both systems may coexist. Even English has one genuine classifier, which can never be marked plural, and which allows both plural count and mass complements:

(44)   The farmer owns two hundred head(#s) of cows/livestock.

It seems that there is greater variation in expressions of countability than has been taken into consideration.

Let us sum up our observations. First, a language may, but need not, encode grammatical countability at the lexical level. Lexically encoded countability results in count nouns. Mandarin is an example of a language which does not allow this and as a result has no mass/count distinction among nouns. Second, in some languages, for example Brazilian Portuguese and Hungarian, all (or almost all) count nouns may be part of a flexible pair. In English, the proportion of flexible nouns is much smaller and is lexically restricted, while in Mandarin, since there are no count nouns, there are also no flexible nouns. Brazilian Portuguese and Hungarian exploit the flexibility of nouns fully in quantity evaluations, while Mandarin exploits the contrast between bare nouns and classifier+N constructions. Third, Hungarian shows that a system of individual sortal classifiers is not incompatible with a lexical count/mass distinction.

Crucially, in all the languages we have looked at, countability is encoded grammatically, whether at the lexical level or by using a system of individuating classifiers, or both. Furthermore, comparing the results here with the data in Chapter 3, we see that classifiers in Mandarin can be categorized as individuating or measuring, just as they can in English, Hungarian, Modern Hebrew and Russian[11], and that the same structural configurations characterize counting as opposed to measuring operations in all languages. In particular, Mandarin showed clearly that counting uses of packaging, container, group and partition classifiers have the same grammatical properties as sortals, while measure heads and measuring uses of ambiguous classifiers pattern in a different way. This suggests that what is

---

[11] I don't have evidence that this doesn't hold for Brazilian Portuguese. In fact, I would expect exactly the same pattern. However, the research hasn't been done yet.

important crosslinguistically is not a lexical division of nouns into (naturally) atomic and substance nouns, but a grammatical distinction into expressions which are countable and those that are not.

Lexical count nouns are one way of encoding countability on bare nouns. Classifiers are another mechanism for encoding grammatical countability phrasally. The data in Section 6.2 shows that Mandarin treats all countable phrases as grammatically equivalent, whether they are grammatically individuating and marked as countable naturally atomic individuals, containers, groups or portioned portions of a substance. We return to these issues in Chapter 8.

6.4 YUDJA

In the final section of this chapter, we examine countability in Yudja, based on Lima (2010, 2012, 2014). Yudja is a Tupi Language spoken by the Yudja people, an indigenous people who live in two areas on the Xingua river in the southern Amazonian basin. In Yudja, nouns are bare, unspecified for either number or definiteness:[12]

(45) Ali   ba'ï   ixu.
      child   paca   eat
      'The/a/child(ren) eat(s)/ate the/a/paca(s).'

(45) literally means 'an undefined number of children eat(s)/ate an undefined number of pacas'. Lima shows that Yudja has no mass/ count distinction and treats all nouns as count nouns, whether or not they are naturally atomic or substance-denoting. She argues this on the basis of elicited judgements and experimental data (for details, see Lima 2014). All nouns can be modified by cardinals, as illustrated in (46,47). In (46), *ba'ï* 'paca' is an easy candidate for a count noun: a paca is a small animal, and the predicate is naturally atomic and easily construed as countable. In (47), however, the nouns modified by a cardinal denote a substance (all data from Lima 2014):

(46) Txabïu ba'ï   wãnã.
      three paca   ran
      'Three pacas ran.'

(47) a Txabïu   asa   he   wï   he.
        three   flour   in   port   in

---

[12] There is a plural suffix which attaches only to [+animate] nouns, which need not concern us here.

'There are three (bags of) flour in the port.'
b Txabïu   uda   apeta   wï.
    three   someone   blood   bring
    'Some brought three (portions of) blood.'
c Maria   yauda   y'a   dju wï.
    Maria   two   water   bring
    'Maria brought two (portions of) water.'

Lima shows that the examples in (47) are all interpreted as making assertions about three (or two) individuated portions of the substance under question which are salient in the specific context. Thus (47c) might be uttered truthfully if Maria brought two individuated quantities of water. The quantities need not be of the same size or in the same kind of containers. Lima shows that this use of number+substance noun is not the same as examples such as *two beers* in English.

In the English examples, substance mass nouns are coerced into a count reading in which they denote individuated servings. These servings must be standardized, and the count usage is felicitous only in the particular context for which that standard is relevant. *Beers* denotes standard servings of beer in a situation in a restaurant or at a party, and it can only be used relative to this situation. Lima shows that, in contrast, in Yudja, nouns equivalent to *blood* and *water* are countable in any situation, and that what are counted are individuated portions possibly of different sizes. In English, in a situation in which a nurse is surveying the scene of an accident and notices three pools or puddles or drops of blood or three drops of water, (48) is inappropriate.

(48)   #There are three bloods/waters on the floor.

In Yudja, this is not so. Suppose that someone brought a container of water and let a drop fall near the school, another drop near the hospital and a last drop near the river, all drops being of different size and form. (49) can be appropriately used to describe the situation (RED marks a reduplicated verb):

(49)   Txabïu y'a   ipide   pe-pe-pe
        three   water on.the.floor drip.RED
        'Three (drops of) water dripped on the floor (in different events).'

The reduplicated verb indicates that there were different events of the water dripping, but this does not mean that (49) is counting events. The sentence is grammatical with a non-reduplicated verb, and, whatever the form of the verb, the cardinal in (49) can only be counting portions of water. Event-counting cardinals are clearly marked as such by the adverbial suffix -ha as in txabïaha 'three times'. So (49) appears to be counting what Lima calls 'concrete portions' of water.

Quantity predicates also show cardinal interpretations of non-atomic, substance mass nouns (which Lima calls 'notionally mass'). The quantity predicate itxïbï, which expresses that a quantity is large, can only have a cardinal interpretation. With a naturally atomic predicate like iidja 'woman' in (50a), it is best translated as 'many'. In (50b), where it modifies y'a 'water', it can only be used to make an assertion about the number of individuated portions of water available and is best translated as 'many portions' (Lima 2014).

(50)   a Itxïbï iidja   a'i.
          many woman here
          'There are many women here.'
       b Itxïbï y'a   a'i.
          many water here
          'There are many (portions of) water here.'

Atomic interpretations of substance nouns occur with the adjective urahu 'big' which distributes over individuals. With substance nouns, urahu can only modify the size of individual portions of N, as in (51):

(51)   Ma de   urahu   asa   dju a'u?
       who   big   flour   have
       'Who has a big portion of flour?'

Lima shows that all nouns, whether or not they are naturally atomic, can be interpreted as denoting individuable entities or quantities, and are countable. Furthermore, quantity evaluations as in (51) are always in terms of cardinality, even if the N denotation is not naturally atomic. So, contextually individuated portions of substance-denoting nouns are perceived as atoms on a par with individual pacas and children. In this sense, all nouns are count nouns or can be used as such. Lima shows that it is not plausible to posit a null syntactic classifier in examples like (40,50b,51), since there is no evidence at all that Yudja is a classifier language. The accumulated evidence points to the fact that Yudja has no way of distinguishing between mass and count nouns, nor does it have a grammatical mechanism for formally encoding countability.

Despite the fact that naturally atomic nouns and substance nouns are both countable, naturally atomic nouns might still have a different grammatical status in Yudja. Suppose that, for naturally atomic nouns, the countable elements are always the natural atoms, independent of context, while for substance nouns, the countable elements are contextually determined. This would mean that at least a notional count/mass distinction could be made, which would presumably reflect the object/substance contrast in the world.

Lima, Li & Snedeker (2014) show that there is evidence that this is not the case. Although naturally atomic predicates like *txabïu ba'ï* 'three pacas' normally involves counting whole pacas, this seems to be a pragmatic phenomenon and not semantic. They show experimentally that adult speakers of Yudja interpret pieces of bananas and pieces of canoe as countable entities in the denotation of the noun.[13] Thus, for many speakers, *txabïu pakua* 'three banana' can refer to three individual bananas, three groups of bananas or three pieces of banana. This implies that, even with naturally atomic count nouns, context may allow pieces of N or parts of an N to be considered countable instances of N, putting all nouns in Yudja on the same semantic footing: they are all countable, and they all allow context to determine what counts as 'one' N.

Lima (2014) suggests a semantics for Yudja nouns based on principles of mereotopology (Casati & Varzi 1999; Varzi 2007). She shows that bare nouns in Yudja can have a kind reading, as has been argued for bare nouns in many languages, including English (Carlson 1977), Mandarin (Krifka 1989, 1995; Chierchia 1998a; Yang 2001; Li 2013) and Brazilian Portuguese (Pires de Oliveira & Rothstein 2011). She suggests that all bare nouns in Yudja are ambiguous between kind-denoting expressions at the type of arguments and predicates at type <e,t>.[14] These predicates are countable. There is an operation which maps the kind denotation N_Σ denoted by the bare noun N, onto the predicate denotation, a set of maximal spatially individuable concrete portions of N_Σ, closed under sum. This set is an atomic Boolean semi-lattice, and the set of minimal elements which generates it is a set of contextually determined, spatially individuable, non-overlapping portions, which can include non-stable entities like drops of blood, puddles of water and pieces of boat. These minimal elements are defined following Varzi (2007) in terms of maximal self-connectedness (see

---

[13] There is evidence that children generally allow parts of objects to count as objects, so that a shoe and two half shoes counts as 'three shoes'. See Srinivasan *et al.* (2013) and references cited there. But adult speakers of English do not show this behaviour.

[14] She also assumes that there is a third possible interpretation, where they denote sets of subkinds, but we will not consider that here.

Lima 2014, Ch. 3.3, and reference cited there for details). Atomic entities, then, are defined in terms of their spatial unity in a particular context. The minimal or atomic portions in the denotation of substance nouns such as *water* and *blood* are spatially self-connected individuable concrete portions, the puddles and drops of water and blood and so on. When a noun is naturally atomic, as in *paca, boat* and *bowl*, the maximally self-connected and individuable concrete portions are normally the atomic pacas, bowls and boats. However, in appropriate contexts, spatially individuated parts may count as countable minimal parts.

Lima's operation mapping from the kind N_Σ onto the set of individuable concrete portions of N has in common with Rothstein (2010) that the atomic elements in the denotation of a count noun are contextually determined. However, this context-dependency is not grammatically encoded, and all count predicates are simply type <e,t>. All nouns have a kind denotation at the argument type, and a count denotation at the predicate type. This predicts that there are no mass predicates at all. And, indeed, there is no evidence that nouns do have a mass interpretation. In fact, the data in (50) and (51), showing that all predicates of quantity and size refer to the quantity of atoms or the size of individual atoms, suggest strongly that there are no mass interpretations.

Lima (2014) discusses a property of Yudja which supports this suggestion. The hypothesis in Chapter 5 was that count predicates denote sets of countable entities, while mass predicates denote mass objects which can be measured. If there are no mass predicates in a language, then this predicts that there should be no explicit measure operations either. Lima presents three pieces of evidence which support this. First, she shows that there are no explicit measure expressions in the language, and reports on informants explaining to her that quantities are always expressed in Yujda via cardinality properties and not in terms of measuring. Lima notes 'the absence in the language of measure words' and continues that 'while constructions with numerals are highly productive in daily activities to refer to portions and number of objects by adults and children, the description of volume (liters, kilos or pounds) is not' (2014: 22). (When quantity expressions are essential, they are borrowed from or expressed in Portuguese.) Her informants made the same points. She reports one as saying that they usually 'count quantities (number of objects or portions), not volume', and another as commenting that 'when the Yudja people can count the produce itself, which is the case with fruits, they count the individual fruits. When they need to count things that are difficult to individuate, they use container words (such as *xãã* 'bowl')' (2014: 23).

Second, Lima reports on a series of experiments she carried out, in which she repeated in Yudja the quantity judgement experiments from Barner & Snedeker (2005) (which we discussed in Chapter 5). In these experiments, the subject is asked to judge *Who has more N?* The results were quite different from the English examples: Yudja speakers consistently favoured comparison according to cardinality, and judged, for example, six small quantities of a substance as 'more' than three big quantities of a substance, indicating that they compare according to number of portions and not overall volume. These results were approximately the same for substance nouns and for naturally atomic nouns. Interestingly enough, when the same experiments were carried out with the question posed in Brazilian Portuguese, which does have a mass/count distinction, noun type did influence the results. Subjects were significantly less likely to judge according to number when asked *Quem tem mais N?* 'Who has more N?' if N was a mass noun. Since noun type (i.e. mass vs count) influences speaker judgements in Brazilian Portuguese, this strongly implies that the lack of variation in judgements in Yudja is evidence of a single noun type, and thus of no mass/ count distinction.

Lima's third point in this respect concerns container expressions. While Yudja does not have expressions for volume or weight, it does optionally use container expressions, as shown in the pair in (52):

(52) a Yauda yukïdï dju wï.
          two   salt   bring
          'Someone brought two (portions of) salt.'
      b Yauda yukïdï xãã   he dju wï.
          two   salt   bowl in bring
          'Someone brought two bowls of salt.'

As we have already seen, in many languages, container expressions are syntactically classifier expressions, ambiguous between an individuating classifier reading, and a measure head interpretation. As already mentioned, Lima argues that there is no productive classifier construction in Yudja, so the question is, how should these be analysed? Lima shows that these container expressions are neither individuating classifiers nor measure phrases but locative adjuncts. The container noun is always followed by the locative preposition *he* 'in', and the locative phrase is always optional. While a container can be used to individuate portions, it is not necessarily used to do so. Consider (53):

(53) Txabïu awïla papera akalikali he wï.
     three honey paper box   in come
     'Three (portions of) honey were brought to the village in (a/the/some) paper box(es).'

While (53) can have the interpretation that each of the three portions of honey was contained in a paper box, Lima's consultant comments: 'We could have a box with three bottles of honey inside it.' So the container term expresses where the three portions of honey are located, either distributively or collectively. These kinds of interpretations were shown experimentally to be generally available.

In sum, then, Lima shows that Yudja has the following properties.

(i) With respect to nouns, all nouns in the language are ambiguous between a kind interpretation and a count predicate interpretation. There is no evidence for mass predicates, and there is no evidence for a mass/count distinction at either the lexical or the syntactic level. Yudja makes a distinction between kind-denoting terms and predicate terms, which are countable, but does not encode a grammatical distinction between countable and non-countable sets.

(ii) There are no measure expressions making reference to a continuous dimension, and lexical expressions of quantity and size make reference to number and size of individuable items.

(iii) Quantity judgements are in terms of cardinality.

I have suggested that measuring is associated with mass nouns analogously to the way in which counting is associated with count nouns. If this is the case, then the combination of properties in (i)–(iii) is not suprising. The lack of a non-countable predicate denotation correlates with the lack of measurement operations, since if there are no measure operations, there is no need for non-countable sets. Our hypothesis about Yudja, then, is that there is no encoding of the countable/non-countable contrast in nouns because there are no lexically expressed measure operations and thus no need for non-countable predicates. All noun predicates are count predicates. Lima's kind-to-predicate operation maps kinds onto sets of countable instantiations of the kind, sets whose members are a set of contextually individuated spatially integral entities closed under sum. In the absence of measure predicates, no other set interpretation is necessary.

This conclusion fits in a clear way into the picture we have been building up. The count/mass distinction is one of a number of possible ways of marking the countable/non-countable opposition between nominal predicates. It may be marked lexically in a count/mass distinction, as in English, or by classifiers as in Mandarin, or by both, as in Hungarian. The contrast is essential because counting operations apply to count predicates (either nouns or classifier phrases), while measuring applies to mass predicates. The fact that count nouns are often naturally atomic reflects the fact that naturally individuable units are good candidates for quantity judgements involving counting. However, the Yudja data suggest that things don't have necessarily have to be this way: natural atoms are only one way of dividing up instantiations of kinds into countable chunks. Furthermore, if quantity evaluations are only cardinal, and counting is the only relevant operation for determining quantity, then there is no need for an opposition between count and mass nouns.

6.5 QUESTIONS FOR FURTHER DISCUSSION AND INVESTIGATION

The suggestion here is very straightforward. Take any language you have access to and investigate how counting and measuring are expressed. Can measure readings of classifiers and count readings of classifiers be distinguished? What tests distinguish between them?

In Section 6.2, I discussed expressions of counting and measuring in Mandarin. I focused on Mandarin because it is the only classifier language that I have studied in any depth. Mandarin is only one out of a huge number of classifier languages, which vary with respect to their morphosyntax. Clearly, we cannot presume from Mandarin anything about the expression of counting and measuring in other classifier languages. So how is counting and measuring expressed in other classifier languages? For the particular language you are studying (classifier, mass/count or mixed, like Hungarian), consider the following:

(i) Are container classifiers ambiguous between a counting and a measuring use?

(ii) Can you disambiguate these uses?

(iii) Is there in general a way to distinguish between counting and measuring uses of classifiers?

(iv) How can classifiers be classified in the particular language under discussion? Sortal vs mensural? [±C,±M] according to what uses they allow?

Please let me know your results!

7 The Universal Grinder

'Spencer Tunick took lots of photos of purple nudists with bits of crushed grape all over their bodies.'

John Parsons, *Wadca Magazine*

7.1 INTRODUCTION

This chapter discusses the semantics of the 'Universal Grinder'. Any theory of mass nouns and count nouns has to deal with cases where nouns shift from count to mass, as in (1) or mass to count, as in (2):

(1) a After the accident there was *dog* all over the road.
     b By two o'clock, the garage floor was covered in *bicycle*.
     c After the paint can fell off the shelf, you couldn't see much *dog* anymore.[1]

(2) a This is an excellent wine, but we still have other *wines* for you to try.
     b They ordered three *waters*, two *beers* and two *coffees*.

In (1), the count nouns are used not to denote individuals, but rather the stuff of which the individuals are made up. Pelletier (1975, 1979) called the operation which derives the stuff interpretation from the individual interpretation the 'Universal Grinder', since, intuitively, (1)

---

[1] This chapter will discuss ground readings of singular count nouns. Landman (2015) points out that singular definite noun phrases headed by count nouns shift to mass interpretations in partitive constructions under the scope of *much* as in (i):

(i)   After the paint-can fell, much of the dog/room was covered in paint.

He suggests that these cases may involve grinding at the DP level. It is not clear to me at this stage whether these cases involve the the same operation as (1), but they do show that count-to-mass shifts occur in different places in the grammar and that (1) may be one case of a wider phenomenon. However, further discussion of these cases is beyond the scope of this chapter.

refers to dog-stuff and bicycle stuff that you get by grinding whole dogs and bicycles into parts. He credits the term to a suggestion by David Lewis. In (1a,c), *dog*, which normally denotes a set of atomic dogs, is understood as denoting a mass of dog-stuff, the material out of which dogs are constructed. The operation responsible for (2a) was called the 'Universal Sorter' in Bunt (1985), and it shifts the mass noun into a count denotation in which it denotes countable subkinds. In (2a), this is a set of different types of wines. (2b) is derived via the Universal Packager (the term is used in Bach 1989, Jackendoff 1991, Landman 1991, but its source is unclear). The Packager allows mass nouns to denote individuated objects, packaged into contextually relevant portions or servings. Packaging most frequently occurs in restaurant contexts, where local constraints indicate what the relevant portions are, but these portions must be standardized. Landman (2011a) points out that *three beers* can only denote three standard portions of beer and not, for example, a teacup of beer, a bottle of beer and a test-tube of beer (though it can denote three standard servings of beer which may not all be of the same size). So this contrasts with the Yudja data discussed in the previous chapter.

All operations are called 'universal', since they are apparently productive. Note that mass nouns can shift to countable types in two different ways – to the subkind reading via the sorter or to the portion reading via the packager, but count nouns shift to mass in only one way, from objects to the stuff they are made of.

Landman (1991) gives a formal account of grinding and packaging, pointing out the asymmetry between the operations. The grinding operation g maps a (possibly plural) individual in the count domain onto a set of the parts of that individual, while the packager p maps a substance onto a plurality of contextually determined atomic individuals. Packaging a body of substance a and then grinding the result gives back the original substance a; however, the same does not hold if the operations are applied in the opposite direction, as expressed in (3).

(3)   a $g(p(a)) = a$
        b $p(g(a)) = a$ does not necessarily hold

Packaging water into standard servings and then taking the set of parts of the servings gives back the original water. In contrast, grinding a stick into sawdust gives sawdust. Packinging the latter gives a package of sawdust, not a stick.

Note that sorting and its inverse, which we can call *shuffling*, are asymmetric in the same way. Sorting a mass denotation into subkinds and shuffling the result back into a mass entity will give back the original mass denotation. However, shuffling a set of subkinds into a mass denotation and then resorting will not necessarily give back the original set of kinds since there may be more than one way of sorting a set into subkinds. While this is not accidental, our focus here is on the individual/substance contrast, and we will not discuss the Universal Sorter any further.

Packaging is a conceptually natural operation, since it essentially mirrors the operation expressed by apportioning classifiers. It has been suggested that in examples like (2b), there is a null classifier mapping substances onto contextually determined standard portions of the substance. Note, though, that packaged mass nouns are marked plural like any ordinary noun, while in classifier + mass noun constructions, pluralization is marked only on the classifier:

(4)   a   three waters
        b   three pieces of cake(#s)

One possibility is that the plural marker shifts to the N when the classifier is empty. Borer (2005) suggests that the plural morpheme is itself a classifier. However, there is evidence that plurality is not a classifier – for example, the only individuating classifier in English, *head* (which cannot itself be marked plural), takes plural nouns as its complement as well as mass nouns, showing that the classifier and plurality must have different functions:

(5)   a   He owns a hundred head of cows/#cow.
        b   'Every head of cows, and every acre of corn, etc. was worth so
            many points, and that was how they determined who could get
            farm deferment.'[2]

Another possibility is that in English, the packaging shift is a lexical operation from a mass noun into a count noun, and that the shifted N is pluralized like any other count noun. There may well be cross-linguistic variation as to whether packaging is a lexical or syntactic operation. In Standard Arabic, *three juices* is expressed using a plural noun (6a) as in English. However, in some dialects of spoken Palestinian Arabic, it is usual to ask for three servings of juice using a singular noun (6b), although *thlatha* normally takes a plural N complement (see Chapter 6).[3] This suggest that a lexical packaging

---

[2] Kansas Historical Society Oral History Project, www.kshs.org/archives/212783. Downloaded 7 June 2015.

[3] These data appear in an unpublished term paper by Aisha Khlaila, Bar-Ilan University, 2014.

operation results in a lexically count noun which pluralizes in the normal way, while a syntactic packaging operation results in a null classifier with a singular N complement.

(6)   a thlatha   a'aseier
          three   juice.PL
          'three glasses of juice / three kinds of juice'
       b thlatha   a'sier
          three   juice.SG
          'three glasses of juice'

Despite these issues, the semantics of the Universal Packager seems relatively straightforward. The Universal Grinder, however, raises different and more complex issues which we will examine in the next section.

7.2   ROOT NOUNS DO NOT HAVE GROUND INTERPRETATIONS

The packaging operation is relatively straightforward, since the output of the operation is a set of individuals that we are familiar with, namely concrete portions of stuff individuated either spatially, or by the container which contains them. The status of the output of the Universal Grinder is more problematic, and so also the status of the operation. Intuitively, *dog* in example (1a) is the stuff you get if individual entities in the denotation of the count noun *dog* are broken into bits. If this 'dog-stuff' is indeed the output of the Universal Grinder, then the operation applies to count noun denotations, and maps the set of individual dogs in the denotation of dog_{count} onto the set of proper parts of the atomic members of dog_{count}. The operation is plausibly the result of coercion in the syntax: in sentence (1a), *dog*, which is specified in the lexicon as singular count, occurs without a determiner. It is in a syntactic context which allows singular nouns only if they are mass, and so *dog* shifts to a mass noun and requires a mass interpretation. Grinding is the semantic operation which gives an appropriate mass interpretation.

While this is very plausible (as argued in Rothstein 2010), it has also been suggested that the 'ground' interpretation is the basic root meaning. The count noun is derived by applying a count operator to dog_{root}, which picks out the individual atomic dogs that are formed out of the stuff. This second approach has become associated with Borer (2005) and Bale & Barner (2009: 242). Borer assumes that the count operator is associated with a classifier position, filled by an explicit classifier, while Bale & Barner posit an empty functional head COUNT. Both proposals are in the spirit of Sharvy (1978), and posit a parallelism between English count nouns and Mandarin classifier constructions, with the null classifier or null head as the analogue of the sortal classifier in Mandarin.

Borer (2005) argues that semantic operations are, as much as possible, expressed by syntactic operators. She assumes that all nouns are unspecified for mass or count properties. Count nouns are derived in the syntax via an operation called 'divide' which is expressed by a syntactic head Cl (for classifier) immediately dominating N (or NP). Number takes ClP as complement. This is illustrated in (7):

(7)   NumPhrase

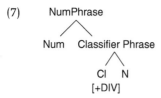

The semantic function associated with the Classifier head is to divide the stuff denoted by N into individuable entities. The default interpretation of the N is mass. Borer suggests that in mass/count languages, plurality functions as a classifier and attaches to a root noun. Count nouns like *dog*, mass nouns like *mud* and 'flexible' nouns like *cake* are generated as roots not specified for mass or count. When marked [+plural] by *-s* or [–plural] by the null singular morpheme, they are interpreted as count, otherwise the default interpretation is mass. *Two dogs* has the structure in (8).

(8)   [_Num two [_Cl -s [_N dog]]]

Plurality, *gè* in Chinese or lexical classifiers such as *piece of* occur in the classifier position, and all have the same function of dividing the denotation of the root noun into units which can be individuated, and thus counted, so, in *two cakes* and *two pieces of cake*, plurality and '*piece*' have the same divisive function.[4] In the absence of a classifier, the default interpretation is mass. In examples like (1a), repeated here as (9), the noun *dog* is not marked [±plural], and is interpreted as mass.

---

[4] It is unclear what exactly the syntactic structure of *two pieces of cake* is in Borer's theory. While *piece* has the semantics of a classifier, it is itself a noun marked plural. Thus, plausibly, the Classifier head takes *piece* as its complement and *cake* is then a nominal complement of the nominal *piece*.

The ground interpretation of the N is taken as evidence to support the account.

(9)   After the accident there was dog all over the road.

Borer's explicit goal is to show the similarities between mass/count languages and classifier languages. (8) seems to be exactly analogous to the Mandarin numerical phrases such as (10), which is predicted if plurality fills the role of the classifier.

(10)   [$_{Num}$wǔ [$_{Cl}$ zhī   [$_{N}$gǒu]]]
         five   Cl$_{small\ animal}$ dog
       'five dogs'

There are a number of questions to raise about this analysis. First, it assumes that there is identifiable 'dog stuff' and 'cat stuff' to be the denotations of the root nouns. While this is just about plausible ('dog-stuff' and 'cat-stuff' can be distinguished by their different DNA), there are other nouns for which it is much less plausible. These are the nouns whose identifying characteristics are only the way that they are put together. As an extreme example, imagine a set of modular furniture parts which can be put together to make bookshelves, tables or stools. (I own such a set of furniture.) While we may point to tables and bookshelves constructed out of these parts and say 'This is a table' and 'This is a bookshelf', it seems very odd to say that the table is a unit of table stuff and the bookshelf is a unit of bookshelf stuff, since we can take a table apart and reconstruct it as a bookshelf and vice versa.

Many more such examples can be constructed – for example, it is difficult to distinguish the stuff out of which an omelette and a scrambled egg are constructed, and yet we would not want *egg*$_{root}$, *omelette*$_{root}$, *scrambled egg*$_{root}$ to have the same denotation. These examples show that information about what constitutes the minimal or atomic parts is part of the root meaning of a noun.

Crosslinguistic data do not support Borer's proposal either. The analysis predicts that bare nouns should display similar properties crosslinguistically. Assume plurality in English is semantically a classifier which applies to the mass, ground, interpretation, and yields atomic entities. We would then expect the same relation between the sortal classifier in Mandarin and its bare nouns complement. However, this is not the case.

First, in English bare singular 'count' nouns can only have a ground reading, and if the ground reading is inappropriate, as in (11), the bare

singular is infelicitous. True count nouns never have an object mass
noun interpretation.

(11)   a #There is not a lot of boy in my class this year.
       b #There is more boy in my class than in your class.
       c #Dog crossed the road.

This correlates with the fact that only inanimate *it* can be anaphorically dependent on a count N with a ground reading. Object mass
nouns prefer *they*:

(12)   a There was dog all over the road. It/#He was airedale. #They were
         airedale.
       b There was livestock grazing in the field. They/?it seemed very
         content.
       c Poultry will consume up to 30% of their/#its body weight in
         forage.

Bare nouns in Mandarin contrast with English ground readings in
two ways. First, they have the natural individuated use that we expect
from object mass nouns. A bare noun like *gǒu* can be used to refer to
individuals (although these individuals cannot be counted, since, as
we saw in Chapter 6, classifiers are necessary to encode countability in
Mandarin).

(13)   wǒ kànjiàn gǒu-le.   tāmen hěn dà.
       I   see   dog-PART. they very big
       'I saw dogs. They were big.'

Predictably, bare nouns can be used felicitously in comparative constructions, where English (11) is infelicitous:

(14)   women bān de   nánshēng bǐ   nǐmen bān de   duō.
       we   class MOD boy   COMP your class MOD more
       'There are more boys in our class than in your class.'

Second, bare *gǒu* can never have a ground interpretation in Mandarin,
as shown in Cheng, Doetjes & Sybesma (2008). Compare the examples
in (15):

(15)   a There was dog all over the wall.
       b qiáng-shàng dōu shì gǒu.
         wall-top   all COP dog
         'There are dogs all over the wall.'

(15b) can never have the interpretation assigned in English to (15a).
(15b) only has what Cheng, Doetjes & Sybesma call a 'wallpaper
reading', in which the sentence means that the wall was covered
with pictures of dogs. This arises as follows: *gǒu* has its standard

interpretation as an object mass noun. *dōu* is a distributive marker which forces N to be witnessed by a plurality. In the context, (15b) is interpreted as meaning that the wall was covered with (pictures of) a plurality of dogs. If we force a reading in which only one dog is involved, we get what you might call the 'cartoon' or 'Tom and Jerry' reading, in which the outline of a single (whole) dog appears on the wall. The only way to get a ground reading is to modify *gǒu* lexically, as in (16a), using *gǒu-ròu* or 'dog meat'. The modified noun has the same distribution as other substance nouns (16b):

(16) a qiáng-shàng dōu shì gǒu-ròu.
     wall-top   all COP dog-flesh/meat
     'There is dog all over the wall.'
   b dì-shàng   dōu shì   shuǐ
     floor-top all COP   water
     'There is water all over the floor.'

Even in a context in which an animal is eaten for food, the bare noun has only an atomic interpretation. (17) is only appropriate if a whole animal is served:

(17) a women zuótiān chī le yú.
     we   yesterday ate PFV fish
     'We ate a fish yesterday.'
   b women zuótiān chī le zhū.
     we   yesterday ate PFV pig
     'We ate a pig yesterday.'

Cheng, Doetjes & Sybesma point out that it is possible to use some fruits in ground readings:

(18) shālā lǐ   yǒu píngguǒ/júzi/#zhū.
     salad inside have apple/orange/pig
     'There is apple/orange/#pig in the salad.'

This supports other crosslinguistic evidence that fruits and vegetables allow both items and stuff in their denotations (see Rothstein 2011; Landman 2011a; Beviláqua *et al.* 2016).

The conclusion is that Mandarin bare nouns do not have the same interpretation as English count nouns with a ground interpretation. *gǒu* 'dog' can never have a substance interpretation. While it is not a count noun, it can only have an object mass noun interpretation and be used to refer to sets of individuals. This extends to examples like (19a), which can only be expressed as (19b) in Mandarin:

(19)   a When I opened the door, I was almost knocked over by 25 kilos
          of dog.
       b ... chà diǎn bèi wǒ nà   zh wǔshí jīn   zhòng de   gǒu
          ... almost PASS my that Cl fifty   pound heavy MOD dog
          bàndǎo.
          knock.over
          '... I was almost knocked over by my fifty-pound dog.'

If, as Borer suggests, Cl+N in Mandarin parallels the English count
noun *dog(s)*, we would expect the English bare or root noun *dog* to
denote a set of singular and plural dog-individuals. However, when
dog in English is used as a mass noun, it can never have an object mass
noun interpretation, but must be interpreted as a substance or stuff-
denoting expression. This is the interpretation which is unavailable
for Mandarin bare nouns.

7.3 THE UNIVERSAL GRINDER AND COERCION

Cheng, Doetjes & Sybesma (2008) give an explanation for the
absence of ground readings in Mandarin in terms of a coercion
theory of grinding (although they don't give an explicit semantics).
They suggest that the ground reading *dog* in English is derived as
a last resort through a coercion to resolve conflict when there is
a mismatch between a count noun and the syntactic context in
which it appears. Only mass nouns can be used as bare singulars in
English, so when a singular count noun is used as a bare singular, it
has to be interpreted as a mass noun. As a last resort, the count noun
is reanalysed as a mass noun and coerced into a mass interpretation,
and the grinding operation is used to derive this interpretation.
In Mandarin, however, as we saw in Chapter 6, all nouns can appear
bare. There is no possibility of a syntactic mismatch occurring, and
no need to coerce a count noun into a mass interpretation. Thus,
grinding is never triggered. In this way, Mandarin provides good
evidence that ground interpretations are not the natural interpretations of the naturally atomic root nouns, but are the result of
coercion.

Modern Hebrew provides further support for a coercion theory of
universal grinder terms. Modern Hebrew is a language with a mass/
count distinction, and classifiers do not occur with bare singular
count nouns. However, unlike English, there is no indefinite article
and bare singular count nouns have a natural indefinite
interpretation:

(20) dani ra'a   namer.
      dani saw.PAST   tiger.SG
      'Dani saw a tiger.'

Further, as Doron (2003) shows, Modern Hebrew allows bare singulars to be used as names for kinds, though the usage is restricted to names of taxonomic species (Rothstein 2013c).

(21) namer hu   min be-sakanat hakxada. (Doron 2003: (1a))
      tiger PRON.SG kind in-danger extinction
      'The tiger is a kind in danger of extinction.'

On the basis of what we have seen so far, we would predict the following. Since bare singular count nouns are licensed and can have both an indefinite and a kind interpretation, there is no position in which we expect a ground reading to be triggered by a syntactic mismatch, and this appears to be the case. (22) does not have a ground reading.

(22) axarey   ha-te'una,   haya   kelev al   ha-šulxan.
      after   DEF-accident was.M   dog.M on   DEF-table
      'After the accident, there was a dog on the table.' (only an individual reading)

However, in non-standard, colloquial Hebrew, ground readings are possible in one configuration. They are triggered by a mismatch, but a morphological mismatch, as in (23):

(23) axarey ha-te'una,   haya   arnevet al (#kol) ha-kir.
      after DEF-accident was.M rabbit.F on (#all) DEF-wall
      'After the accident, there was rabbit all over the wall.'

arnevet is the Hebrew word for 'rabbit', and it is inherently feminine, marked with the feminine suffix *-et*. Unlike pairs like *kelev/kalba* 'dog.M/dog.F', there is no masculine counterpart, i.e. no lexical item *arnav*. In (23), the copula is in the masculine. There is a morphological gender mismatch between copula and bare singular count noun which follows it, and in colloquial Hebrew, this triggers a shift to the ground reading. As soon as the copula is changed to the feminine *hayta* and the morphological mismatch disappears, the universal grinder reading is impossible.

(24) #axarey ha-te'una,   hayta arnevet al (#kol) ha-qir.
      after   DEF-accident was.F rabbit.F on (#all) DEF-wall
      'After the accident, there was a rabbit on the (#whole) wall.'

(24) has its normal indefinite reading (the most natural context is the 'Tom and Jerry' reading described above). The quantifier *kol* is

infelicitous, since *arnevet* has only its normal count singular interpretation, and the context requires *al kol ha-qir* 'over the whole wall' to have either a mass or plural antecedent.

The universal grinder reading in (24) is possible only if the gender mismatch is unavoidable, because of a lexical gap in the language. The gender mismatches in (25) are simply judged as 'mistakes' and not assigned an alternative interpretation.

(25) #axarey ha-te'una,   haya   kalba / hayta kelev al kol ha-qir.
      after   DEF-accident was.M dog.F / was.F dog.M on all DEF-wall
      'After the accident, there was dog on the whole wall.'

These data support the claim that grinder readings are triggered by a mismatch which makes the normal interpretation unavailable.

Brazilian Portuguese adds an interesting twist to the discussion. Ground interpretations are possible in examples like (26):[5]

(26) Tinha   cachorro pela   parede toda.
      was.IMPFV dog.SG   across.the wall   whole
      'There was dog all over the wall.'
      Or 'There were dogs all over the wall.'

Unlike the examples we have seen above, (26) can have both a ground interpretation and a plural, Mandarin-like 'wallpaper' interpretation. However, the plural interpretation is strongly preferred. A possible explanation is as follows: *cachorro* in (26) is a bare object mass noun and can be used to make reference to a plurality of instantiations, as in Mandarin. Like the Mandarin example in (15), it has the 'wallpaper' interpretation. Suppose the plural or kind interpretations are not available. Unlike Mandarin, *cachorro* can also be analysed as a singular count noun. In this case, there is a syntactic mismatch, since N does not have a determiner. As a last resort, grinding allows a ground reading. Preliminary results (Beviláqua *et al.* 2016) suggest that this may be the case. More research is necessary to find out exactly what triggers these ground readings in Brazilian Portuguese. However, it is unlikely to be coincidental that, of the languages we have looked at, the only one that allows an ambiguity between a ground reading and a wallpaper reading is the only language in which bare N is ambiguous between a mass and a count interpretation.

---

[5] Thanks to Roberta Pires de Oliveira for the example and for discussing these data with me. Note that the ground reading is more easily available with an imperfective copula than a perfective copula.

7.4 ANALYSIS OF THE UNIVERSAL GRINDER

We have looked at four languages (English, Mandarin, Modern Hebrew and Brazilian Portuguese), and have seen that ground readings are available in three of them, but under different conditions.

Ground readings are completely unavailable in Mandarin. So arguing that ground readings are mass (or root) noun interpretations would leave us with the conclusion that root nouns have different interpretations in Mandarin and English. Furthermore, in Brazilian Portuguese, mass nouns have similar properties to Mandarin bare nouns, as we saw in Chapters 5 and 6. However, ground readings are available and are distinct from mass noun interpretations. This strongly suggests that they are derived from count nouns and not from root interpretations. In all three of the languages which do allow ground readings – English, Modern Hebrew and Brazilian Portuguese – they are only possible when there is some kind of mismatch between the 'normal' use of the count noun and the syntactic context in which it is used. This strongly supports a coercion-based analysis of grinding, where the ground reading is derived from the count noun when syntactic context makes the count noun interpretation impossible.[6]

The operation which derives the readings we want maps a set of atomic individuals onto a set of proper parts of those individuals. Of course, atomic individuals don't have (visible) parts, so we need the set of proper parts of the mass stuff of which each dog is made up (since we want to exclude whole dogs from the ground interpretation of *dog*). The operation in (27) maps an atom a in k onto the mass parts of a, excluding a itself.[7]

(27) $\downarrow$ is a function that maps every a $\in$ ATOM onto the sum of its mass parts. We impose here a minimal constraint: if a $\in$ ATOM: $\downarrow$ (a) $\neq 0$ and $\downarrow$(a) $\notin$ ATOM and $\downarrow$(a) $\sqcap$ a $= 0$ (and assume further constraints locating a and the sum of its mass parts in the same space, etc.). With this we define operation $\downarrow_k$ which specifies the set of mass parts for the atoms in context k. Let $\sqsubset$ be the proper part-of relation, k a context, and z a variable over objects: If a is a *natural* atom, i.e. a $\in$ k $\cap$ ATOM, then $\downarrow_k$(a) $= \lambda z.z \sqsubset \downarrow$(a), the set of a's proper mass parts (and $\sqcup\downarrow_k$(a) is $\downarrow$(a), the sum of a's mass parts).

If x is a *contextual* atom, i.e. x $\in$ K – ATOM, then $\downarrow_k$(x) $= \lambda z.z \sqsubset$ x, the set of x's proper parts (and $\sqcup\downarrow_k$(x) $=$ x).

---

[6] Landman (p.c.) points out that (i) grinding may not be a last-resort operation crosslinguistically, and that (ii) even if it is a last-resort operation at the bare N level, it may be freely available in the case of DPs (see footnote 1 above). It would make perfect sense for grinding at the bare N level to make use, under coercion, of an operation which is freely available at the NP level.

[7] Thanks to Fred Landman for clarifying this and for the formulation of (27) and (28).

We can now define GRIND as in (28), P_x a predicate of type $\langle e \times k, t \rangle$:

(28) $GRIND(N_k) = \lambda P_x \lambda x. \exists y [y \in \pi_1(P_x) \wedge x \in \downarrow_k(y)]$

What happens is the following.

GRIND applies to a (singular) count predicate and maps it onto the set of proper parts of the elements in its denotation which are not naturally atomic, and parts of the mass correlates of the entities in the denotation that are naturally atomic. Thus, contextually atomic fences are mapped onto proper fence-parts, naturally atomic dogs are mapped onto their grind, their mass correlates. The proper parts of the k-indexed elements are not themselves k-indexed and so the output of GRIND is a mass noun. The entire derivation for the ground interpretation of dog_{ground} is as follows:

dog_{root} is a naturally atomic root noun denoting DOG_{root} the set of singular dogs closed under sum.

DOG_k is the result of applying COUNT to DOG_{root}. It is the set of individual dogs which count as atomic in context k:

$DOG_k = COUNT(DOG_{root}) = \{\langle x, k \rangle : x \in DOG_{root} \cap k\}$

Note that, given the natural atomicity, and the fact that sums of dogs do not count as semantic atoms of dogs, this is just:

$\{\langle a, k \rangle : a \in ATOM \text{ and } a \in DOG_{root} \cap k\}$

Applying GRIND gives you:

$DOG_{ground} = GRIND(COUNT(DOG_{root}))$
$= GRIND(\{\langle a, k \rangle : a \in ATOM \wedge a \in DOG_{root} \cap k\})$
$= \lambda x. \exists y [y \in \pi_1(\{\langle a, k \rangle : a \in ATOM \wedge a \in DOG_{root} \cap k\}) \wedge x \in \downarrow_k(y)]$
$= \lambda x. \exists a \in ATOM[a \in DOG_{root} \cap k \wedge x \in \downarrow_k(a)]$
     The set of mass parts of naturally atomic dogs in k

In the mass denotation imposed via $GRIND(N_k)$, the individual dogs are no longer the minimal parts of the denotation; in fact, the theory is neutral as to whether there are minimal parts in the ground denotation.

The shift operation only applies to count noun denotations, hence, we predict that naturally atomic mass nouns do not have grinding readings. (29a) contrasts with (29b):

(29)   a   There is jewellery/clothing all over the floor.
       b   There is dog all over the floor.

(29b) only has a ground reading, excluding 'whole' dogs, but (29a) has the natural interpretation in which whole pieces of clothing or jewellery are scattered over the floor. Pieces of clothing and jewellery may be included if they are big enough to count as instances of clothing or jewellery, for example, a necklace which is in two pieces and needs repairing may still be 'jewellery'. However, it does not have the 'stuff' reading associated with grinding. To get that interpretation, we need a lexical operator or classifier, similar to the Mandarin example in (16a):

(30)   a There are bits of jewellery all over the floor.
        b There are shreds of clothing all over the floor.

If GRIND(N_k) is triggered by a syntactic mismatch between the count properties of the N_k and the syntactic environment which is appropriate for a mass noun, GRIND will never be triggered when N is mass, even if it is a naturally atomic mass noun, just in the same way that it is not triggered in Mandarin. So, indeed, we would predict Mandarin-like interpretations for English object mass nouns.

7.5   QUESTIONS FOR FURTHER DISCUSSION AND INVESTIGATION

1 Close examination of the lexicon suggests that many mass nouns have 'packaged' counterparts, especially abstract nouns as in (31):

(31)   a Passion / a passion / his two great passions
        b Attention / the attentions they paid her
        c clarification/clarifications

What criteria of individuation are involved? Do you find patterns?
2 Cases like (32) suggest that bare count nouns in English may have a kind interpretation in certain contexts, rather than a ground interpretation.

(32)   During the apple harvest, apple is eaten in some form or another at every meal.

Are there ways to distinguish between bare kind readings in English and ground readings? Are there other contexts in which a kind interpretation is possible?
3 Explore the hypothesis that nouns denoting food show grammatical patterns which distinguish them from other nouns.
4 Explore the suggestion in footnote 1, that there are other syntactic contexts in which coercion from count to mass is possible.

8 Classifiers

'[F]or every collection of beasts of the forest and for every gathering of birds of the air, there is their own private name so that none may be confused with another.'

Arthur Conan Doyle, *Sir Nigel*, quoted in J. Lipton,
An Exaltation of Larks

8.1   INTRODUCTION

This chapter explores the semantics of individuating classifiers in English, and in particular how they are used to create complex countable phrases. I will not give a semantic analysis of the whole range of individuating classifiers, since it would take us far beyond the scope of this book.[1] Instead, I want to focus on the role of classifiers in a mass/count language, and what the contrast is between classifiers in a 'classifier language' and in a 'non-classifier' language.

English, and languages like it, are often termed 'non-classifier' languages, because count nouns can be modified directly by numericals, as in (1a,b), in contrast to so-called 'classifier languages' like Mandarin, where, as we have seen, counting is impossible without a sortal or other individuating classifier (1c,d):

(1)   a   three women   b   five cats
       c   sān   gè   rén   d   wǔ zhī   gǒu
           three Cl$_{general}$ person   five Cl$_{small\ animal}$ dog
           'three people'   'five dogs'

Obviously, English does use classifiers of many different kinds. A list of classifier types will include at least those listed in I and II. This list follows Allan (1977, 1980) and Lehrer (1986), but, unlike them, and based on the results in Chapters 3 and 6 of this book, it

---

[1] For a detailed technical analysis of the semantics of different classifiers, see Landman (2015).

distinguishes between counting classifiers and measures.[2] As argued in Chapter 3, counting classifiers combine with a complement to form a phrase which is modified by a numerical, while measure classifiers combine with a numerical to form a measure predicate, which modifies the complement noun.

I **Counting classifiers**

- (a) unit classifiers which pick out individual entities, such as **unit** *(of furniture)*, **item** *(of clothing)*, **head** *(of cattle)*;
- (b) apportioning or partition classifiers which divide masses into individual portions, such as **piece** *(of cake)*, **puddle** *(of water)*, **grain** *(of rice)*, **chunk** *(of wood)*, **quantity** *(of sand)*;
- (c) container classifiers, such as **box** *(of books)*;
- (d) group or collective classifiers which allow individuals to be grouped into higher-order entities, such as **group** *(of children)*, **herd** *(of elephants)*;
- (e) 'arrangement' classifiers (Allan 1977, 1980), such as **row** *(of books)* and **pile** *(of magazines)*;
- (f) kind classifiers which individuate kinds, such as **kind** of *(dog)*.

II **Measuring classifiers**

- (a) lexical measures, such as **kilo** *(of flour)*, **litre** *(of wine)*;
- (b) measures derived from containers, such as **bottle** *(of wine)*, **glass** *(of whisky)*;
- (c) measures derived explicitly via the suffix *-ful*, such as **pocketful** *(of rye)*, **busful** *(of tourists)*;
- (d) measures derived explicitly via the suffix *-worth*, such as ten **dollarsworth** /ten **poundsworth** *(of petrol)*.

---

[2] There are several different categorizations. Chao (1968), writing about Mandarin, gives six different types of classifier expressions: individual classifiers, group classifiers, partition classifiers, container classifiers, temporary classifiers and standard measures. The first three of these would be counting classifiers in our terms, the last two would be measures, and the fourth group, containers, is ambiguous between count and measure. Allan (1977) distinguishes five types of classifiers in English: unit counters such as *piece (of equipment)*, collective classifiers as in *herd (of animals)*, varietal classifiers, e.g., *kinds/species (of wheat)*, measure classifiers as in *pound/box (of candy)* and 'arrangement classifiers' such as *row/stack (of books)*. He also considers approximatives such as *hundreds (of cats)* as classifiers, as well as fractions such as *three-quarters (of the cake)*. The last is best considered a partitive construction, since, unlike true classifiers, it cannot take a bare NP as a complement.

In this chapter, I will discuss classifiers of type I. In the next chapter, I will discuss measure heads (often called 'mensural classifiers') and explore the relation between measure heads and individuating classifiers.

Some uses of counting classifiers are illustrated in (2):

(2)   a three grains of rice
      b three pieces of furniture
      c three glasses of wine/lentils
      d three puddles of water
      e three groups/classes of children
      f three boxes of books
      g three heaps of sand/mud/books

Counting classifiers head countable NPs. They are individuating classifiers, since they map mass or plural predicates onto sets of discrete countable units. They do this in one of two ways. They map mass predicate denotations onto countable predicates by picking out discrete units in the denotation of the mass N. For example, in (2c), *wine* is not countable, but *glasses of wine* are countable. Counting classifiers may also 'repackage' plural count predicates into higher-order non-overlapping countable units. *Children* and *books* are count predicates, so they do not need classifiers to be countable. However, the classifier allows collections or groups of children (or of books) to be counted, rather than counting the children or books themselves. Most classifiers seem to apply to both mass and plural NPs, although there may be semantic restrictions (e.g. *puddle* presupposes that its complement is liquid). *Group* seems to apply only to count nouns, as shown by the contrast between *a group of guests* and the infelicitous #*a group of company*, but other group classifiers are more permissive.

Different classifiers map NP denotations onto countable units in different ways. *Grain* in (2a) is a sortal classifier. *Glass/group/box* in (2c,e,f) illustrate the container classifiers discussed in Chapter 3, which individuate discrete units of stuff / plural objects via the objects which contain them. *Piece* in (2b) is an apportioning or partition classifier, as are *puddle* and *heap*. Classifiers like *heap/stack/pile* were called 'arrangement classifiers' in Lehrer (1986). (2e) is a 'group' classifier which repackages count nouns and naturally atomic mass nouns into groups.

Given these data, why does Mandarin count as a classifier language while English does not? We shall show that in Mandarin, classifiers are an independent functional category, while the classifiers in (2) are relational count nouns. English can do without a functional category of classifiers because it can exploit the count properties of relational nouns to produce complex count phrases.

Before we continue, we need a pretheoretic definition of 'classifier' which makes it possible to distinguish classifiers from other relational nouns. I suggest the following:

(3)   N is a classifier if [(Num) N NP] denotes countable sums of NP-stuff/ entities.

(3) is purposely vague in order to allow a variety of classifier constructions, including both measuring and counting classifiers. *Class* as a relational noun can be used as a classifier since *three classes of students* can be used to give indirect information about the quantity of students. *Class* contrasts with nouns like *examination*. *Examination* is a relational noun, but not a classifier since *examination of the students* denotes a set of **events** of examining the students, and does not give us any information about the quantity of students in the denotation of NP. *Three examinations of the students*[3] gives us only information about how many examination events there were and not about the number of students. *Kilo* is a not a classifier in the sense of (3), since, on the analysis we have been giving, *kilos of flour* is not countable. While this may not answer all questions as to whether an N has a classifier interpretation, it is a good enough working definition for us to use here.

8.2   SOME SYNTACTIC PROPERTIES OF COUNTING CLASSIFIERS

8.2.1   Counting Classifiers Are Count Nouns

We begin by showing that only count nouns (and not mass nouns) can be used as classifiers. Classifiers and other relation nouns appear in the *N of NP* construction, but a classifier interpretation is possible only when N is count. Take near-synonyms such as *mess* and *untidiness*, where the first is count, but the second is mass, as witnessed by *a mess* vs #*an untidiness*. The first can have a classifier interpretation, on which it denotes a quantity of books as in (4a), while the second is infelicitous as a classifier, as in (4b). If *untidiness* has (marginally) an

---

[3] 'There shall be **three examinations of the students** in the course of the session; one immediately before the Christmas recess – one in the last week of March – and another before the close of the session in June' (*Journal of the House of Delegates of the Commonwealth of Virginia*, 1835, p. 28).

interpretation as a relational noun, it can only be in a sentence like
(4c), where it denotes a particular kind of untidiness, the untidiness
caused by books, but it does not have a quantity reading:

(4)   a I moved the mess of books out of the room.
       b #I moved the untidiness of books out of the room.
       c The/#that untidiness of books horrifies me.

Dutch shows the absence of mass classifiers even more clearly since
classifier constructions are syntactically distinct from other relational
nouns. A classifier directly precedes an NP, as in (5a), whereas other
relational nouns take PP complements (5b):

(5)   a een glas   water
          a   glass water
          'a glass of water'
       b de verwoesting van de stad
          the destruction of the city
          'the destruction of the city'

Only count nouns can appear in the [N NP] configuration. Fred
Landman (p.c.) gives the following illustration. The noun *smurrie*,
a mass noun meaning 'dirty mess', can be used as in (6a), and in
a mass noun compound *verf-smurrie* 'paint mess' as in (6b). *Verf-
smurrie* can be modified by a measure predicate.

(6)   a Wat heb je nou voor smurrie aan je   schoen?
          What have you now for   mess   on your shoe
          'What is that dirty mess on your shoe?'
       b Ik   heb in   drie uur tijd   ongeveer vier kilo/ de
          I   have in   three hour time   about   four kilo/ the
          hele verf smurrie van de   grond   verwijderd.
          whole paint mess   from the ground removed

          'It took me about three hours to remove about four kilos of / the
          whole paint mess from the ground.'

However, (7) shows that *smurrie* cannot be a classifier in the
N-N structure used in (5a). (7) contrasts with (6b), and with the felicitous English classifier construction headed by the count noun *mess*, as
in *the whole mess of paint* and in (4a) above.

(7)   #Ik heb in   drie uur tijd de hele *smurrie verf* van
          I have in   three hour time the whole mess paint from
          de grond   verwijderd.
          the ground removed
          Intended: 'It took me three hours to remove the whole mess of paint
          from the ground.'

Coercion of *smurrie* into a count noun is (very) marginally acceptable. To the degree that it can be coerced into a count noun, it can also be used as a classifier, leading to the contrast between (7) and (8):

(8) ???Ik heb in drie uur tijd drie smurries verf van de
     I   have in three hour time three messes paint from the
     grond verwijderd.
     ground removed
     'It took me three hours to remove three messes of paint from the ground.'

The conclusion is that mass nouns cannot be classifiers. Intuitively, this is not surprising, and we will give an explanation later in this chapter.

8.2.2 The Category of Classifiers

The next important question is: what category are classifiers? It has been argued extensively that individuating classifiers in Mandarin form a closed class of functional heads, independent of nouns. Li (2013: ch. 2) summarizes these arguments, showing that classifiers and nouns have different properties. First, many individuating classifiers do not have a nominal use. (9) and (10) show that *ba*, the classifier which indicates that an object that can be picked up in the hand, and *zhi*, the classifier used for counting small animals, never have a nominal use, even if preceded by the general classifier *gè*. *gè* itself cannot be used as a noun, either preceded by a classifier (11a) or in a bare numeral + Cl phrase (11b):

(9) a yì bǎ yǐ zià
        one Cl_{grip} chair
        'one/a chair'
     b #yí gè bǎ
        one $Cl_{general}$ Cl_{grip}
        Intended reading: 'One grip'

(10) a sān zhī gǒu
        three $Cl_{small\ animal}$ dog
        'three dogs'
     b #sān gè zhī
        three $Cl_{general}$ $Cl_{small\ animal}$
        Intended reading: 'three small animals'

(11) a #sān gè gè
        three $Cl_{general}$ $Cl_{general}$
     b #sān gè
        Intended reading for both: 'three objects/things'

Second, Li shows that, even when classifiers are apparently derived from nouns[4], they have different grammatical properties as classifiers and as nouns. As classifiers, they combine with nouns and allow the noun to be counted. As nouns, they are as uncountable as any other noun, and require an appropriate classifier in order to combine with a numeral. Crucially, in Modern Mandarin, a single lexical item cannot be interpreted as a classifier and an N in one classifier phrase.[5] For example, *shàn* has a classifier use in which it individuates *mén* 'door' and *chuāng* 'window', as, for example in (12a). As a noun it means 'fan', as in (12b), and is used with the classifier *bǎ* which individuates items that you can grip or hold in your hand, as illustrated in (9a) above. *shàn* cannot be used to 'classify' itself (12c). This pattern holds for container classifiers like *píng* 'bottle', as illustrated in (13). In (13a), *píng* is a classifier for *jiǔ* 'wine'. In (13b) it is a noun, denoting a particular kind of object, a bottle, in contrast to a cup or a bowl. Note the added detail that, in some dialects, in particular in the more northern ones, *píng* in its nominal use has to be marked with the nominalizer *-zi*.

(12) a wǔ shàn mén
         five Cl_{fan} door
         'five doors'
      b wǔ #(bǎ) shàn
         five Cl_{grip} fan
         'five fans'
      c #wǔ shàn shàn

(13) a sān   píng   jiǔ
         three Cl_{bottle} wine
         'three bottles of wine'
      b sān gè   píng(-zi)
         three $Cl_{general}$ bottle(-nom)
         'three bottles'
      c #sān píng píng(-zi)

Bare *wǔ shàn* or *sān píng* are possible only if *shàn* and *píng* are interpreted as classifiers in a context in which the N complement of the classifier is elliptical and can be supplied contextually, as in (14), or when the N complement has been fronted, as in (15):

---

[4] Cheng & Sybesma (1999) argue that 'massifiers', i.e. non-sortal classifiers, start off syntactically as N and raise to classifier position, incorrectly predicting that all non-sortals are derived from nouns. But it seems plausible that in some cases there is a lexical relation. See also Cheng (2012).

[5] In oracle bone Mandarin, there are examples of N being used as a classifier. See Peyraube (1999).

(14) a Q: nǐ cā le jǐ shàn chuānghu?
          you clean PFV how-many Cl_fan window
          'How many windows did you clean?
       A: wǔ shàn.
          five Cl_fan
          'Five.'
      b Q: zhuō shàng fàng le jǐ píng hóngjiǔ?
          table on put PFV how-many Cl_bottle red wine
          'How many bottles of red wine were put on the table?'
       A: sān píng.
          three Cl_bottle
          'Three.'

(15) píngguǒ, wǒ zhǐ chī le sān gè
      apples, I only eat PFV five Cl_general
      'As for apples, I only ate three.'

Some classifiers never have a nominal use:

(16) a yì kǔn dàocǎo a' #yí gè kǔn
         one Cl_bundle straw   one Cl_general bundle
         'one bundle of straw' Intended: 'one bundle'
      b yì zhāng zhǐ b' #yí gè zhāng
         one piece paper   one Cl_general piece
         'one piece of paper' Intended: 'one piece'

The classifiers exemplified in (9)–(16) include individuating classifiers like *gè*, partition (or apportioning) classifiers like *zhāng* and *kǔn*, and container classifiers like *píng*. The same behaviour characterizes other classifiers, including group classifiers and measure classifiers.

The third argument is that classifiers are not a productive class in Mandarin. Group classifiers include expressions such as *qún*, used for a group of people or animals, *bān*, used for a group of people, *huǒ*, used for hooligans, *duī* 'pile', used for discrete or homogeneous entities, *dié* 'pile', used for a stack of books or plates or other thin objects, but the list is limited. Similarly, my informants tell me that container nouns cannot be shifted productively into classifiers. This is what we would expect if classifiers are a functional category, and thus a closed class, rather than an open lexical class.

Fourth, modification of classifiers by adjectives is highly restricted. Classifiers can be modified only by dimensional adjectives such as *dà* 'big' and *xiǎo* 'small', but not by other adjectives, and the adjectives have a different interpretation when they modify classifiers from when they modify nouns. As nominal modifiers, they give a property of the N in the expected way, while as modifiers of classifiers, they express the speaker's perspective on the object. See Li (2011) for more discussion.

In contrast, classifiers in English show all the characteristics of relational count nouns. *Piece, group* and *box* illustrate partition, group and container classifiers respectively, and have a wide range of nominal properties. They obligatorily agree with a numeral, as in (17):[6]

(17)   a a piece of silverware / three pieces of silverware
          b a group of children / three groups of children
          c a box of chocolates / three boxes of chocolates

They can be freely modified by adjectives, as shown in (18):

(18)   a three wedge-shaped pieces of wood/cake
          b 'Nothing moved except the wind and a few dried pieces of mud which rolled into the shaft.'[7]
          c 'several round, flat, pieces of white and red metal[8]
          d a noisy/unruly group of children
          e a beautifully wrapped box of chocolates

The classifiers in (18) can all be used as non-relational intransitive nouns as in (19):

(19)   a The puzzle came in fifteen pieces and had to be assembled.
          b The divisions between spectators and performers became unclear as both groups mingled together.
          c The boxes were waiting to be filled.

They can also be used in subject-predicate construction as in (20):

(20)   a These three pieces are gold, while these four pieces are silver.
          b These groups are highly skilled.
          c These boxes are cardboard.

They can take DP complements as well as NP complements:

(21)   a This jersey collage contains a piece of every jersey he has ever worn for the US.[9]
          b A group of some twenty very loud teenagers came into the room.
          c Buy a box of our hand-made, creamy pralines.

---

[6] The only exception to this is *head* which, as mentioned in Chapter 6, is probably the only genuine classifier in English. It does not agree in number with a numerical, as in (i), and it cannot be used as a sortal without changing its meaning (ii).

(i)   three head(#s) of cattle/livestock
(ii)   how many heads do you have?

As discussed in Chapter 6, there is nothing to prevent a language having sortal classifiers as well as a mass/count distinction.

[7] Brian Croasdell, *High Cross*, iUniverse 2006, p. 90.
[8] Jonathan Swift, *Gulliver's Travels*, Ware: Wordsworth Editions, p. 23.
[9] Based on http://the18.com/news/farewell-captain.

Strikingly, classifier+NP phrases can be used as bare kind-denoting terms, as in (22), which is not surprising if the classifier is an N. In Mandarin, this is impossible, and a bare classifier +NP can only denote a singular term (Li & Bisang 2012).

(22)   a 'If you are looking for pieces of gold, you are going to require a metal detector'.[10]

        b 'However, pieces of coal are widespread in the soil.'[11]

        c 'They looked for groups of stars which seem to form patterns in the sky.'[12]

        d Groups of tourists are rare in December.

        e Boxes of good chocolates are difficult to find!

Finally, classifiers are a productive class in English. We can replace *piece* in *piece of wood* with nouns such as *fragment, splinter, chip, log, twig, chunk* and *plank*, and many others depending on the context, and each of them can be used to determine some set of individuable entities. Semantically, at least some of the content of *piece of* contributes to the truth conditions of the sentence, as (23) shows, and, in this, English contrasts with Mandarin, where, as we saw in Chapter 6, all information contributed by the individuating classifier is presuppositional.

(23)   I asked for two pieces of wood. Instead they gave me two splinters.

Group classifiers are similarly an open class. Beyond general terms such as *group of N, collection of N, assembly of N, flock of N* and so on, English has a vast collection of so-called 'company terms', where the group term is specific to the particular group members, such as *pride of lions, gaggle of geese,* and new items are easily added to the language (Lipton 1993). The conclusion is, then, that English classifiers are nouns, and thus different from Mandarin classifiers which are an independent syntactic category.

8.3   *THE INTERPRETATION OF ENGLISH COUNTING CLASSIFIERS*

In Chapter 3, we argued that container classifiers like *glass* and *bottle* are relational nouns derived from one-place sortal nouns, and that in classifier phrases they head an NP. In this sense they are analogous to inherently relational nouns like *mother (of)* as well as relational nouns

---

[10] www.metaldetectorsonline.net/goldmetaldetectors/gold-metal-detectors.html.

[11] http://nzetc.victoria.ac.nz/tm/scholarly/tei-NHSJ04_05-t1-body1-d1-d4.html.

[12] www.yourarticlelibrary.com/essay/essay-on-our-universe-definition-stars-and-solar-system/31857.

derived from other sources, for example nouns derived from verbs, such as *performance* or *gift*. Relational nouns usually are of type <e,<e,t>>, analogous to transitive verbs, with the internal argument syntactically licensed (i.e. case-marked) by a preposition, as in *mother of John* and *gift to John*. However, in Chapter 3, we treated classifiers as heads which took NP complements, and we now review the evidence which supports that move.

The contrast between classifiers and other relational nominals is masked in English by the fact that *glass, box* and *set* can take definite DP complements. However, when the complement is definite, the reading must be partitive. On the classifier reading, the NP complement of the classifier denotes the material(s) packaged by the classifier, as in (24).

(24)   a I drank two glasses of wine.
        b We mailed twenty boxes of books.
        c He ate two pieces of cake.

In the partitive reading, the definite NP complement denotes a particular quantity of N, and the complex NP denotes a subset (though not necessarily a proper subset) of that specific quantity. This is illustrated in (25).

(25)   a I drank two glasses of the red wine (and indeed that was all that there was).
        b We mailed twenty boxes of those books.
        c He ate two pieces of the chocolate cake.

The similarity between the two readings is a language-specific property of English, due to the multipurpose use of *of* to divide a head from its complement, as a result of which *bottles of wine* and *bottles of the wine* look superficially very similar. But this is a property of English. As we already saw, Dutch classifiers take NP complements and do not allow definites or partitive readings (26).

(26)   a twee flessen   wijn
           two bottle.PL wine
        b #twee flessen   van de wijn/Chablis
           two   bottle.PL of   the wine / of the Chablis

Relational nouns must take PP complements and cannot take bare NP complements, as shown in (27a–d). A classifier with a PP complement must be reinterpreted as a (non-relational) sortal, as in (28).

(27)   a twee zusters van het slachtoffer
           two   sisters of   the victim

    b #twee zusters slachtoffer
       two   sisters victim
    c twee uitvoeringen van de symfonie
       two perfomances of the symphony
    d #twee uitvoeringen symfonie
       two   perfomances symphony

(28)   Twee nieuw flessen van/uit de Chablis Collectie zijn deze maand
      two new   bottles of/from the Chablis Collection are this month
      verschenen.
      appeared
      'Two new bottles in the Chablis Collection appeared this month.'

Classifiers, then, generally take NP complements, but these can be modified nouns. The complement of the classifier can be a plural count noun modified by a numerical, shown in (29a–d), or by temporal and stage-level modifiers, as in (29e–f).[13]

(29)   a six boxes of twenty chocolates
      b six packets of five hundred sheets of paper
      c two sets of fifteen pieces of silverware
      d a pile of twelve books / a heap of a hundred Smarties
      e six slices of yesterday's bread / stale bread
      f three sheets of tomorrow's newspaper

(30) below also shows that the classifier complement is an NP. In (30a), a singular count noun is infelicitous as a classifier complement (unless it can be reinterpreted as mass). This cannot be because N is singular, since *one chocolate* is a felicitous complement in (30b). But if the classifier complement is an NP, (30a) is predicted to be infelicitous, since a singular count N in English needs to be preceded by a determiner.

(30)   a #six boxes of book
      b We supply boxes of one chocolate for party favours.

Classifiers, then, are relational count nouns which apply to the NP predicate denotation and map it onto a count predicate. The restrictions on what predicate a classifier can apply to are complicated and are a mixture of semantic restrictions and pragmatic restrictions which are hard to disentangle.

---

[13] Note that the facts are not the same in Dutch, where modification of the complement of the classifier is much more restricted. None of the examples in (29) is acceptable in Dutch except for the adjectival modification in (29e):

   (i)   een stapel oud brood
            a   heap   old bread
            'a   heap of stale brea'

In some cases, the constraints are clear. Container classifiers apply equally well to mass and count predicates as in *jar of sand / jar of oil / jar of cookies*. Container classifiers 'repackage' quantities into countable quantities defined by the container they fill. It is immaterial whether the contents of the container are countable (denoted by a count noun) or non-countable (denoted by a mass noun). Arrangement classifiers are similarly acceptable with count and mass complements, but may presuppose physical properties of their complements. *Pile*, as in *pile of sand/cookies*, presupposes that the complement must denote something which is physically able to keep the shape expressed by the classifier. So, *pile of oil* is infelicitous, while *pile of mud* implies that the mud is thick and dry enough to keep its 'pile' shape.

Apportioning or partition classifiers also presuppose the physical properties of their complements. They apply usually to substance mass nouns, and their semantic effect is to divide substances into countable discrete pieces or quantities. Like arrangement classifiers, partition classifiers presuppose the physical nature of the substance they classify. So, *chunk* presupposes that its complement denotes a physically stable substance, while *drop* presupposes that its complement is a liquid. As a result, *chunk of wood* and *drop of water* are felicitous, while #*chunk of water* and #*drop of wood* are infelicitous. *Chunk of mud* presupposes that the mud is solid and dry, and *drop of mud* presupposes that it is liquid. While the physical properties of the complement are presupposed, the quantity properties of the unit are asserted. *That is a pile of oil* is always infelicitous, but *That is a pile of mud* is false if there isn't enough mud to constitute a 'pile'.

Group predicates naturally apply to count nouns, since they map pluralities of individuals into groups, but they also allow naturally atomic mass nouns as in *class of pupils / class of youth, herds of cows / herds of livestock*, although *group* seems to prefer count noun complements.

Classifiers such as *item/unit/piece* pose a different set of problems. They apply to naturally atomic mass predicates, and map them onto countable predicates as in *item of furniture*. However, in certain circumstances, they may take plural count predicates, as in (31).

(31)   This library has over 10,000 items of books.

(30) may not be truth-conditionally equivalent to *This library has over 10,000 books* since the *Encyclopedia Britannica* may count as one item, but consists of thirty-two separate volumes or books.

Note that some classifiers may look as if they belong to more than one category. For example, *piece* looks like a sortal classifier in *piece of furniture*, where *piece* maps the mass denotation of the naturally atomic predicate *furniture* onto a count set of countable individual units of furniture. In *piece of chair* it has a different use. The bare singular *chair* can only have a mass denotation, denoting chair-stuff, and the classifier has a partitioning use, mapping the mass denotation of *chair* onto countable pieces of chair-stuff.

However, we do not need to assume more than one meaning for *piece*. Assume that *piece* maps a mass predicate onto a set of salient individuable countable parts. When the mass predicate is naturally atomic, like *furniture*, the salient individuals are (normally) the natural atoms, and the classifier looks like a sortal. If the mass predicate is a substance predicate, like *chair* on its mass interpretation, the salient individuals will be contextually salient portions of chair-stuff and *piece* looks like a partitioning classifier.

So while we can identify categories of classifiers, reflecting the different ways in which we individuate countable units, and while we may even be able to propose general semantic characteristics associated with the different categories, they do not correspond to rigid lexical templates with non-overlapping properties.

This suggests that, beyond a very general level, the semantic interpretation of classifiers needs to be worked out on a classifier-by-classifier basis. It is beyond the scope of this chapter to do this, and instead I shall give some examples of interpretations, trying to show what the general properties associated with certain classifier types are, and focusing on the question of how the classifier usage is derived from the N usage.

Container classifiers are among the most familiar of classifiers. They apply to mass and plural count predicates, and partition the NP denotation into units which can be individuated via the container which contains them. For the sake of simplicity, I will give derivations for examples with mass noun complements, but adapting the derivations for count noun complements is straightforward. (Rothstein 2010 shows how adjectives can modify both count and mass nouns, and classifier meanings are flexible in the same way.)

Classifiers like *box* and *glass* begin as sortal count expressions of type $\langle e \times k, t \rangle$ as in (32a), but shift to relational expressions as in (32b).

Let x,y be variables of type e, x a variable of type $e \times k$, π_n the nth member of an ordered tuple.

(32)   a $\lambda\mathbf{x}.\text{GLASS}(\mathbf{x})$
      b $\lambda P\lambda\mathbf{x}.\text{GLASS}(\mathbf{x}) \wedge \exists y[P(y) \wedge \text{CONTAIN}(\pi_1(\mathbf{x}),y)]$

While the sortal in (32a) denotes a set of countable objects, the relational classifier denotes a relation between a predicate P and the set of countable glasses which contain some P-stuff. *Glass of wine* then has the interpretation in (33a), denoting sets of countable glasses, each of which contains some wine. The plural operator applies to the relational predicate (see Chapter 3), and (33b) is the denotation for *three glasses of wine*.

We repeat some definitions:

Let $\mathbf{a}$, $\mathbf{x}$, $\mathbf{y}$ be a variable of type $e \times k$
$\mathbf{x} \sqsubseteq \mathbf{y}$ iff $\pi_1(\mathbf{x}) \sqsubseteq \pi_1(\mathbf{y})$ and $\pi_2(\mathbf{x}) = \pi_2(\mathbf{y})$
$\mathbf{a} \sqsubseteq_k \mathbf{x}$ iff $\pi_1(\mathbf{a}) \in k$ and $\mathbf{a} \sqsubseteq \mathbf{x}$
$|\mathbf{x}|_k = |\pi_1(\mathbf{x})|_k$ if $\pi_2(\mathbf{x}) = k$; undefined otherwise

(33)   a $\lambda\mathbf{x}.\text{GLASS}(\mathbf{x}) \wedge \exists y[\text{WINE}(y) \wedge \text{CONTAIN}(\pi_1(\mathbf{x}),y)]$
      b $\lambda\mathbf{x}.\forall\mathbf{a}[\mathbf{a} \sqsubseteq_k \mathbf{x} \rightarrow \text{GLASS}(\mathbf{a}) \wedge \exists y[\text{WINE}(y) \wedge \text{CONTAIN}(\pi_1(\mathbf{a}),y) \wedge$
        $|\mathbf{x}|_k = 3]]$

Glass as a classifier allows us to say how much wine there is by counting the glasses which contain the wine.

In general, counting classifiers in English are relational nouns derived from sortals, with different relational clauses replacing CONTAIN. Partitioning classifiers apply to a predicate and partition the NP denotation into non-overlapping portions. The properties of the portion are derived from the semantics of the original sortal, while CONSTITUTED-FROM replaces CONTAIN in (32b). For example, *chunk* as a sortal denotes a set of solid, stable individuable objects of contextually appropriate (but not necessarily uniform or regular) size, as in 'This chocolate comes in chunks.' Similar nouns are *lump*, *chip*. The relational count noun *chunk* denotes a relation between these objects and the stuff of which the chunks are constituted. The stability of *chunk*-objects means that relational *chunk* presupposes that the complement NP denotes stuff solid enough to hold a stable shape.

(34)   a $\lambda P\lambda\mathbf{x}.\text{CHUNK}(\mathbf{x}) \wedge \exists y [P(y) \wedge \text{CONSTITUTED-FROM}(\pi_1(\mathbf{x}),y)]$
      b   three chunks of wood:
        $\lambda\mathbf{x}.\forall\mathbf{a}[\mathbf{a} \sqsubseteq_k \mathbf{x} \rightarrow \text{CHUNK}(\mathbf{a}) \wedge \exists y[\text{WOOD}(y)$
               $\wedge \text{CONSTITUTED-FROM}(\pi_1(\mathbf{a}),y) \wedge |\mathbf{x}|_k = 3]]$

Importantly, it is not necessary to use an explicit partition operation in (34). Since *chunk* is a count noun and denotes a set of contextually determined non-overlapping semantic atoms, the partitioning of the NP denotation *wood* is done indirectly. *Wood* is effectively partitioned into non-overlapping quantities by identifying a set of non-overlapping chunks which are constituted from the wood.

Puddle, also a partition classifier, has the same basic semantics as *chunk* but, since the sortal denotes a set of small pools, relational *puddle* presupposes a complement denoting a liquid. These natural presuppositions can be overridden, so, in the right context, *a puddle of Smarties* can have a felicitous interpretation.

Khrizman *et al.* (2015) argue that partition classifiers are portion classifiers in that they map their input onto sets of disjoint portions. They argue that portion classifiers are widespread. Portion classifiers differ from container classifiers in that, if the classifier is a container classifier, the complex expression *classifier of N* denotes a set of objects in the denotation of the sortal interpretation of the classifier (glasses of wine are glasses), while, if the classifier is a portion classifier, the complex expression *classifier of N* denotes a subset of the denotation of N (puddles of water are water).

There are many classifiers which individuate portions, including containers like *glass*. In (35a), *fifteen* is counting portions of beer individuated via the glasses which contain them:

(35) a I drank fifteen glasses of beer, five flutes, five pints, and five steins. I drank five of the fifteen glasses of beer before my talk and the rest after it. (From Khrizman *et al.* 2015)
      b Hungry Goldilocks ate three bowls of porridge: Daddy Bear's big bowl of porridge, Mummy Bear's middle-size bowl of porridge and Baby Bear's little bowl of porridge.

Fifteen glasses of beer in (35a) cannot have a measure interpretation, since the individuated portions are of different sizes. But it also cannot have a container-classifier interpretation, since it is, crucially, the portions of beer which are being drunk and not the glasses with the beer they contain. (35b) makes the same point. Khrizman *et al.*, adapting a suggestion in Partee & Borschev (2012), propose an additional classifier interpretation for container classifiers, the *contents interpretation*, to account for these readings. On this operation, the sortal GLASS shifts to a relational interpretation, and is then passivized, as in (36a) (which recasts the analysis of Khrizman *et al.* in the present framework).[14]

---

[14] Khrizman *et al.* give an intersective semantics for partition classifiers. They analyse *hunk of meat* as denoting (i), and the classifier *hunk* as in (ii):

(i) $\lambda x.\text{HUNK}(x) \wedge \text{MEAT}(x)$
(ii) $\lambda P \lambda x.\text{HUNK}(x) \wedge P(x)$

(36)   a $\lambda \mathbf{y}.\exists \mathbf{x}[GLASS(\mathbf{x}) \wedge CONTAIN(\pi_1(\mathbf{x}),\pi_1(\mathbf{y})) \wedge \pi_1(\mathbf{y}) \in k]$
       b $\lambda P\lambda \mathbf{y}.\ P(\pi_1(\mathbf{y})) \wedge \exists \mathbf{x}[GLASS(\mathbf{x}) \wedge CONTAIN(\pi_1(\mathbf{x}),\ \pi_1(\mathbf{y})) \wedge \pi_1(\mathbf{y}) \in k]$
       c $\lambda \mathbf{y}.\ BEER(\pi_1(\mathbf{y})) \wedge \exists \mathbf{x}[GLASS(\mathbf{x}) \wedge CONTAIN(\pi_1(\mathbf{x}),\ \pi_1(\mathbf{y})) \wedge \pi_1(\mathbf{y}) \in k]$

(36a) is a singular count predicate. As Khrizman *et al.* argue, its denotation is a set of *disjoint* portions: disjoint, because (in a given context)
different glasses have disjoint contents. The classifier interpretation is
(36b), which combines with the interpretation of mass noun *beer* to
give (36c). (36c) denotes the set of countable portions of beer that are
the contents of glasses.

Note that, in this case, we specify singularity of the predicate in
(36a) (in particular, $\pi_1(\mathbf{y}) \in k$), since we cannot derive that semantically
from the classifier itself. But we assume that it is licensed by the one-to
-one mapping between containers and their contents, so that, in
a specific context, if the container is in k, the sum of the contents of
the container, by extension, are in k too. In all the other cases discussed here, the singularity of the predicate can be derived directly
from the classifier interpretation. Khrizman *et al.* (2015) show that
measure heads like *kilo* and *litre* can also be shifted to a portion interpretation in contexts such as (37):

(37)   I bought three litres of milk. But I broke one of them.

For details, see the paper.

Individuating classifiers such as *item* map predicate denotations
onto countable salient units. Again, the relational use is derived
from the sortal use, and again each classifier needs to be analysed
individually. *Item* is derived from a sortal use in which it denotes a set
of enumerable entities, as in *How many items are there on your list of things
to buy?* As a relational classifier, it maps sets on to sets of enumerable
atoms. These atoms may be single units, but they may also be more
complex – for example, a suit may be one item of clothing, although it
may have two or three parts. Assume that the interpretation of the
sortal *item* is constrained as in (38a). The classifier in (38b) maps
furniture on to a set of items of furniture:

(38)   a   If ITEM($\mathbf{x}$) then $\exists \mathbf{y}$ [LIST($\mathbf{y}$) $\wedge$ IS AN ENTRY ON($\pi_1(\mathbf{x}),\pi_1(\mathbf{y})$)]
       b   *item*: $\lambda P\lambda \mathbf{x}.ITEM(\mathbf{x}) \wedge P(\pi_1(\mathbf{x}))$
       c   *item of furniture*: $\lambda \mathbf{x}.ITEM(\mathbf{x}) \wedge FURNITURE(\pi_1(\mathbf{x}))$

We would expect *item* to occur with mass nouns since (38c) seems
only to be adding countability. However, *item* can also take a plural
count noun complement, as in *The library has 10,000 items of books.* This is
not semantically equivalent to *The library has 10,000 books*, since *item* is
defined in (38a) in terms of a list. Thus, while the thirty-two volumes of

the *Encyclopedia Britannica* and the two volumes of *War and Peace* may together be thirty-four books, they may well only be two items of books, if the *Encyclopedia Britannica* and *War and Peace* are entered as 'items' on the list which is the library's catalogue.

Two other kinds of classifiers which we mention, but do not discuss in detail, are group classifiers and kind classifiers. Group classifiers apply mostly to plural count nouns as in *a group of guests, a flock of birds*. Some, but not all, group nouns can also take naturally atomic mass noun complements. *Group* cannot, as is shown by the infelicity of #*group of company* (in contrast to *group of guests*). On the other hand, both *a herd of cows* and *herd of livestock* are possible, and so is *flock of poultry*.

English has a particularly wide repertoire of group terms, with many classifiers lexically restricted for the NP that they classify (Lipton 1993). Their semantic function is to repackage pluralities of individuals into higher-level atomic entities (groups) whose members are instances of the complement NP. Unlike other classifiers, the atomic individual entities in the denotation of the complement remain grammatically accessible. Thus, the examples in (39) contrast sharply:

(39) a The group of children were playing with each other.
      b #The box of books were stacked on top of each other.

In (39a), the definite DP *the group of children* takes a plural verb and *children* can provide the antecedent for the reciprocal. In (39b), the singular container classifier does not allow either the plural verb or the reciprocal. In this respect, group classifiers behave like group nouns such as *committee* and *family*:

(40) a The committee are quarrelling with each other.
      b The family is/are arriving soon.

The semantics of group classifiers is part of the wider issue of group nouns, and I am not going to explore it any further here. Kind classifiers, like *kind, type, genre, sort*, which make it possible to count subkinds, are also beyond the scope of this chapter. Kind classifiers have very different properties from the other classifiers discussed so far, as shown by the fact that they take bare singular count complements as in *that kind of jacket, three kinds of dog*.[15] *Three kinds of dog* counts three subkinds of the dog-kind, and suggests that, as complements of kind classifiers, English bare singular count nouns have a kind interpretation.

---

[15] See Wilkinson (1995) for a semantic analysis of *kind* as a classifier.

8.4 CLASSIFIERS IN MASS/COUNT LANGUAGES VS CLASSIFIERS IN 'CLASSIFIER' LANGUAGES

We now return to our original question: what is the difference between classifier constructions in English and in Mandarin? The simple answer is that classifiers in English are nouns, while classifiers in Mandarin are an independent functional category. But it is important to spell out exactly what this means and how it is connected to the fact that English has a lexical distinction between mass and count nouns.

As we saw in Chapters 4 and 6, in a language with a mass/count distinction count nouns are derived in the lexicon and form a lexical category in which disjointness and/or countability are grammatically encoded. In Mandarin, countability is not encoded lexically, and is expressed via individuating classifiers which introduce in the syntax the grammatical feature which allows counting.

In the theory I have been using, countable N predicates are of type $<e \times k, t>$. In English, count nouns emerge from the lexicon at this type, while in Mandarin, where bare nouns are kind-denoting terms, individuating classifiers are of type $<\Sigma, <e \times k, t>>$, and apply to bare nouns at type Σ, to yield countable expressions at type $<e \times k, t>$. This is shown in (41):

(41) a sān   [zhī$_{<\Sigma, <e \times k, t>>}$ gǒu$_\Sigma$] $_{<e \times k, t>}$
          three   Cl$_{small\ animal}$ dog
          'three dogs'
      b one [dog] $_{<e \times k, t>}$

Unlike (41), the Mandarin and English examples in (42) look like word-for-word translations, with the Mandarin classifier *jiàn* directly analogous to English *piece*.

(42) a yí   jiàn   jiājù
          one   Cl$_{item}$ furniture
          'one piece of furniture'
      b one piece of furniture

However, despite the similarity, the two sentences in (42) have different structures, since *jiàn* is a classifier at type $<\Sigma, <e \times k, t>>$, while *piece* is a relational noun at type $<<e, t> \ <e \times k, t>>$, derived from the sortal *piece*:

(43) a yí   [jiàn $_{<\Sigma, <e \times k, t>>}$ jiājù$_\Sigma$]$_{<e \times k, t>}$
      b one   [piece$_{<<et>, <e \times k, t>>}$ (of) furniture$_{<e, t>}$]$_{<e \times k, t>}$

The countability of *piece of furniture* follows from the fact that *piece* is a count noun. The same is true for all the examples discussed in the Section 8.3. In Mandarin, classifiers are necessary to map kind terms onto countable predicates. In contrast, English can exploit the possibility of shifting sortal nouns to relational nouns to build complex countable NPs with mass or bare plural complements. In (43b), the relational N *piece* yields a countable set of furniture-pieces by introducing a relation between a countable entity and a non-countable body or sum. Put differently, *jiàn jiājù* denotes a set of countable furniture atoms. *Pieces of furniture*, in contrast, denotes a set of countable piece-atoms, each of which is a pair $<x, k>$, where x is in the denotation of *furniture*. Grammatical countability is not added directly via the classifier (as it is in Mandarin), but is a by-product of the fact that the relational noun head is inherently count.

So the presence or absence of a lexical mass/count distinction has ramifications at the classifier level, beyond the question of whether a language has sortal classifiers. English has a count/mass distinction and therefore does not need a grammatical category of sortal classifiers.

It does not need a grammatical category of group, partition or container classifiers either, since it can use relational count nouns derived from count sortals to introduce countability at the level of containers, groups and portions. In Mandarin, there are no count sortals, and therefore there are no count relational nouns derived from them. Classifier heads must be used to introduce countability at all levels: countability of groups, of portions, of kinds, of containers.[16] A language which does not have count nouns will need a syntactic category of classifiers in order to count both at the individual level as well as at the level of groups, portions, containers and so on.

Note that, in principle, a language can have relational nouns which act as nominal classifiers as well as a syntactic category of Classifier heads, in the same way that a language with a mass/count distinction can also have sortal classifiers. We have already seen in Chapter 6 that Hungarian may well have this kind of 'dual' system. Gil (2013) in the *World Atlas of Language Structures Online* claims that, out of 400 languages investigated, individuating classifiers were obligatory in counting contexts in 78 languages, and optional in 62 languages. This suggests that dual systems of marking countability may well be

---

[16] In fact, with the exception of kinship terms, Mandarin does not generally have relational nouns at all (XP Li, p.c.).

quite common. In such a language, we would expect two different kinds of syntactic and semantic classifier behaviour, depending on whether the classifier is an N or a Cl. Whether this is indeed the case remains to be seen.

8.5   QUESTIONS FOR FURTHER DISCUSSION AND INVESTIGATION

1 Can you identify other kinds of classifiers, beyond those listed in Section 8.1?
2 How might you analyse *a number of* in *a number of cats*, discussed in Akmajian & Lehrer (1976)? Note that, unlike with other classifiers, the verb must agree with the plural *cats* and the indefinite cannot be replaced by a numeral.

   (44)   a #two numbers of cats
             b A number of cats are/#is in the garden.

3 All counting classifiers are individuators, but not all individuating classifiers allow counting. In particular, classifiers which take abstract mass nouns as complements may not allow modification by numericals. However, they allow indefinite determiners and even universal quantifiers. This seems to be related to the properties of the N complement, since (45c) contrasts with (45d). Note that the classifiers themselves are clearly count nouns.

   (45)   a an element of suspicion / #two elements of suspicion
             b This is bound to eliminate every element of suspicion.
             c a touch of dislike / #two touches of dislike
             d The room was white, with one or two touches of colour.

   What classifier–NP combinations produce these effects? Do you see any patterns?

9 Measures

Ian, who's translating, stops to explain this archaic spiral of language as an eighteenth-century legal description of the amount of land, measured by how long it would take two oxen to plough it. We have, it seems, two plowing days worth of property.

Frances Mayes, *Under Tuscan Sun*

9.1 MEASURE HEADS AND MEASURE PREDICATES

In the previous chapter, we discussed counting classifiers, classifiers which package noun denotations in a variety of forms in which they can be counted. We showed how sortals shift to a classifier interpretation. We also pointed out that measure heads such as *kilo* can shift to a portion-classifier interpretation, as shown in Khrizman *et al.* (2015). But this is not the only kind of shift operation which is necessary to construct the full range of pseudopartitives. Pseudopartitives can also be headed by measure heads at type <n,<e,t>>. As we saw in Chapter 3, there are two kinds of measure head, lexical measures such as *kilo* which are born at this type, and nouns such as *glass* which start off as sortals but end up as measure heads. So the question we address here is: how does this happen?

In the rest of this section, we review briefly the range of nouns which can be used as measure heads in English. In Section 9.2, we discuss how nouns are interpreted as measure heads.

Measure heads like *kilo* are born at type <n,<e,t>> as in (1a), and combine with a numerical as in (1b) to form a measure predicate. They can shift to a modifier at type <<e,t>,<e,t>> as in (1c). This expression can then modify a mass noun or a plural count noun which has shifted to a mass denotation (1d).

(1) a kilo$_{<n,<et>>}$: $\lambda n\lambda x.\text{MEASURE}_{\text{WEIGHT,KILO}}(x) = n$
     b two kilos$_{<e,t>}$: $\lambda x.\text{MEASURE}_{\text{WEIGHT,KILO}}(x) = 2$

  c two kilos$_{<<e,t>,<e,t>>}$: $\lambda P\lambda x.P(x) \wedge \text{MEASURE}_{\text{WEIGHT,KILO}}(x) = 2$
  d two kilos of flour$_{<e,t>}$: $\lambda x.\text{FLOUR}(x) \wedge \text{MEASURE}_{\text{WEIGHT,KILO}}(x) = 2$

Measure predicates have a variety of usages, although these may vary from language to language. In English, as well as heading pseudopartitives such as *two kilos of flour/apples* in (2a), they have an attributive, or adjectival, use, as in (2b), and they can be sentential predicates as in (2c). We will discuss these uses of measure phrases in Chapter 10. Measure predicates may also may modify verb and path arguments, as in (2d,e), but we will not discuss these uses in this book.

(2) a two kilos of apples/flour
  b three two-kilo apples
  c This dog is/weighs twenty kilos!
  d He drove two kilometres on.
  e The theatre is two kilometres from here.

While (2) illustrates uses of the standard measure *kilo*, nouns in general can be used as measure heads. Chapter 3 showed that classic container nouns can have measure interpretations, illustrated in (3).

(3) a This punch is made with two litres of orange juice and *two bottles* of white wine.
  b I am mopping up about *two buckets* of water, which has leaked out of the fridge.

In addition to container nouns such as *bucket* and *bottle*, many other nouns can also have a measure interpretation. Some examples are given in (4). Note that in these examples, where the use of the N as a measure head is not usual, a measure suffix is either obligatory or highly preferred. As the use of N as a measure head becomes less canonical, the more the use of a measure suffix is preferred. The primary measure suffixes are *-ful* and *-worth*, but some others, such as *-load*, can be used, as in (4b).

(4) a '... *three roomfuls* of pupils of a given chronological age'[1]
  b 'Mulberry bushes ... attracting *treefuls* of happily chirping silver eyes.'[2]
  c 'That's about *two busloads* of people dying every day ...'[3]
  d '... *nine tablefuls* of guests gathered for a Cantonese-inspired dinner banquet ...'[4]

[1] M. Ediget, *Elementary Curriculum Improvement*. New Delhi: Discovery Publishing House, 2003, p. 40.
[2] T'ien-hsin Chu, *The Old Capital: A Novel of Taipei*. New York: Columbia University Press, 2007, p. 25.
[3] www.shoctober.org.au/2014-09-06-03-24-46/media-resources.
[4] http://kindlyyours.blogspot.co.il/2010/09/to-hayley-melbourne-and-more.html.

e *a pocketful of* rye, *a thimbleful* of whisky, *two handfuls* of flour
f Add *a glug* of oil /*several glugs* of oil …
g I have two *classes(worth)* of material prepared.
h When my computer crashed, I lost *ten hours* of work.
i The route saved us *two blocks* of walking.
j She bought *ten dollars(worth)* of *gas* / *ten pounds(worth)* of *petrol*.
k 'So a 50lb bag will have roughly *137.5 cups worth of flour*.'[5]

The measure predicates express a quantity property of the stuff or sums denoted by N. (4a) comes from a piece of writing on elementary education, and is discussing how many pupils of a particular age are necessary in a school in order to divide them into groups according to ability. *A roomful of pupils* determines a quantity of pupils in terms of how many pupils are on average assigned to a single classroom. (4b) tells us that the quantity of birds attracted by the mulberry bushes was enough to fill several trees. In (4c), *two busloads* gives the quantity of people dying. Note that 'about' modifies the number of people and not the number of buses: we are told that the number of people dying was about the number sufficient to fill two buses and not that it was sufficient to fill about two (i.e. two or three) buses. Note, also, that some of these measures, in particular *busload* and *tableful*, express measures on a cardinality scale, giving you quantity properties of sums of individuals or natural atoms.

In Rothstein (2009), I suggested that container classifiers on their measure interpretation have a meaning directly parallel to the meaning of a lexical measure head such as *kilo*, with the N substituting for the unit as in (5):

(5)   bottle$_{<n,<et>>}$: $\lambda n \lambda x.\text{MEASURE}_{\text{VOLUME,BOTTLE}}(x) = n$

But this avoids the question of how the N meaning is incorporated into the measure expression.

Intuitively, nouns can be used as measures in different ways. Some of the more obvious ones include:

(i) **Containers.** A bottle, as a container, has a volume property. So while a *two-kilo bottle* naturally means a bottle which weighs two kilos, a *two-litre bottle* is naturally interpreted as a bottle which can contains two litres of liquid.

Casati & Varzi (1999) develop a theory of *holes* or empty spaces. They explain informally that a hole is part of an object's complement (i.e. not part of the object itself) which is 'encompassed by the object's containing parts' (p. 139). This informal explanation is

---

[5] www.amazon.com/ask/questions/asin/B00993BW7Y.

supported by a formal definition. The advantage of allowing objects to have holes is that holes themselves are objects with properties. Thus a *two-litre bottle* is an object with a hole, where the volume of the hole is two litres. In *a two-kilo bottle*, *two-kilo* is the property of the bottle, while in *a two-litre bottle*, *two-litre* is a property of the hole associated with the bottle. A *two-kilo jar of flour* is three-ways ambiguous, depending on whether *two-kilo* gives the weight of the jar empty, the jar full, or the weight of the flour that the jar can contain. The notion of 'hole' allows us to define canonical containers as objects associated with holes.

We can state the following principle:

(6)   a   A container is an object associated with a hole (in the sense of Casati & Varzi 1999).
      b   If CONTAINER(x)
          then $\forall U$: MEASURE$_{VOLUME,U}$(x) = MEASURE$_{VOLUME,U}$(HOLE(x)).

Containers can naturally be used as measures because, if x is a container, then its volume can be used to define a unit of measure. Canonical containers like *cup*, *bottle*, *jug* are frequently used without measure suffixes.

(ii) **Quasi-containers.** Many Ns used as measure heads are treated as quasi-containers. This is the case with the examples in (4a–e). A schoolroom or classroom can contain, or seat, a certain number of students in (4a). *Two busloads of people* in (4c) treats 'bus' as a container which can contain, or seat, a certain number of travellers, and gives a quantity of tourists in terms of the number of buses which would be needed to transport them. This is a genuine measure and no actual buses need be involved. (7) can be true if about 120 kids are going through a museum, even if they arrived by foot:

(7)   There must have been two busloads of schoolchildren in the museum that day.

Treeful in (4b) presupposes that trees have place for a certain quantity of birds, while *tableful* presupposes that a table can seat a certain quantity of diners. *Pocketful, handful, thimbleful* express that *pockets, hands* and *thimbles* can be used as containers.

However, the concept of containment is interpreted very loosely. While a bus can be seen as having a 'hole' in the sense of Casati & Varzi, the spatial dimensions of the hole are not what is used in determining how many tourists constitutes a busload. How big a quantity *a busload of people* is is determined by how many seats (and possibly standing places) a bus has and not directly by its volume (though the two properties are connected).

Quasi-containers lie on a continuum from true containers such as *bottle* to objects which can only be seen as containers metaphorically. *Busload* is nearer to a true container-measure than *treeful* since a bus does have an 'inside' and is able to contain a specific number of people. A tree does not have an inside, nor can the space within its perimeter be assigned to a specific number of birds. Arguably, in *two classes(worth)*, (4g) *class* can be seen as an abstract container for a quantity of material that can standardly be taught in a single class.

(iii) **Temporal measures.** When the measure N is temporal, the notion of containment is understood by analogy. *Ten hours work* is enough work to fill ten hours, *three days journey* is a journey long enough that it will fill three days.

(iv) **Value measures.** These are often marked by *-worth* as in *ten dollars(worth) of gas*, and allow us to measure stuff in terms of its monetary value. *Worth* can also be used on non-monetary scales. (4k) gave an example for a concrete measure, *cupsworth of flour. Ten hoursworth of work* is work which is valued at ten hours of time, though in practice it may take much longer. *Ten hoursworth of work may often take fifteen hours* is not a contradiction.

(v) **Other measures.** While (i)–(iii) are the major types of *ad hoc* measures, English allows quite creative use of nouns to create measure predicates. Here are some examples: *two blocks of walking, enough for two meals of fresh meat, a finger of whisky, a glug of oil, a trickle of oil.*

9.2 BUILDING MEASURE HEADS FROM SORTALS

How do we build measure heads from sortals? There is very little discussion about this in the literature, but a notable exception is Partee & Borschev (2012), who discuss sortals used as measures in Russian, and propose a semantic interpretation for *stakan* 'cup'. They distinguish three different measure uses which are shown in (8), (transcribed into the current framework):

(8) a standard measure:
$stakan_{<n,<e,t>>}$: $\lambda n \lambda x.\text{MEASURE}_{\text{VOLUME,STAKAN}}(x) = n$
   b ad hoc measure:
$stakan_{<n,<e,t>>}$:
$\lambda n \lambda x.\text{GLASS}(\mathbf{y}_1) \wedge$
$\forall U[\text{MEASURE}_{\text{VOLUME,U}}(x) = n \times \text{MEASURE}_{\text{VOLUME,U}}(\mathbf{y}_1)]$
      (where $\mathbf{y}_1$ is a free variable)

c   concrete measure:

stakan$_{<n,<e,t>>}$:

$\lambda n \lambda x. \exists \, \mathbf{y} \forall \, \mathbf{a}[\mathbf{a} \sqsubseteq_k \mathbf{y} \rightarrow \text{GLASS}(\mathbf{a})] \wedge |\, \mathbf{y}\,|_k = n \wedge \text{FILL}(x, \pi_1(\mathbf{y}))$

The standard measure reading in (8a) is the interpretation of *stakan* when it is used in the precise sense equivalent to *cup*, i.e. 284 millilitres (= UK) or 236.48 millilitres (= US). In this use, the meaning of *stakan* is determined lexically, just like any other measure unit. We assume that in this use *stakan/cup* is born at type $<n <e,t>>$, just like *kilo*, *litre* and so on. Like other measure heads, it combines with a number and gives a property of stuff which measures n cups on the scale of volume.

In contrast, (8b,c) do not assign a quantity some value on a dimensional scale. They give an indirect quantity property of x in terms of its relation to an entity in the denotation of *stakan*. Partee & Borschev assume that the noun *stakan* at type $<e,t>$ shifts to the measure type $<n,<e,t>>$ and applies to a number to give a relation between a quantity of stuff and the *stakan* entity. They identify two such uses. In the concrete measure reading in (8c), the result of applying *stakan* to *dva*, which denotes the number 2, is a predicate which denotes stuff which fills 2 specific glasses, as in (9). Existential quantification over the y variable means that (9) entails the existence of two glasses in the domain which contain milk.

(9)   concrete portion reading: *dva stakana moloka*

$\lambda x. \text{MILK}(x) \wedge \exists \mathbf{y} \forall \mathbf{a}[[\mathbf{a} \sqsubseteq_k \mathbf{y} \rightarrow \text{GLASS}(\mathbf{a})] \wedge |\, \mathbf{y}\,| = 2 \wedge \text{FILL}(x, \pi_1(\mathbf{y}))]$

under the natural condition: $\text{FILL}(x, \pi_1(\mathbf{y}) \sqcup \pi_1(\mathbf{z}))$ iff $\text{FILL}(x, \pi_1(\mathbf{y}))$ and $\text{FILL}(x, \pi_1(\mathbf{z}))$

The *ad hoc* measure in (8b) combines with a number to give the quantity property that a body of stuff has if it will, in principle, fill a contextually relevant or stereotypical glass n times. (8b) does not require some actual glass to be present.

(10)   ad hoc measure reading: *dva stakana moloka*

$\lambda x. \text{MILK}(x) \wedge \text{GLASS}(\mathbf{y}_1) \wedge$

$\forall U[\text{MEASURE}_{\text{VOLUME},U}(x) = 2 \times \text{MEASURE}_{\text{VOLUME},U}(\iota(\mathbf{y}_1))]$

The milk that would fill glass $\mathbf{y}_1$ 2 times

I have already argued in Chapter 8, following Khrizman *et al.* (2015), that the concrete portion reading is in fact a count reading and not a measure reading. This is supported by the data from Hungarian which show that, in portion readings, the *-nyi* suffix marking a measure reading is impossible. Schvarcz (2014) shows that, in contexts in which a specific container is made salient, *-nyi* is infelicitous, strongly supporting the argument that these are counting readings.

(11) Három pohár(#-nyi)   pezsgő-t   ittam   a   partin,
      three glass.SG(#-NYI) champage-ACC drank1.SG.PST the party
      a   tálcá-ról   vettemel   őket.
      the tray-from took.1.SG.PST them
      'I drank three glasses of champagne at the party, I took them from the tray.'

Furthermore, (12) clearly shows that it is the portions which are being counted and not the glasses. (12) assert that a single glass is filled three times, resulting in three countable portions, and, as in (11), the *-nyi* is ungrammatical:

(12) Három pohár(#-nyi)   pezsgő-t   ittam   a   parti-n,
      three glass.SG(#-NYI) champagne-ACC drink.1.SG.PST the party-on
      a   pincér kétszer töltötte   újra a   pohar-am-at.
      the waiter twice   fill.2.SG.PST again the glass-1.POSS.SG.-ACC
      'I drank three glasses of champage at the party. The waiter refilled my glass twice.'

If portion readings are count readings, then (8c) should be excluded from the measure uses of *stakan*, and this leaves us with two kinds of measure readings, the standard measure in (8a) and the *ad hoc* measure in (8b).

The Partee & Borschev analysis suggests that these are different kinds of measurement, and that n has a different role in each case. In (8a), the standard measure assigns x a value on a dimensional scale, and n is the numerical value of the measure. In contrast, (8b) does not name a value on a scale but specifies a quantity indirectly in terms of the relation between the measure of x and that measure of a salient (possibly stereotypical) object in the denotation of N_k: for some y in the denotation of N_k, the measure of x on a scale in terms of unit u is n times the measure y on the same scale in terms of unit u. The volume of y is given indirectly in terms of the volume of the container, and the numerical n gives a property of the relation between the body of stuff measured and the N_k entity being used to measure.

So there is a contrast between direct measure-predicates, which map sums of stuff directly onto a scalar value measured in terms of canonical units and thus directly express a quantity property, and *ad hoc* measure-predicates, where the scalar measure value in canonical units is calculated indirectly.

Partee & Borschev are, of course, discussing measurement in Russian, and I am not going to discuss their data here. But, it seems to me that (8b) does not accurately capture the semantics of *ad hoc* measurement, either in English or, as we will see, in Hungarian. English does allow indirect measurement, and this is associated with use of the suffix *worth* as in example (4k): The big bag of flour contains *roughly 137.5 cups worth of flour*. Here the measure of the flour is given indirectly in terms of the measure of the cup: whatever a cup of flour is worth on the scale of volume, the bag of flour contains 137.5 times as much.

(13)   *137.5 cups worth of flour:* $\lambda x.\text{FLOUR}(x) \wedge \text{CUP}(y_1) \wedge$
          $\text{MEASURE}_{\text{VOLUME},u}(x) = 137.5 \times \text{MEASURE}_{\text{VOLUME},u}(\pi_1(y_1))$

However, *ad hoc* measurement usually does not work this way. Treating *ad hoc* measurement as indirect measurement as in (8b) implies that the *y* entity in terms of which x is measured is in context more easily assigned a measure value than x itself, and that using N_k as an *ad hoc* measure is an indirect way of measuring in canonical units. But *ad hoc* measurement is productive and involves a wide variety of count nouns which cannot easily be assigned a measure in terms of canonical units, and in fact the point of *ad hoc* measurement is not doing so.[6] Take, for example, *a glug of olive oil*.[7] *Glug* is derived from the onomatopoeic *glug-glug* which describes the sound that liquid makes when it is poured relatively slowly from a bottle into a container. However, *pour a glug of olive oil into the pan* is not instructing you to 'count glug sounds', nor it is instructing you how to measure out indirectly *n* millilitres or *m* tablespoons of olive oil. Instead, it is using an imprecise measure unit, the approximate value of which you are supposed to learn through experience. To quote an expert: 'So how much is a glug? 'A glug is, um, a glug,' replied Oliver's spokesman Peter Berry. 'There's no real 'definition,'' as such but everyone knows what a glug is.'[8] Crucially, when you add several glugs of oil to what you are cooking, you decide how big a glug of oil is not by using measuring scales but by using your eyes, your ears, your sense of smell, and your sense of context. *A drizzle of oil* raises similar problems: it is also a quantity on the volume scale, but how much it is depends

---

[6] A similar problem arises when discussing how themes are used to 'measure out' the progress of an event. See Rothstein (2004: ch. 4).

[7] 'Heat a generous glug of oil in a wide frying pan and saute the onion, garlic and chilli until soft' (http://thecolourofpomegranates.blogspot.de/2011/05/ottolenghis-open-kibbeh.html).

[8] http://californiaoliveranch.com/what-does-jamie-oliver-mean-by-a-glug-of-olive-oil.

on the size of the portion of food or of the pan that you are drizzling the oil onto. So it seems that what we are doing with this kind of *ad hoc* measurement is calibrating our dimensional scales in terms of *ad hoc* units which may be vague, and which allow us to remain imprecise in our measurements. An *ad hoc* unit can be given an approximate value in terms of canonical units ('If you really must have measurement: A glug of oil is probably just over a tablespoon'[9]). But we usually don't want to specify this, because, in context, the size of the unit is actually determined in much more complex ways.

Schvarcz (2014) discusses this point in some detail in her discussion of Hungarian measure phrases. In Hungarian, non-container nouns used as measure heads are obligatorily marked by the suffix *-nyi* in a productive operation which allows almost any N to be used to express an approximate, *ad hoc* unit of measurement. These measure phrases are used in a wide variety of grammatical constructions, as shown in (14):

(14) a egy   kellemes   két   fizetés-nyi vakáció
         a   pleasant   two   salary-NYI   holiday
         'a pleasant two-salary holiday'
      b egy malomkő-nyi   sajt
         a   millstone-NYI cheese
         'a millstone of cheese'
      c A szőlőskert-ünk két domb-nyi-ra   van a   ház-unk-tól.
         the vineyard-our   two hill-NYI-sublative is the house-our-from
         'Our vineyard is two hills away from our house.'

Schvarcz shows that the value of these measure heads is an approximate value supplied contextually in varied ways, and that, even in a specific context, it may be underspecified how exactly the N_k is to be used as a unit of measurement.

In (14a), where the measure is used adjectivally, the holiday is measured in terms of how much it cost, with the price being specified as being approximately equivalent to the value of two (contextually relevant) salaries. (14b) suggests that the cheese is equivalent in weight and/or shape to a particular kind of millstone, and leaves it to context to determine which property of a salient or stereotypical millstone is relevant. (14c) specifies a distance in terms of numbers of hills, but does not indicate whether the two hills have to be crossed, or driven round or flown over to reach the vineyard. An appropriate interpretation for *két domb-nyi* will therefore need to indicate that the distance is measured in terms of hills, while leaving unspecified

---

[9] www.aglugofoil.com/p/print-conversion-chart.html.

what aspect or aspects of contextually relevant hills are to be taken in consideration in deciding how far a hill-unit-away is. The millstone, the salary and the hills name vague units in terms of which the objects are measured, but leave unspecified what the measure value of the N-entity is.

This suggests that we do not want to assume that standard measurement and *ad hoc* measurement are two different kinds of operations. *Ad hoc* measurement allows us to calibrate particular dimensional scales in terms of non-standard, and often vague, units of measurement. These can be given very approximate values in terms of canonical units, since any unit of measurement on a dimension can be given a value in terms of another unit of measurement on the same dimension. But these values may remain 'ball-park values', and very approximate. So *ad hoc* measurement allows us to remain relatively uncommitted as to what the value of the *ad hoc* unit is. This gives us a new way to give approximate measurements: we approximate not by being vague or imprecise about the numerical value of a measure, but by using an imprecise unit of measure.

Grammatically then, there are two kinds of measure heads, those born as measure heads, and those derived from a noun. Lexical measure heads are born at the type $\langle n, \langle e,t \rangle \rangle$ and they denote standard fixed measures. As we saw in Chapter 3, in the discussion of examples (4–7), they may have grammatical properties which distinguish them from measure heads derived from nouns. Their value is specified lexically, and the value of *one litre* is part of our lexical knowledge, as is the value of *one cup* on its standard measure interpretation. A lexical entry for *cup* on its standard measure reading might look like (15):

(15)　$\lambda n \lambda x. \text{MEASURE}_{\text{VOLUME,CUP}}(x) = n$:
　　　　$\langle \text{VOLUME, CUP, 1} \rangle = \langle \text{VOLUME, MILLILITRE, 240} \rangle$
　　　　where:　$\langle M, U_1, n \rangle = \langle M, U_2, m \rangle$ iff
　　　　　　　　$\forall m \forall n \forall x [\text{MEASURE}_{M,U1}(x) = n$ iff $\text{MEASURE}_{M,U2}(x) = m]$

Since *cup* has a precise equivalent in terms of millilitres, it can be used to calibrate the scale of volume precisely.

Ad hoc measure heads do not have this lexicalized interpretation. When N is used as an *ad hoc* measure, as in *two glasses of wine* / *several glugs of oil*, entities, either concrete or abstract, are being used to supply a unit in terms of which a scale can be calibrated, but the unit itself is left imprecise, the degree of imprecision being context-determined.

Following the suggestion in Schvarcz (2014), we can assume that a measure suffix, possibly unexpressed, denotes an operation which applies to a singular count noun N_k to yield an ad hoc measure reading. This operation -FUL is given in (16a) and has the interpretation in (16b):[10]

(16) a $FUL_{<<e \times k,t>,<n,<e,t>>>} (N_k) = \lambda n \lambda x.MEASURE_{M,Nk}(x) = n$
          where M is a dimension suitable for N_k as a unit, and N_k satisfies
          a constraint like the following:
      b For some $y \in N_k$ there is contextually determined unit U for M such
          that:
          $MEASURE_{M,Nk}(x) = 1$ iff $MEASURE_{M,U}(x) \approx MEASURE_{M,U}(M(\pi_1(y)))$
          where $\approx$ means: is approximately equal to and $(M(\pi_1(y)))$ is the
          relevant dimensional property of **y**.

FUL applies to a count noun to give a measure head. If a measure head is derived from N_k, then there is some entity in N_k which is used to determine a unit of measure on a particular dimension which is calibrated in terms of a familiar unit, so that one N-unit can be given an approximate value in terms of U. This leaves it entirely up to context how the unit value associated with N_k is determined, and how wide the approximation band is.

Sometimes, the value of an *ad hoc* unit is explicitly given, as in (17), which gives a value for *box* on the scale of weight.

(17) Ten boxes of books at five kilos a box is fifty kilos.

Here, *box* is given an *ad hoc* value in terms of kilos, in the same way that *kilo* itself can be specified in terms of grams. If a kilo is a thousand grams, and a box is five kilos, then five boxes is five thousand grams.

In contrast, in (18), the value of *cup* on the scale of volume is not specified:

(18) The correct proportions are four cups of flour to one cup of sugar.
      It doesn't matter what size cup you use, but the ratio must be
      correct.

(16) allows us to treat *ad hoc* measure phrases as direct measures. Like standard measures, they map a quantity onto a numerical value on a scale. The difference between standard and *ad hoc* measures is in the status of the unit in terms of which the scale is calibrated.

---

[10] Measure classifiers, like counting classifiers, are derived from count nouns. (16) stipulates this by making *-ful* apply to a singular noun of type $<e \times k, t>$. However, it is plausible that only semantically atomic entities can be used to define one unit, which is necessary for calibrating a scale.

In standard measures, the unit has a fixed value independent of context, while in *ad hoc* measures, the scale is calibrated in terms of an *ad hoc* unit, derived from a contextually relevant entity in the denotation of the measure N_k, and may remain imprecise. This predicts correctly that *ad hoc* measures allow scalar comparisons with the same ease that standard measures do, as in (19), and they may also be directly compared with other measures as in (20):

(19) a I put five glasses of vodka in the punch, that is about two more than I usually add.
      b There are ten shelves of books in the bedroom, two more than in the kitchen.

(20) Two glugs is much less than two cupfuls.

9.3   QUESTIONS FOR FURTHER DISCUSSION AND INVESTIGATION

1 On some occasions, classifiers are not followed by *of*. In (21a,b) *of* is impossible. In (21b,c), it is optional, but arguably affects the meaning.

(21) a It is two days journey to Rio.
      b He lives two streets walk from here.
      c I lost two hours work / two hours of work.
      d It took about three days discussion / three days of discussion to come to a decision.

Consider under what conditions *of* is (i) impossible and (ii) optional. Note that the factors involved include the dimension of the scale of measurement and the syntactic position of the measure phrase. Can you come to any conclusion about the difference of interpretation in (20c) and (20d)?

2 In English, you often find (22) as orthographic variants of (21):

(22) a It is two days' journey to Rio.
      b He lives two streets' walk from here.

The apostrophe in (22) suggests that *days'* and *streets'* are being treated as genitives, while the lack of apostrophe in (21) suggests that they are simple plurals. Can you find any arguments to decide between these two variants?

3 What is the difference in meaning (if any) between the following:

(23) a two hoursworth of work
      b two hours of work
      c two hours work

4 Are there other kinds of measure heads, beyond those listed in Section 9.1?

5 How might you analyse *a number of cats* discussed in Akmajian & Lehrer (1976)? Is *number* a measure or a classifier? Note that unlike other classifiers, the verb must agree with the plural *cats* and *a* cannot be replaced by a numeral.

(24) a #two numbers of cats
      b A number of cats are/#is in the garden.

5 Are there any predictable patterns of agreement with measure heads? We find examples like (23) where both singular and plural agreement are possible. Does context affect whether the verb is plural or singular?

(25) a Three hundred kilos of cocaine were/was seized this morning by the police.

10 Additive and Attributive Uses of Measures

'Use two strands of six-strand floss in an embroidery needle.'
E. Sienkiewicz, *Baltimore Elegance: A New Approach to Classic Album Quilts*

10.1 ATTRIBUTIVE VS PSEUDOPARTITIVE MEASURE PREDICATES

This chapter examines and contrasts two different uses of measure predicates in English nominal constructions, illustrated in (1) and (2).[1]

(1)   a Please buy *two kilos* of cheese/apples.
      b We ate *two kilos* of the cheese/apples.

(2)   a Please buy a *two-kilo* cheese / two *two-kilo* cheeses.
      b This is *eighteen-carat* gold.

The measure heads a pseudopartitive in (1a) and a true partitive in (1b), while the predicates in (2) are inside the NP, below the scope of the determiner in the position in which we find attributive adjectives; they are often called 'attributive measure phrases' (Schwarzschild 2006). Note the lack of plural marking on *kilo* and *carat* in (2), which is characteristic of the attributive use in English.

---

[1] In this chapter, I only discuss measure predicates as modifiers in the nominal domain. There are other uses for measure predicates, many of which are discussed in Jackendoff (1977). These include expressions of degrees in comparisons (i), predicate complements of verbs (ii), modifiers of adjectives (iii) and partitives (iv).

   i   This box of apples is two kilos heavier than that one.
   ii   This box weighs two kilos.
   iii   This wall is two metres high.
   iv   I want to buy two kilos of those apples.

I argue in this chapter that measure predicates denote properties of individuals, but I am only concerned with the nominal domain. Plausibly, the measure predicates in (i)–(iii) denotes properties of scales. I assume that in (iv), however, the predicate has the same interpretation as in (1) and (2).

Schwarzschild (2006) discusses contrasts between these two uses of measure predicates, and proposes an account in which the measure predicate in the (pseudo)partitive denotes a property of scalar intervals, while the attributive measure phrase denotes a property of individuals. In the earlier chapters of this book, I have treated measure predicates in pseudopartitives as denoting properties of individual entities or sums of entities. In this chapter I want to show, *contra* Schwarzschild, that measure predicates have this denotation both in (1) and (2), but that, despite this, we can explain the differences between the two uses. We will restrict our discussion to the pseudopartitive/attributive contrast, but I assume that the crucial aspects of the account of pseudopartitives extend naturally to partitives.

The measure predicates in (1) and (2) have different semantic functions, depending on their position. In the pseudopartitive, the measure expresses a property of the bodies or sums of stuff in the denotation of the NP. As an attributive, it predicates a property of the minimal parts of that sum. So *two kilos of apples* denotes pluralities of apples which all-in-all weigh two kilos, while *two-kilo apples* denotes pluralities of apples, in which each atomic apple weighs two kilos. The two measure phrases can be combined in one phrase as in (3).

(3)   I bought ...
      a ... ten kilos of two-kilo apples. (That was five apples!)
      b ... a two-kilo bag of flour.
      c ... two ten-kilo crates of two-kilo watermelons.
          (= two crates each with five watermelons)

The simplest analysis of these measure phrases is that they have the same denotation in both positions and that the difference in interpretation follows from the difference in syntactic position. A measure predicate like *two kilo(s)* has the denotation in (4):

(4)   *two kilo(s)*: $\lambda x.\mathrm{MEASURE}_{\mathrm{WEIGHT,\ KILO}}(x) = 2$

As an attributive modifier, it distributes over the atomic entities in the denotation of its complement, as in (5a). In a pseudopartitive, it intersects with the set of pluralities in the denotation of NP non-distributively and gives the set of pluralities of apples which have an overall weight of two kilos (as in 5b).

Let **a**, **x**, **y** be variables of type e × k.
If X is a set of type <e × k, t> such that
    for all $\mathbf{x_1}, \mathbf{x_2} \in X$: $\pi_2(\mathbf{x_1}) = \pi_2(\mathbf{x_2}) = k$, for some k:
Then *X = {**z**: $\exists \mathbf{Y} \subseteq \mathbf{X}$:z = $<\sqcup\{\pi_1(\mathbf{y}): \mathbf{y} \in \mathbf{Y}\}$, k>} (closure under sum)

(5)   a *two-kilo apples*:
           $\lambda x.^*\text{APPLE}(x) \land \forall a[a \sqsubseteq_{\text{ATOMIC}} x \to \text{MEASURE}_{\text{WEIGHT, KILO}}(\pi_1(a)) = 2]$
        b *two kilos of apples*:
           $\lambda x.^*\text{APPLES}(x) \land \text{MEASURE}_{\text{WEIGHT, KILO}}(\pi_1(x)) = 2$

As Schwarzschild (2006) points out, attributive measure phrases
are very similar to dimensional adjectives such as *heavy*, which
also have distributive interpretations in prenominal position.
Attributive measures permute with these adjectives, as in (6a–c),
and are optional (6d), so they do look semantically like intersective
adjectives.

(6)   a Please give me that heavy, canvas, five-kilo bag.
        b Please give me that heavy, five-kilo, canvas bag.
        c Please give me that five-kilo, heavy, canvas bag.
        d Please give me that heavy, canvas bag.

Distributivity seems then to follow from the 'height' in the structure.
Measure phrases within NP modifying N (or N') distribute, while
measures in pseudopartitives modifying NP do not.

Schwarzschild (2006) shows that there are a number of points that
this simple theory of measure phrases does not immediately answer.

The first point concerns the contrast between extensive and non-
extensive measures. Extensive measures, discussed in Krifka (1990),
are measures for which the value grows as the object measured
grows. As Krifka (1990: 494) expresses it: 'measure functions
are homomorphisms which preserve an empirical relation in an
arithmetical relation.'

If a is heavier than b, then $\text{MEASURE}_{M,U}(a)$ will be a numerical value
that is higher on the scale than $\text{MEASURE}_{M,U}(b)$. Further, an extensive
measure is *additive*, which means that (7) holds:

(7) $\text{MEASURE}_{M,U}$ is **additive** iff:
        $\forall a \forall b[\text{if } a \sqcap b = 0 \text{ then}$
        $\text{MEASURE}_{M,U}(a \sqcup b) = \text{MEASURE}_{M,U}(a) + \text{MEASURE}_{M,U}(b)]$

Kilo denotes an extensive measure since, if a sum of apples a weighs
n kilos and I put that sum together with non-overlapping sum of
apples b weighing m kilos, the resulting plurality $a \sqcup b$ will weigh
n + m kilos.

Non-extensive measures do not meet either of these criteria. For
example, *carat* measures the purity of gold (and diamonds). But the
purity of the gold does not increase as the quantity of gold increases,
and if a and b are non-overlapping portions of eighteen-carat gold,

then a ⊔ b will also be a portion of eighteen-carat gold. Non-additive measures are *cumulative*:

(8)   P is a cumulative predicate iff ∀x ∀y[x ∈ P ∧ y ∈ P → x⊔y ∈ P]
       P is a cumulative predicate iff when x and y are in P, then the sum of x and y is also in P.

Two kilos is not cumulative, since, if a and b each have the property of weighing two kilos, the sum of a and b will not weigh two kilos but four kilos.[2]

The contrast between extensive and non-extensive measures shows up in their distribution. While extensive measures can occur either as pseudopartitives, as in (1), or as attributives as in (2), non-extensive measures can be attributives, but cannot head pseudopartitives or partitive constructions, as shown in (9).

(9)   a some eighteen-carat gold
       b #eighteen carats of gold
       c #eighteen carats of the gold

This is quite general, as the following examples show. (10) and (11) show that both extensive and non-extensive measures occur as attributives and sentential predicates, while (12)–(13) show that only extensive measures head pseudopartitives and partitives:

(10)   a three-inch rope
       b thirty-degree water, three-ply tissue

---

[2] Note that there are two kinds of additive measures: strict additive measures and conventional additive measures. With strict additive measures, MEASURE$_{\text{DIMENSION, UNIT}}$(a) is strictly dependent on the value of the parts of a. For example, weight is strictly additive, since MEASURE$_{\text{WEIGHT,U}}$(a) is strictly dependent on the weight values of a's material parts, and MEASURE$_{\text{WEIGHT,U}}$(a) increases or decreases in direct proportion to the way in which a's material parts grow or shrink. Conventional additive measures also increase and decrease depending on the extent of the object measured, however, since the measure values are conventional, they can be overridden by stipulation. For example, cost is additive, since, if a shirt costs \$5, then, without other stipulations, two shirts of the same kind will cost \$10. But, this can be overridden, as in 'Shirts are \$5 apiece, three for \$12.' We still recognize the inherent additivity of cost, since we can still say 'I bought \$15 worth of shirts for only \$12.' Or, if a watermelon weighs 4 kilos, then half a watermelon will weigh 2 kilos and two watermelons will weigh 8 kilos. But if the same watermelon costs 5 euros, the price of either half a watermelon or two watermelons cannot be predicted. And if a shirt costs \$5, then half a shirt will not cost \$2.50, it will probably be worthless, although it will still weigh half of what the whole shirt weighed. However, the distinction between material and conventional additive measures will not concern us here.

(11) a The length/diameter of that rope is three inches.
      b The apples cost five euros.
      c The temperature of the water is thirty degrees.
      d All our gold is eighteen carat.
      e Those tissues are three-ply.

(12) a three inches of rope, five dollars of gas
      b #thirty degrees of water, #three-ply of tissue

(13) a three inches of the rope, five dollars of the gas
      b #thirty degrees of the water, #three-ply of the tissue

Second, Schwarzschild (2006) notes that extensive measure predicates like *two-kilo* are more natural as attributive modifiers of count nouns than of mass nouns, while non-extensive measures are natural modifiers of mass nouns as well as count nouns.

(14) a some two-kilo apples
      b #some two-kilo gold
      c some eighteen-carat gold
      d twenty-four-carat diamonds

Third, Schwarzschild notes that extensive measure predicates seem to lose their properties of extensivity in attributive position, as (15) shows. *Two-kilo* in (15a) seems to be cumulative in the same way that *thirty-degree* is in (15b):

(15) a If a is a plurality of two-kilo apples and b is a plurality of two-kilo apples, then the sum of a and b will be an (even bigger) plurality of two-kilo apples.
      b If a is a body of thirty-degree water and b is a body of thirty-degree water, then the sum of a and b will be an (even bigger) body of thirty-degree water.

The sum of two pluralities of apples each weighing two kilos does not weigh two kilos, but the sum of two pluralities of two-kilo apples is also a plurality of two-kilo apples. This is summarized in (16):

(16) a If a and b are each in the denotation of *two kilos of apples*, $a \sqcup b$ is not in the denotation of *two kilos of apples*.
      b If a and b are each in the denotation of *two-kilo apples*, $a \sqcup b$ is also in the denotation of *two-kilo apples*.

Schwarzschild discusses and rejects, correctly, the suggestion that (16b) follows because the attributive *two-kilo* is a kind modifier, and that *two-kilo apples* denotes a subkind of apples. Dimensional properties can be purely stage-level, transitory properties as in (17), and are not kind modifiers:

(17) a He tried to lift a forty-pound suitcase, but it was too heavy so he
          emptied out some of the contents.
      b She gave birth to a two-kilo girl.

Schwarzschild's analysis of attributive measures focuses on the fact that all attributive measures seem to be cumulative, as in (15), and thus non-extensive. What we have called *additivity* above, Schwarzschild calls *monotonicity* (in other words, his definition of *monotonicity* is the above definition of additivity under (7)). To avoid confusion, I will use *additive* rather than *monotonic* in this discussion.

As Schwarzschild puts it, additive measure functions track the part–whole structure of a quantity, since they grow as the quantity increases. Un-additivity (his *non-monotonicity*) is defined as follows.

(18) MEASURE$_{M,U}$ is **un-additive** iff
      $\forall x \forall y [x \sqsubseteq y \rightarrow \text{MEASURE}_{M,U}(x) = \text{MEASURE}_{M,U}(y)]$
      MEASURE$_{M,U}$ is un-additiive iff x is part of y, x and y have the same measure.

30° is un-additive, since, if a quantity of water has the property of being 30 degrees in temperature, its parts have the same temperature (that is, according to Schwarzschild).[3] *Two kilos* in *two kilos of apples* fails to be un-additive since, if b_2 is in the denotation of *two kilos of apples*, and b_1 a sum of apples which is a proper part of b_2, then b_1 will not also weigh two kilos.

Focusing on the data in (15) and (16), Schwarzschild argues that the syntactic position of a measure phrase determines whether it has an additive or an un-additive interpretation. All measures which head pseudopartitives are additive, while all attributive measures are un-additive. This leads to the contrasts in (20):

(19) a Three centimetres of wire and three centimetres of wire is six
          centimetres of wire (and not three centimetres of wire).
      b Three-centimetre wire and three-centimetre wire is three-
          centimetre wire (and not six-centimetre wire).

Schwarzschild proposes to strengthen the generalization that only extensive measures can head pseudopartitives to a syntax–semantics map concerning additive and un-additive measure heads. He proposes the linking rules in (20) (Schwarzschild 2006: (28,29)).

---

[3] In fact, *30° water* is only thirty degrees on average. So a pool of 30° water will have warmer water at the end where the pump is pumping warm water into the pool, and colder water at the other end.

(20)   a When a measure phrase is combined with a substance noun in
           the [pseudo] partitive, the interpretation is one in which the
           dimension is additive on the relevant part–whole relation in the
           domain given by the noun.
       b When a measure phrase is combined with a substance noun in
           the attributive, the interpretation is one in which the dimen-
           sion is un-additive on the relevant part–whole relation in the
           domain given by the noun.

Note that 'substance noun' in (20) means merely the noun modified,
irrespective of whether it is or is not a naturally atomic predicate.

The un-additivity condition on attributives is easily satisfied when
the measure predicate modifies a mass noun or a bare plural.

  – In *thirty-degree water, thirty-degree* is a property of a body of water
     and its parts (and the sums of those parts).
  – The parts of a body of *two-kilo apples* are also two-kilo apples, down
     to the atomic apples out of which the plurality is composed.
  – Natural atoms only have themselves as $\sqsubseteq$-part, contextual count
     atoms only have themselves as $\sqsubseteq_k$-part, hence singular predi-
     cates, such as *(a) two-kilo apple* or *(a) four-kilo baby* satisfy un-
     additivity trivially (Schwarzschild has a constraint to this effect,
     but in the present framework this just follows).

Attributive measure phrases then are properties of individuals or
individual sums. The measure phrase modifies a noun, and un-
additivity follows from distributivity.

Schwarzschild's analysis of pseudopartitives and an explanation of
their additivity is formulated in an interval semantics for measures,
where measures relate individuals not to measure points, but to measure intervals. However, the details of the interval semantics are highly
complex and completely irrelevant for the issues that I am interested in
here. So, rather than giving an exegesis of Schwarzschild's analysis,
I present a reconstruction in the framework presented in this book of
the compositional gist of Schwarzschild's proposal.

Schwarzschild's analysis of pseudopartitives such as *three ounces of
gold* is as follows. He proposes an additive head, Add°, expressed in
English by *of. Of* relates the complement *gold* to the higher number–unit
phrase *three ounces*. Since we only deal here with the simple expression
three ounces of gold, we will assume that *three ounces* denotes the
unit–number pair <OUNCE,3>, and we will use variable Z as
a variable over such pairs.

The Add° head *of* is interpreted as a function that maps noun
interpretations and unit–number pairs onto NP interpretations

(sets). This function is indexed for a contextually provided measure dimension M. And the requirement of Add° is that MEASURE$_M$ is an additive measure.

The interpretation of the classifier is then as in (21):

(21) Let M be a measure dimension, Z a variable over unit–number pairs.
 $of = Add^0$: $\lambda P\lambda Z\lambda x.P(x) \wedge MEASURE_{M,\pi_1(Z)}(x) = \pi_2(Z)$
 Constraint: MEASURE$_{M,U}$ is additive, for every unit U.

(22) two ounces of gold:

gold:	GOLD
two ounces:	<OUNCE,2>
of:	$\lambda P\lambda Z\lambda x.P(x) \wedge MEASURE_{M,\pi_1(Z)}(x) = \pi_2(Z)$
of gold:	$\lambda Z\lambda x.GOLD(x) \wedge MEASURE_{M,\pi_1(Z)}(x) = \pi_2(Z)$
two ounces of gold:	$\lambda x.GOLD(x) \wedge MEASURE_{M,OUNCE}(x) = 2$
	$\lambda x.GOLD(x) \wedge MEASURE_{WEIGHT,OUNCE}(x) = 2$

The last step fills in WEIGHT as the proper measure dimension for the unit OUNCE, checking, of course, the presupposition that the measure is additive. Add° constrains the dimension M to dimensions such that MEASURE$_M$ is additive. This is, of course, a stipulation.

This analysis makes *of*, as an expression of Add°, look like a real lexical preposition since it has semantic content. This is very surprising. In English, *of* is a usually regarded as an element without semantic content, and, as we saw in Chapters 3 and 6, it has no correlate in languages such as Modern Hebrew, Dutch, Hungarian or Mandarin, where the putative additive head can never be lexically expressed. Even more strongly, we saw that, in Modern Hebrew, measure pseudopartitives are only possible in construct state phrases where no lexical material at all can intervene between the measure phrase and its complement. So this raises the question of whether there is crosslinguistic justification for positing such a (quasi)-prepositional account of an Add° head for pseudopartitives.

Before offering an alternative account of the contrasts between attributive and pseudopartitive measure phrases, we look briefly at the contrast in languages other than English.

10.2 CROSSLINGUISTIC DATA

Pseudopartitives and attributive measures have different characteristic properties in different languages. Schwarzschild cites a number of examples of different ways in which this contrast is expressed crosslinguistically. For example, in Dutch, a measure classifier directly precedes the NP, without any correlate of the English *of*, while the attributive is expressed by post-nominal modification by a prepositional phrase:

(23) a een centimeter staaldraad   (Schwarzschild 2006: (53b))
         one centimetre wire
         'one centimetre of wire'
      b staaldraad **van** een centimeter   (Schwarzschild 2006: (54b))
         wire   VAN one centimetre
         'one centimetre wire' (= wire one centimetre in diameter)

Like Dutch, Russian uses a bare measure phrase for the classifier construction (24a), but with genitive case on the NP, while attributives have adjectival inflection (24b):

(24) a dva   kilogramma   knig
         two   kilo.SG   books.GEN.PL
         'two kilos of books'
      b tri   dvux.kilogrammovye   knigi
         three two.kilo.ADJ. PL   books.OM.SG
         'three two-kilo books'

In Hebrew, pseudopartives are expressed in construct state phrases, (as in 25a), while attributives are expressed by prepositional phrases, which occur post-nominally in the standard position for adjectival modification. Note that, in (25a), *avatiax* must be interpreted as a mass noun, and in (25b), it is count.

(25) a šney   kilo   avatiax /   tapux-im
         two   kilo   watermelon.SG   apple-PL
         'two kilos of watermelon/apples'
      b avatiax/tapuax   šel šney kilo
         watermelon.SG/ apple.SG   of two kilo
         'a watermelon/apple of two kilos' or 'a two-kilo watermelon/
         apple'
      c šloša avatix-im   šel šney kilo (kol   exad)
         three watermelon-PL   of two kilo (each one)
         'three two-kilo watermelons'

Two things are clear:

  (i) pseudopartitives and attributives have different structural positions in many languages;
 (ii) there is structural parallelism between attributive measure phrases and both adjectives and PP modifiers of nouns.

We support this observation with data from Mandarin and Hungarian.

i Mandarin

Tang (1990, 2005) discusses examples like (26):

(26) a liǎng   mǐ   (de)   bù   [mass classifiers]
         two   metre   DE   cloth
      b liǎng   bàng   (de)   ròu
         two   pound   DE   meat

mǐ and *bàng* are measure classifiers. As we saw in Chapter 6, these may optionally be followed by *de*, which occurs at the right edge of predicate phrases (see also Paul, in press). Tang shows that in (26), when *de* is present, the measure phrase is ambiguous between a pseudopartitive reading and an attributive reading: *liǎng mǐ de bù* can mean either 'two metres of cloth' or 'cloths packaged in two-meter lengths', and *liǎng bàng de ròu* is ambiguous between 'two pounds of meat' and 'two-pound packs of meat'. However, *de* is obligatory for the attributive reading, and if it is dropped, only the pseudopartitive reading is possible. Since *de* is often required to mark an AP modifier phrase, this is not surprising. Note also that, while *de* cannot follow an individuating classifier which heads a classifier phrase, as we saw in Chapter 6, it can follow the same classifier used in an attributive, as shown in the contrast between (27) and (28):

(27) a liǎng běn   (#de) shū
         two   Cl$_{book}$ DE   shu
         'two books'
      b wǔ gè   (#de) píngguǒ
         five Cl$_{general}$ DE   apple
         'five apples'

(28) a liǎng běn   DE shū
         two   Cl-volume DE book
         'books that are sorted in twos / books that come in two volumes'
      b wǔ gè   de píngguǒ
         five Cl DE apple
         'apples that are sorted into fives / five-apple packs of apples'

As in English, attributive and classifier measure phrases may be used in the same sentence (example from Li & Rothstein 2012):

(29) wǒ mǎi le   yì   xiāng de liǎng cè   de   shū.
      I   buy PFV one   Cl$_{box}$ DE two   Cl$_{volume}$ DE   book
      'I bought a box of two-volume books.'
      Impossible: 'I bought a box with two books in it.'

(29) would be true if I bought a box of books which come in two volumes (e.g. a box of sets of two-volume dictionaries). A stacked

classifier reading is impossible, and (29) cannot mean that I bought a box containing two books.

Jiang (2008) shows that, when a measure is inherently non-extensive, only an attributive reading is possible: *de* is obligatory:

(30)   sān   dùn   #(de) shuǐ
        three degree DE   water
        'three-degree water'

So *de* is clearly obligatory when the measure phrase is attributive, and this suggests that the attributive and pseudopartitives have different structures, although in both constructions *de* marks them as predicates.

ii Hungarian

Schvarcz (2014) shows that Hungarian measure heads occur as classifiers and in attributive measure phrases. As attributives, the adjectival properties of the measure phrase are clearly indicated. As we saw in Chapter 3, examples like (31a) are ambiguous between a counting and a measure reading, but are unambiguously measure when *-nyi* is added to the classifier, as in (31b):

(31)   a két pohár bor
           two glass wine
           'two glasses of wine'
        b két pohár-nyi bor
           two glass-NYI wine
           'two glasses-ful of wine'

While the *-nyi* suffix is optional when a pseudopartitive is headed by a container expression, the measure head must be morphologically marked if the measure phrase is attributive. There are several possibilities: either *-nyi* is used, as in (32), or the adjectival marker *-s* is used, as in (33). In some cases, it is possible to use a possessive, as in (33c) (all examples from Schvarcz 2014):

(32)   a egy kellemes két fizetés-#(nyi) vakáció
           a   pleasant two salary-NYI   vacation
           'a pleasant two-salary vacation'
        b egy két arasz-#(nyi) küszöb
           a   two span-NYI   doorstep
           'a two-span doorstep'

(33)   a egy két kötet-es könyv
           a   two volume-S book
           'a two-volume book'

   b egy hat szirm-os virág
      a   six petal-S flower
      'a six-petal flower'
   c egy hat szirm-ú   virág
      a   six petal-POSS flower
      'a six-petal flower'

Lexical measures like *kilo* can only have adjectival morphology in attributive position:

(34)   egy három kiló-#(s) kenyér
      a   three kilo-S   bread
      'a three-kilo (loaf of) bread'

Schvarcz (2014) shows another contrast. Hungarian nouns modified by quantity predicates (cardinals or measures in pseudopartitives) are always singular, as in (35a). Bare NPs (and demonstratives) are plural when they have a plural denotation. Schvarcz shows that bare nouns modified by attributive measures are marked singular or plural depending on whether they denote sets of atoms or sets of pluralities.

(35)   a három kiló cseresznye-(#k)
        three   kilo cherry-(#PL)
        'three kilos of cherries'
     b egy három kiló-s cseresznye
        one three   kilo-S cherry
        'a three-kilo cherry'
     c három kiló-s cseresznyé-k
        three   kilo-S cherry-PL
        '(some) three-kilo cherries'

These data suggest that, also in Mandarin and Hungarian, attributive measure phrases are adjectival and are within the NP, while pseudopartitives have scope over the whole NP.

10.3   *THE SEMANTICS OF ATTRIBUTIVE MEASURE PHRASES*

In Section 10.1, we raised three issues:

- Why does the measure head of a pseudopartitive denote an extensive measure function?
- Why is the attributive measure predicate apparently divisive?
- Why do attributives based on extensive measures occur more easily with count nouns?

Schwarzschild's suggestion is that attributives denote properties of objects or entities, while measure phrases in pseudopartitives denote measure properties (properties of scale intervals – unit–number pairs in our reconstruction). The un-additivity of attributive predicates follows from their syntax position, and the additivity of pseudopartitives follows from Add°.

In this section, we will give an alternative account which allows measure predicates to have the same denotations in both positions, and we show that the so-called 'un-additivity' of attributives is a more subtle phenomenon that it has so far appeared.

The problem with Schwarzschild's account is that additivity is a property of measure operations, and should thus be independent of syntactic position. *Degree (centigrade)* denotes an un-additive measure function, since incrementally increasing the size of the object measured does not predictably affect its temperature, while *pound* and *kilo* are additive since weight-in-pounds grows predictably as the extent of the object measured grows. Given this, we do not expect the syntactic position of the measure predicate (relating to an Add° head or not) to change the (un)-additive nature of the measure. We would rather expect that differences between extensive and non-extensive measures will show up in attributive position as well, even though they may not be as obvious as in pseudopartitives.

In fact, this is what we do find. Measure predicates are additive or un-additive independent of their syntactic position.

We already saw that the attributive modifier distributes over the atomic entities in the N that it modifies, while the pseudopartitive is intersective on the whole NP denotation, as shown in (5) above.

(36)   a   *two-kilo apples*:
          $\lambda \mathbf{x}.{}^*\text{APPLE}(\mathbf{x}) \wedge \forall \mathbf{a}[\mathbf{a} \sqsubseteq_{\text{ATOMIC}} \mathbf{x} \to \text{MEASURE}_{\text{WEIGHT,KILO}}\,(\pi_1(\mathbf{a})) = 2]$
       b   *two kilos of apples*:
          $\lambda \mathbf{x}.{}^*\text{APPLE}(\mathbf{x}) \wedge \text{MEASURE}_{\text{WEIGHT, KILO}}\,(\pi_1(\mathbf{x})) = 2$

The properties of the measure function do not change in the two cases: what changes is the object of measurement. The apparent un-additivity, or cumulativity, of the measure predicate in (36a) follows directly from its distributivity. *Two-kilo* is a property of individual apples, *two-kilo apples* denotes a plurality of individual apples each of which weigh two kilos, and *kilo* is a function whose domain is individual apples and not pluralities. Since, in (36a), *kilo* applies to the atomic apples, increasing the cardinality of the set of atomic apples doesn't increase the value on the measure *kilo*. If a sum of apples, $\mathbf{x}$, is in the denotation of *two-kilo apples* (36a), then we know almost nothing about the value of $\text{MEASURE}_{\text{WEIGHT,KILO}}(\pi_1(\mathbf{x}))$, except that it is a multiple of 2, since $\mathbf{x}$ is a sum of entities that each weigh two kilos. *Two kilo* involves the normal additive measure function *kilo*, but checking whether it is additive on the domain of pluralities of apples is something of a category mistake, since that is not, semantically, what it applies to in the first place. We can show that it is truly an additive measure in several ways.

First, with an additive measure, growth in the object measured should lead to increase in the measure value. This holds for objects within the domain of the attributive, as in (37):

(37)   a The candles I was making were supposed to be 500-gram candles. This one was only a 400-gram candle, so I added another 100 grams of wax to make it a 500-gram candle.
       b The journal was soliciting ten-page articles. I wrote a ten-page article to submit, but then I wrote another five pages. So it wasn't a ten-page article any more, but a fifteen-page article.

In both these cases, the attributive measures distribute over the individual atomic entities. *500-gram* distributes over individual candles, and *ten-page* distributes over the individual articles. The measure is additive because, when the extent of the object is increased appropriately, the value of the measure increases in exactly the right additive way. What is important in showing its additivity is increasing the extent of the object measured and not the cardinality of the set of measured objects.

Second, strictly additive attributive measures are sensitive to fractions. If the attributive were an un-additive predicate, (38) would be unexpected.

(38)   If *a* is a two-pound apple, then half of *a* weighs one pound.

Lastly, we can see the effects of additivity in attributive predicates in accumulation entailments. Accumulation entailments are entailments of the form in (39).

(39)   a Three two-kilo apples is six kilos of apples.   TRUE
       b Three 500-metre skeins of yarn is 1,500 metres of yarn. TRUE
       c Three ten-dollar tanks of gas is thirty dollars worth of TRUE
          gas.

The attributives here are clearly additive because they contribute to the measures through which the measure of the overall quantity is computed.

Un-additive measures in attributive position contrast with *two-kilo*. When modifying count nouns, they distribute over the atomic entities in the denotation of N, since these atoms are the minimal elements in N. Examples of un-additive measure predicates modifying count nouns are given in (40):

(40)   a   a 70° sauna
       b   three-ply tissues
       c   eighteen-carat rings

Unlike the measures discussed above, these measures show up in all three tests as un-additive. (41a) contrasts with (37). Statements like (41b), following the template in (38), are invalid, since a three-ply tissue is three-ply along its entire plane.

(41)   a   I made this piece of eighteen-carat gold heavier by adding more
           eighteen-carat gold. It is still eighteen-carat gold.
       b   If a is a three-ply tissue, then half of a is one-and-a-half ply.

Finally, accumulation entailments following the template in (39) are not valid when the attributive is un-additive. The examples in (42) are infelicitous, and, to the degree that they can be interpreted, they are false.

(42)   a   #Two 70° saunas is 140° of saunas.
       b   #Three three-ply tissues is nine-ply of tissues.
       c   #Two eighteen-carat rings is thirty-six carat of rings.

The contrast between additive and un-additive attributive measures shows up in the mass domain in the same way. Un-additive measures are divisive and cumulative. Parts of *thirty-degree water* are also thirty-degree water (on the average). Increasing the quantity of thirty-degree water does not result in increasing its temperature and the accumulation entailment in (43) is invalid:

(43)   Thirty-degree water plus thirty-degree water is sixty-degree water.

Additive measure predicates also occur as attributives in the mass domain, although less frequently than in the count domain. As Schwarzschild shows, they distribute over salient discrete quantities or natural atoms. They occur naturally with object mass nouns, as in (44a,b), where they distribute over individual entities, as discussed in Chapter 5. They also occur with substance mass nouns, when they distribute over salient entities or discrete units, as in (44c,d) (examples from Schwarzschild (2006)). *Ten-dollar wine* is wine that costs ten dollars a bottle, and *twenty-pound paper* weighs twenty pounds per 500 standard-size sheets.

(44) a fifty-kilo furniture
      b five-dollar jewellery
      c ten-dollar wine
      d twenty-pound paper

As we predict, the three tests used above show them to be additive. If I add shelves incrementally to a piece of fifty-kilo furniture, it will no longer be a piece of fifty-kilo furniture, while half of a piece of fifty-kilo furniture will weigh less than fifty kilos. Accumulation entailments like those in (39) are also valid:

(45) a Three pieces of 50-kilo furniture is 150 kilos of furniture.
      b Three pieces of five-dollar jewellery is fifteen dollars(worth) of jewellery.
      c Three bottles of twelve-dollar wine is thirty-six dollars(worth) of wine.

Finally, note that, like other prenominal adjectives, attributive measure phrases, though primarily distributive, do also allow collective interpretations. The ambiguity in question is illustrated for ordinary prenomimal adjectives with *successful*: (46) is ambiguous between a distributive interpretation, where the adjective *successful* distributes over each individual girl, triggered by continuation (a), and a collective interpretation, triggered by continuation (b).

(46) The *successful* girls   (a) each received a scholarship.
                               (b) together received a prize.

Landman (1995) argued that collective interpretations occur when pluralities of individuals are mapped onto singular groups. The collective interpretation of (46) is possible if the successful girls form a team or a group which allows them to receive a prize together.

Collective readings of attributive measures are possible in the same circumstances, namely when a sum can be reanalysed as a singularity or group. (47a) has a natural distributive reading, but it can also have a collective reading, when the price is per collection, per group, or possibly per kilo. In the up-market delicatessen, (47b) may well have the distributive interpretation, where it means that I bought five packs of, say, 4 apples which each cost 5 euros, and I pay 100 euros; in the supermarket opposite, it is more likely to have the collective interpretation, where it means that each pack of, say, 4 apples costs 5 euros, and I pay 25 euros.

(47) a I bought the five-euro apples, not the three-euro apples.
      b I bought five packs of five-euro apples.

Together, these data show that there is good evidence that additive measures do not lose their additivity in attributive position, and that the contrast between additive and un-additive measures is present both in pseudopartitives and attributives.

In the next section, we discuss two kinds of apparent counterexamples to this claim.

10.4 AXES OF ACCUMULATION

The first kind of counterexample is illustrated in (48). While accumulation entailments like (41a) are natural, examples like (48), which use the same kind of additive measure predicates, seem unnatural to many.

(48) a #Three three-pound babies is nine pounds of babies.
      b #Five two-metre basketball players is ten metres of basketball players.

Intuitively, this is because we don't naturally measure the accumulated weight of three babies as if they were a single unit, nor do we normally measure the extended length of two basketball players. In a context in which five basketball players can be considered a single measurable quantity, the examples improve, as in (49a), while (49b) is a quote from an internet article on a travelling inflatable castle:

(49) a When the team lay down head to foot on the playing field, there was 10 metres of basketball players ready for the photographer.
      b How many kilos of children can this particular [inflatable] castle withstand?[4]

We can also reformulate (48) felicitously as in (50).

(50) a Three three-pound babies together weigh nine pounds
      b Five two-metre basketball players together measure ten metres.

This supports the idea that the unnaturalness of (48) is caused by the implausibility of considering five basketball players or three babies as a single measurable unit, and not because of the semantics of measurement.

The second problem concerns examples like (51). *Centimetre* in (51) is apparently un-additive, since it distributes to any length of wire cut from a coil of three-centimetre wire:

---

[4] http://yabangee.com/2014/10/yellow-bouncy-castle-coming-istanbul.

(51)   A part of a piece of three-centimetre wire is itself three-centimetre
        wire.

Furthermore, we do not get the accumulation entailments that we
expect. (52) is repeated from (19) above. While we judge (52a) true,
(52b) is naturally judged false and (52c) seems true.

(52)   a Three centimetres of wire and three centimetres of wire is six
           centimetres of wire (and not three centimetres of wire). (TRUE)
        b Three-centimetre wire and three-centimetre wire is six-
           centimetre wire. (FALSE)
        c Three-centimetre wire and three-centimetre wire is three-
           centimetre wire. (TRUE)

(53), from Schwarzschild (2006), shows the same problem:

(53)   For good fishing you need an acre of five-foot water.

In (53), the quantity of the water is given by the classifier *an acre*,
which specifies the area covered by the water, while the attributive
five-foot gives the depth-property which holds at every contextually
relevant 'slice' of the water, and is apparently un-additive.

   Crucially, we get these un-additivity effects only with measurement
on spatial dimensions, in contrast to measures on other dimensions,
such as *two-kilo* (weight), *three-litre* (volume) or *ten-dollar* (cost).

   The explanation is as follows.

   Additive measures such as *kilo* and *litre* measure objects on a scale
with only one dimension. This is why $MEASURE_{M,KILO}(x)$ can only have
one dimension: WEIGHT. On the other hand, additive measures of
distance like *centimetre* are compatible with several possible measure
dimensions, because, for any object x, there are several axes along
which distance can be measured. So, for example, the measure unit
kilo assigns to a box of candy only one weight value, *litre* assigns only
one volume value, and *euro* only a cost value, but *centimetre* assigns
values on different measure scales relative to different dimensions: it
can be measured along the different axes, including length, breadth
and height (or depth). This means that a spatial measure head cannot
just apply to an object x, but must apply to x relative to a particular
dimensional axis. This means that a spatial distance measure will
measure different axes in different contexts. Often the choice of axis
is given by context. In everyday contexts, a four-foot or four-metre
pole is naturally a pole which is four foot/meters in length, while
a four-inch pole is naturally four inches in diameter. A ten-foot ladder
will normally be ten foot in length, and a twelve-inch ladder will be
normally be twelve inches in width. But this is because of our

expectations about ladders and poles, not because of grammar. If I am buying a ladder for a Lego set, I may well buy a twelve-inch ladder and be referring to length.

A consequence of this is that measures of spatial distance, unlike measures on other dimensions, can be felicitously stacked in attributive position. Talk of a *two-kilo, four-kilo watermelon* does not make sense. But in (54), N is modified by multiple distance modifiers representing different spatial axes, and in (55), the classifier and the attributive make reference to different dimensions of spatial measurement.

(54)   a For this you will need twenty six-foot, two-by-four planks.
        b They ordered a twenty-foot, twelve-inch ladder.

(55)   She needed ninety centimetres of three-centimetre wire.

So, when a nominal includes only one spatial distance measure predicate, it must be assigned to a particular spatial axis, and when it includes more than one spatial distance measure predicate, each one must be assigned to a different spatial axis.

The multiplicity of axes of spatial measurement explains why, in (52b), we do not get the accumulation entailments that are normally associated with additive measures.

We have already seen that calculating the value of an accumulation depends on concatenating entities into a single measurable accumulation. When there is only one possible axis of measurement, giving a value for an accumulation does not depend on how the parts of the accumulation are put together, but only on whether they can plausibly be put together into a single measurable body. If I have two piles of two-pound apples, and I want to know the combined weight, then how I put them together is completely irrelevant as long as I treat them as a sum. However, when the measure is a spatial distance, then how a plurality of quantities or entities is concatenated is a crucial factor in the calculation.

Suppose I have three planks which are six foot in length and four inches in width. Put together 'end to end', the accumulation will grow incrementally along the axis of length. Three six-foot four-inch planks is eighteen feet of planks. However, if I put the planks together long side by long side, then three six-foot four-inch planks will grow incrementally along the width axis and give me 3×4 inches, which is twelve inches of planks. So, concatenation must choose an axis of accumulation in the same way that attributive spatial measures must be matched with a spatial axis.

Accumulation entailments hold for distance measures in attributive position as long as the axis of accumulation is the same as the axis modified by the attributive. In (56a), the attributive modifies the axis of accumulation, and accumulation entailments, like those in (39), are valid. In (56b), the attributive modifies the contextually salient axis of width, which is not the axis of accumulation. Accumulation entailments hold, but only relative to the length axis. The attributive is irrelevant for the measure value of the accumulation, but it is still additive.

(56) a Climbing three ten-foot ladders means climbing thirty foot of ladders.
      b Climbing three (ten-foot,) eight-inch ladders means climbing thirty foot of very narrow ladders.

In many cases there is a default axis of accumulation. For wire, rope and ladders, this tends to be length, which is why distance properties of diameter or width seem to be irrelevant for accumulation. But this too depends on context. Stranded wire is constructed out of bunches of thin wires, and the gauge of the stranded wire is determined by its diameter. This in turn is dependent incrementally on the diameter of the strands out of which it is constructed as in (57):

(57)   One example is a 2/0 wire [= 9.2 mm wire] made from 5,292 strands of #36 gauge wire [.13 mm wire].[5]

Of course, we can measure the result of concatenating three planks by adding the length of a, the width of b and the depth of c. Even if we were to write this as MEASURE$_{LENGTH}$(a) + MEASURE$_{WIDTH}$(b) + MEASURE$_{DEPTH}$(c), we have to realize that this is not accumulation in the sense of (39), since a different operation of + is involved: one that is not simple arithmetic addition within one scale, but one that combines values in different dimensions, different axes of accumulation (i.e. some form of vector addition).

In conclusion, spatial measure predicates are additive, both in attributive and in classifier position, like other additive measure predicates. Attributive additive predicates generally contribute to accumulation calculations just as we would expect, with the caveat that spatial measure units are compatible with more than one measure dimension, since one-dimensional measuring in three-dimensional space takes place along an axis.

---

[5] https://en.wikipedia.org/wiki/Wire. Accessed 18 October 2016.

The general conclusion is that additivity is a property of measures which, *contra* Schwarzschild, is not dependent on syntactic position, even though syntactic position may influence how entailments relating to additivity can be expressed.

10.5   THE SEMANTICS OF MEASURE CLASSIFIER PHRASES

We are left with one more question: why are only additive measures possible as heads of complex NPs, as illustrated in (58)? This restriction holds for both partitive and pseudopartitive constructions, and, although we will only discuss pseudopartitives here, the explanation that we give extends to partitives too.

(58)   a three kilos of (the) tissues/apples
        b three litres of (the) water
        c #three-ply/plies of (the) tissues
        d #thirty-degrees of (the) water

For the sake of simplicity, we will discuss classifiers with count noun complements, though mass nouns work in the same way.

We have argued that pseudopartitives and attributives have the same interpretation, and that the difference between attributive measure predicates and classifier measure predicates lies not in the meaning of the predicate itself, but in the properties of the predicates they modify. We use this to suggest an explanation for the infelicity of (58c,d).

We have assumed that our interpretation domain for mass nouns and count nouns is a complete Boolean algebra M, and we interpreted root nouns as generated ideals in M: sets X such that $X = \{x \in M: x \sqsubseteq \sqcup X\}$. This means that all root noun interpretations themselves form complete Boolean algebras. Lexical mass nouns are interpreted as root nouns; lexical plural nouns as sets generated from sets of atoms in a counting context k. The latter makes the denotations of lexical plural nouns complete atomic Boolean algebras.

Additive measure functions are defined on the Boolean structure: additivity in (59b) follows the Boolean equation in (59a):

(59)   a $x \sqcup y = \quad (x-y) \sqcup \quad (y-x) \sqcup \quad (x \sqcap y)$
        b $MS_{M,U}(x \sqcup y) = MS_{M,U}(x-y) + MS_{M,U}(y-x) + MS_{M,U}(x \sqcap y)$

Let us think about the difference between pseudopartitive measures and attributive measures.

An attributive modifier is dominated by NP and is the sister of N (or a non-maximal N', if N is modified by an adjective). As we have seen, when an attributive modifies a plural count noun, its interpretation distributes over the atomic entities in the denotation of the plural N. Thus, while the plural noun denotes a Boolean algebra, the attributive modifier ignores the Boolean structure and goes for the atoms. From there on, the denotation of *two-kilo apples* results from intersecting the Boolean denotation of *apples* with the set of entities whose atoms weigh two kilos. This is equivalent to intersecting the non-Boolean denotation of *apple*, the set of atomic apples, with the set of entities that weigh two kilos, and pluralizing the result. *Two-kilo apples* denotes a plurality of apples where each atomic atom weighs two kilos. While the measure is extensive, the measure value of the atoms is given in terms of structure that is not directly semantically accessible (since atoms have no parts).

Measure heads of pseudopartitives are outside NP and modify the whole (mass or bare plural) NP.[6] (As we saw in Chapter 8, a singular count noun is not an NP, and thus it cannot be modified by a classifier.) The measure operation in the pseudopartitive takes place outside the NP: it combines with the Boolean interpretation of the NP. At this level, it cannot apply distributively. So in *two kilos of apples*, *two kilos* intersects with the Boolean interpretation of NP and divides the pluralities of apples into those that weigh (overall) two kilos and those that don't. The measure value of each plurality in the NP denotation is given in terms of its (semantically accessible) Boolean structure, following the equation in (59). In this way, *two kilos of (N)* differs from normal adjectives, but patterns with numerical phrases. In (60), the adjective *beautiful* distributes over individual flowers, but *three* can only be true of a plurality of flowers and doesn't distribute to the atoms.[7]

(60)   three beautiful flowers

Crucially, for additive measures, the same measure phrase applied to a set of atoms (as an attributive) and to a Boolean algebra (as

---

[6] I suggested in Chapter 5 that all bare plurals modified by classifiers have a mass interpretation. The argument that I make in this section is not dependent on that claim.

[7] As Fred Landman (p.c.) points out, *three* can only be true of pluralities. So #*three committee* can never have the interpretation 'a committee of three'.

a pseudopartitive) give different results. Assume that *apple* denotes the set {a, b, c}, and that a and b weigh one kilo, while c weighs two kilos. Then the denotation of *two-kilo apples* is {c}, while the denotation of *two kilos of apples* is {c, a⊔b}.

However, the attributive and the pseudopartitive will only yield different results when the measure is additive, i.e. defined on the Boolean structure in the way that additive measures are.

Compare *eighteen carat* as an attributive in (61a) and in the infelicitous pseudopartitive in (61b):

(61)   a eighteen-carat gold
        b #eighteen carats of gold

The crucial observation is the one we made earlier: *eighteen-carat gold* in *eighteen-carat gold rings* patterns with normal adjectives: it allows for distributive and collective interpretations. And, like normal adjectives, since it is non-additive, *eighteen-carat* does not have an interpretation where the measure is sensitive to the Boolean structure.

Sums of eighteen-carat gold will also be eighteen-carat gold, i.e. if MEASURE$_{\text{PURITY, CARAT}}$ applied to a and to b gives the value 18, then MEASURE$_{\text{PURITY, CARAT}}$(a⊔b) will also have the value 18. This is no different from normal adjectival behaviour: if a and b are both beautiful, then we expect the sum of a and b to be beautiful too. Thus, putting *eighteen carats*, with un-additive measure *carat*, in the pseudopartitive construction is similar to putting the adjective *beautiful* in that position. The infelicity of (61b) is no more surprising than the infelicity of (62).

(62)   #beautiful of gold (rings)

So, given the theory of counting and measuring developed in this book, it is not clear that we need to give a special explanation for why (61b) is infelicitous: the non-additive measure predicate is constrained to be inside the NP just like any other predicate modifier.

But explaining the felicity of *three kilos of gold* has been one of the tasks of this book, and we have found a satisfactory explanation. The felicity of non-distributive additive measuring requires the measuring operation to apply to a complete Boolean structure, and pseudopartitives are the structures which allow measures access to this structure.

10.6   QUESTIONS FOR FURTHER DISCUSSION AND INVESTIGATION

1 For any other language that you have access to, how are attributive modification and classifier modification by measure predicates expressed?

2 Can you find other ways in which the contrast between additive and non-additive measure operations is expressed linguistically?

3 Is there an explanation for why *two kilos* is marked plural in pseudo-partitives like *two kilos of apples* and singular in attributives like *two-kilo apples*?

11 In Conclusion

'Die ganzen Zahlen hat der liebe Gott gemacht, alles andere ist
Menschenwerk.' ('God made the integers, all the rest is the work
of man.')

Leopold Kroneker

It is time to take stock of where we are and what (I hope) we have seen.
In the first place, we have seen good evidence that a number of
typologically diverse languages distinguish grammatically between
counting and measuring, and that there are syntactic parallels crosslinguistically between counting structures and measuring structures.
We have seen the fruitfulness of a Boolean semantics for plurality,
which has enabled us formulate semantic operations of counting and
measuring, and allowed us to explain their syntactic properties.
We have shown what counting and measuring have in common.
From the beginning of this book, we have been arguing that the
felicity of counting depends on the counting operation applying to
a complete atomic Boolean structure, since it must access the atoms in
the structure, and the structure of the sums based on the set of atoms
must be the correct structure for counting (e.g., below each sum must
sit the correct number of atoms.)

In the previous chapter, we showed that measuring pluralities or
accumulations of stuff also requires access to a complete Boolean
structure, and that this underlies the generalization that pseudopartitive measuring is additive. Neither counting nor pseudopartitive
measuring allows distributive interpretations in the way that adjectives do.

We have also, from Chapter 3 on, been arguing that counting and
measuring are different, with different syntactic structures, and this
too has an explanation. Counting must access grammatically encoded
atomic structure, while measuring is possible in the absence of this
structure. This leads to a syntactic contrast between pseudopartitive
measure predicates which are outside the NP, and cardinals which are

left-peripheral adjectives inside NP, the highest adjective inside the maximal projection of N. We can explain this too. Neither counting nor pseudopartitive measuring is distributive, and so neither cardinals nor measure predicates are low modifiers, since low modifiers are (at least potentially) distributive. Pseudopartitive measures, as NP modifiers, have access to the NP denotation, which is what they need. But cardinal predicates are predicates of countable pluralities, and they must have access to the atoms of the pluralities and be able to count them. So they must be inside the NP, so as to have access to the atomic structure, but higher than attributives, since they do not distribute to atoms. The left-most or highest adjectival position directly dominated by NP meets these criteria exactly. This suggests a picture where modifiers are adjoined as high in their structure as their semantics allows. It also explains why *one* is so often a 'real' adjective in contrast to other cardinals. It is the only cardinal that distributes to atoms.

A second theme of the book has been the requirement in very many languages that countability is grammatically encoded, or, put differently, that a grammatical encoding of countability is a prerequisite for explicit linguistic counting. I have suggested that this underlies the contrast between count and mass nouns: count nouns encode countability at a lexical level. This, though, is only one way of encoding countability, and languages which do not have a lexical count/mass distinction encode countability in different ways, often using functional heads or classifiers. However, nouns are not the only predicates which can be counted. NP predicates also divide into countable and non-countable, and languages with a lexical count/mass distinction need to mark countability at the NP level too. They do this by using nominal classifiers, as we saw in Chapter 8. So, even in count/mass languages, sortal count nouns are only one way of encoding countability.

Thinking of count nouns as one way of encoding countability leads to the very natural suggestion that measuring is associated with mass denotations analogously to the way in which counting is associated with count denotations. This is supported by the contrasts discussed just above: counting requires access to grammatical encoded atoms, while measuring operates on a structure where the atoms are grammatically inaccessible and lexical counting is impossible. We saw empirical evidence in support of this in Chapter 5, where we looked at quantity comparisons with minimally contrasting object mass nouns and count nouns. And, as we saw in Chapter 6, languages may encode countability in different ways, but the sensitivity to the contrast between measuring and counting seems to transcend the particular mechanisms of encoding countability. Strikingly, the only language we looked at in which counting is not explicitly encoded grammatically, Yudja, is a language which apparently does not have ways of expressing measure operations.

I want to end by mentioning some of the most obvious unanswered questions which have been raised by this current study, but that must be left for further research. Note that this is only a partial list.

(i)   Pires de Oliveira & Rothstein (2011) showed that there is good evidence that bare singulars are kind-denoting mass nouns in Brazilian Portuguese. But the same kind of arguments show that mass noun interpretations of flexible nouns in Hungarian do not denote kinds. This means, apparently, that there is no relation between the flexibility of N in choosing a count or mass denotation and the choice between kind interpretations or predicate interpretations for mass nouns. So what is the choice of mass denotation determined by?

(ii)   Almost all accounts of counting and individuation focus on concrete nouns. In these cases, in English, properties such as pluralization, determiner selection, and modification by cardinals seem to cluster together. But, as I have pointed out, mainly in questions at the end of chapters, in the domain of abstract nouns things are very different. We seem to be able to individuate units in N and mark abstract nouns grammatically with count syntax without being able to use cardinals to count. The topic of count nouns with abstract denotations is almost entirely uncharted.

(iii)   The discussion in this book has not touched on the question of why there is crosslinguistic variation as to which nouns are mass and which are count (in count/mass languages). But I hope that establishing the link between count syntax and countability has opened new ways to think about this problem.

(iv)   We have focused almost entirely on cardinal numerals in this book, and on the contrasts between counting and measuring. But there are, of course, many other contexts in which numericals are used and many kinds of numericals. (A particularly interesting group are fractions.) There are also many different kinds of approximation contexts. All these need to be explored.

(v)   Above all, there are so many languages! We have focused on a small group of languages. Within this group of languages, we have seen striking diversity in the lexical and morphosyntactic mechanisms used to encode countability and enable measurement. In each case, the semantic contrast between counting and measuring interacts with the specific morphosyntactic structure of the language in ways which we have only just touched on. I very much hope that this book will encourage linguists to investigate these issues further in these and in other languages, and, bit by bit, we may be able to build a more general picture of how counting and measuring work crosslinguistically.

Envoi

一只青蛙一张嘴，
两只眼睛四条腿，
扑通一声跳下水。
两只青蛙两张嘴，
四只眼睛八条腿，
扑通扑通两声跳下水。

yì   zhī qīngwā,   yì   zhāng zuǐ
one Cl frog,   one Cl   mouth

liǎng zhī yǎnjīng,   sì   tiáo tuǐ
two Cl eyes,   four Cl legs

pūtōng, yì   sheng tiào xià   shuǐ
pit-a-pat one sound jump down water

liǎng zhī qīngwā,   liǎng zhāng zuǐ
two Cl frog,   two Cl   mouth

sì   zhī yǎnjīng,   bā   tiáo tuǐ
four Cl eyes,   eight Cl legs

pūtōng pūtōng, liǎng sheng   tiào   xià   shuǐ
pit-a-pat pit-a-pat, two sounds jump down water

Traditional Mandarin counting rhyme

References

Acquaviva, P. 2008. *Lexical Plurals: A Morphosemantic Approach*. Oxford: Oxford University Press.

Aikhenvald, Alexandra, 2003. *Classifiers: A Typology of Noun Categorization Devices*. Oxford: Oxford University Press.

Akmajian, Adrian, and Adrienne Lehrer, 1976. NP-like quantifiers and the problem of determining the head of an NP. *Linguistic Analysis* 2, 4, 395–413.

Alexiadou, Artemis, 2011. Plural mass nouns and the morpho-syntax of number. In Mary Byram Washburn, Katherine McKinney-Bock, Erika Varis, Ann Sawyer and Barbara Tomaszewicz (eds.), *Proceedings of the 28th West Coast Conference on Formal Linguistics*, pp. 33–41. Somerville, MA: Cascadilla Press.

Allan, Keith, 1977. Classifiers. *Language* 53, 2, 285–311.

1980. Nouns and countability. *Language* 56, 3, 541–67.

2006. A 'just that' lexical meaning for *most*. In K. von Heusinger and K. Turner (eds.), *Where Semantics Meets Pragmatics*, pp. 49–91. Amsterdam: Elsevier.

Bach, Emmon, 1989. *Informal Lectures on Formal Semantics*. Albany: SUNY Press.

Bale, Alan C., and David Barner, 2009. The interpretation of functional heads: using comparatives to explore the mass/count distinction. *Journal of Semantics* 26, 3, 217–52.

Bale, Alan, and Jessica Coon, 2014. Classifiers are for numerals, not for nouns: consequences for the mass/count distinction. *Linguistic Inquiry* 45, 4, 695–707.

Bale, Alan, and Hrayr Khanjian, 2008. Classifiers and number marking. In T. Friedman and S. Ito (eds.), *Proceedings from Semantics and Linguistic Theory XVIII*, pp. 74–88. Ithaca, NY: Cornell University.

Barner, David, and Jesse Snedeker, 2005. Quantity judgments and individuation: evidence that mass nouns count. *Cognition* 97, 1, 41–66.

Barnes, Julian, 2003. *The Pedant in the Kitchen*. Revised edn published 2012. London: Atlantic Books.

Barwise, Jon, and Robin Cooper, 1981. Generalized quantifiers and natural language. *Linguistics and Philosophy* 4, 2, 159–219.

Beviláqua, Kayron, Roberta Pires de Oliveira and Suzi Lima, 2016. Bare Nouns in Brazilian Portuguese: an experimental study an grinding. In S. Rothstein and J. Šķilters (eds.), *The Baltic International yearbook of Cognition, Logic and Communication*, Volume XI: *Number: Cognitive, Semantic and Crossliguistic Approaches*, Kansas: New Prairie Press. http://dx.doi.org/10.4148/1944-3676.113. [Online publication]

Bisang, Walter, 2012. Numeral classifiers with plural marking, a challenge to Greenberg. In D. Xu (ed.), *Plurality and Classifiers across Languages in China*, pp. 23–42. Berlin: Mouton de Gruyter.

Borer, Hagit, 1989. On the morphological parallelism between compounds and constructs. In G. Booij and Jaap Van Marle (eds.), *Yearbook of Morphology 1989*, pp. 45–64. Dordrecht: Foris.

1999. Deconstructing the construct. In K. Johnson and I. Roberts (eds.), *Beyond Principles and Parameters*, pp. 43–90. Berlin: Springer (Kluwer).

2005. *Stucturing Sense*. Oxford: Oxford University Press.

2009. Compounds: the view from Hebrew. In R. Lieber and P. Stekauer (eds.), *The Oxford Handbook of Compounding*, pp. 491–511. Oxford: Oxford University Press.

Borges, Jorge Luis, 1999. *Collected Fictions*, translated by Andrew Hurley. New York: Penguin Books.

Borschev, Vladimir, and Barbara H. Partee, 2004. Genitives, types, and sorts: the Russian genitive of measure. In Ji-yung Kim, Yury A. Lander and Barbara H. Partee (eds.), *Possessives and Beyond: Semantics and Syntax*, UMOP 29, pp. 29–43. Amherst, MA: GLSA Publications.

Borschev, Vladimir, Elena V. Paducheva, Barbara H. Partee, Yakov G. Testelets and Igor Yanovich, 2006. Sentential and constituent negation in Russian BE-sentences revisited. In James E. Lavine, Steven L. Franks, Mila Tasseva-Kurktchieva and Hana Filip (eds.), *Formal Approaches to Slavic Linguistics: The Princeton Meeting 2005*, pp. 50–65. Ann Arbor: Michigan Slavic Publications.

2008. Russian genitives, non-referentiality, and the property-type hypothesis. In A. Antonenko, J. F. Bailyn and C. Bethin (eds.), *Formal Approaches to Slavic Linguistics: The Stony Brook Meeting 2007*, pp. 48–67. Ann Arbor: Michigan Slavic Publications.

Bunt, Harry, 1985. *Mass Terms and Model-theoretic Semantics*. Cambridge: Cambridge University Press.

Carey, Susan, and Fei Xu, 2001. Infant's knowledge of objects: beyond object files and object tracking. *Cognition* 80, 179–213.

Carlson, Gregory N., 1977. Reference to Kinds in English. Unpublished Ph. D. dissertation, University of Massachusetts, Amherst.

Casati, Roberto, and Achille C. Varzi, 1999. *Parts and Places: The Structures of Spatial Representation*. Cambridge, MA: MIT Press.

Chao, Yuen-Ren, 1968. *A Grammar of Spoken Chinese*. Berkeley: University of California Press.

Cheng, Lisa L.-S., 2012. Counting and classifiers. In D. Massam (ed.), *Count and Mass across Languages*, pp. 199–219. Oxford: Oxford University Press.

Cheng, Lisa L.-S., and Rint Sybesma, 1998. Yi-wan tang, yi-ge tang: classifiers and massifiers. *Tsing Hua Journal of Chinese Studies* 28, 3, 385–412.

1999. Bare and not-so-bare nouns and the structure of NP. *Linguistic Inquiry* 30, 4, 509–42.

2005. Classifiers in four varieties of Chinese. In G. Cinque and R. S. Kayne (eds.), *The Oxford Handbook of Comparative Syntax*, pp. 259–92. Oxford: Oxford University Press.

2012. Classifiers and DP. *Linguistic Inquiry* 43, 4, 634–50.

Cheng, Lisa L.-S., Jenny S. Doetjes and Rint Sybesma, 2008. How universal is the universal grinder? In M. van Koppen and B. Botma (eds.), *Linguistics in the Netherlands 2008*, pp. 50–62. Amsterdam: John Benjamins.

Chierchia, Gennaro, 1984. Topics in the Syntax and Semantics of Infinitives and Gerunds. Unpublished Ph.D. dissertation, University of Massachusetts, Amherst.

1985. Formal semantics and the grammar of predication. *Linguistic Inquiry* 16, 417–43.

1998a. Plurality of mass nouns and the notion of 'semantic parameter'. In S. Rothstein (ed.), *Events and Grammar*, pp. 53–103. Berlin: Springer (Kluwer).

1998b. Reference to kinds. *Natural Language Semantics* 6, 339–405.

2004. Scalar implicatures, polarity phenomena, and the syntax/pragmatics interface. In A. Belletti (ed.), *Structures and Beyond, the Cartography of Syntactic Structures 3*, pp. 39–103. Oxford: Oxford University Press.

2010. Mass nouns, vagueness and semantic variation. *Synthese* 174, 99–149.

Chierchia, Gennaro, and Raymond Turner, 1988. Semantics and property theory, *Linguistics and Philosophy* 11, 3, 261–302.

Chomsky, Noam, 1981. *Lectures on Government and Binding*. Dordrecht: Foris.

Cohen, Ariel, and Manfred Krifka, 2010. Superlative quantifiers as modifiers of meta-speech acts. In *Baltic International Yearbook of Cognition, Logic and Communication*, Volume VI. http://newprairiepress.org/biyclc/vol6/iss1/11.

Comrie, Bernard, 2011. Numeral bases. In M. S. Dryer and M. Haspelmath (eds.), *The World Atlas of Language Structures Online*. Leipzig: Max Planck Institute for Evolutionary Anthropology, ch. 131, http://wals.info/chapter/131. Accessed on 21 August 2013.

Corbett, Greville, 2000. *Number*. Cambridge: Cambridge University Press.

Croft, William, 1994. Semantic universals in classifier systems. *Word* 45, 145–71.

Csirmaz, Anikó, and Éva Dékány, 2014. Hungarian is a classifier language. In S. Raffaele and F. Masini (eds.), *Word Classes: Nature, Typology and Representations*, pp. 141–60. Amsterdam: John Benjamins.

Danon, Gabi, 2008. Definiteness spreading in the Hebrew construct state. _Lingua_ 118, 7, 872–906.

2012. Two structures for numeral–noun constructions. _Lingua_ 122, 12, 1282–1307.

Dantzig, Tobias, 1954. _Number, the Language of Science: A Critical Survey Written for the Cultured Non-mathematician_, 4th edn. Doubleday. Reprinted in 2007. Middlesex: Penguin Books.

David, Elizabeth, 1999. _French Provincial Cooking_. London: Penguin.

Dehaene, Stanislas, 2010. _The Number Sense: How the Mind Creates Mathematics_, 2nd edn. Oxford: Oxford University Press.

Dékány, Éva, 2011. A Profile of the Hungarian DP. Unpublished Ph. D. dissertation, Center for Advanced Study in Theoretical Linguistics, University of Tromsø.

Dočekal, Mojmír, and Markéta Ziková, 2013. Semantic opacity of collective nouns and transparency of group numerals. Paper presented at Formal Description of Slavic Languages 10. Leipzig, December.

Doetjes, Jenny S., 1997. Quantifiers and Selection: On the Distribution of Quantifying Expressions in French, Dutch and English. Unpublished Ph.D. dissertation, Leiden University.

2012. Count/mass distinctions across languages. In C. Maienborn, K. von Heusinger and P. Portner (eds.), _Semantics: an International Handbook of Natural Language Meaning, Part III_, pp. 2559–80. Berlin: de Gruyter.

Doron, Edit, 2003. Bare singular reference to kinds. _Proceedings of Semantics and Linguistic Theory_ 13, 73–90.

Doron, Edit, and Irit Meir, 2013a. Construct state: modern Hebrew. In G. Khan (ed.), _The Encyclopedia of Hebrew Language and Linguistics_, pp. 581–9. Leiden: Brill. http://referenceworks.brillonline.com/entries/encyclopedia-of-hebrew-language-and-linguistics/construct-state-modern-hebrew-EHLL_COM_00000681?s.num=0&s.f.s2_parent=s.f.book.encyclopedia-of-hebrew-language-and-linguistics&s.q=constructs.

2013b. Amount definites. In C. Bessayde and R. Pires de Oliveira (eds.), _Weak Definites across Languages – Theoretical and Experimental Investigations_, Recherches Linguistiques de Vincennes 42, pp.139–65. Saint-Denis: Presses Universitaires de Vincennes.

Doron, Edit, and Ana Müller, 2013. The cognitive basis of the mass–count distinction: evidence from bare nouns. In P. Cabredo Hofherr and A. Zribi-Hertz (eds.), _Crosslinguistic Studies on Noun Phrase Structure and Reference_, pp. 73–101. Leiden: Brill.

Epstein-Naveh, Noa, 2015. Pluralization and mass nouns – can they go together in modern Hebrew? Unpublished MA thesis, Bar-Ilan University, Ramat Gan.

Erbaugh, Mary S., 2002. Classifiers are for specification: complementary functions for sortal and general classifiers in Cantonese and Mandarin. _Cahiers de Linguistique-Asie Orientale_ 31, 1, 33–69.

Farkas, Donka, and Henriette de Swart, 2003. *The Semantics of Incorporation*, Stanford Monographs in Linguistics. Stanford: CSLI Publications.

Feigenson, Lisa, Stanislas Dehaene and Elisabeth Spelke, 2004. Core systems of number. *Trends in Cognitive Sciences* 8, 7, 307–14.

Franks, Steven, 1995. *Parameters of Slavic Morphosyntax*. Oxford: Oxford University Press.

Frege, Gottlob, 1884. *Grundlagen der Arithmetik / The Foundations of Arithmetic*. Translated from the German by J. L. Austin. Oxford: Wiley-Blackwell.

    1892. Über Begriff und Gegenstand. *Vierteljahresschrift für Wissenschaftliche Philosophie* 16, 192–205. Translated as 'On concept and object'. In P. Geach and M. Black (eds.), *Translations from the Philosophical Writings of Gottlob Frege*, pp. 42–55. Oxford: Basil Blackwell.

Gadzar, Gerald, 1979. *Pragmatics: Implicature, Presupposition and Logical Form*. New York: Academic Press.

Gafni, Chen, and Susan Rothstein, 2014. Who has more N? Context and variety are both relevant. Paper presented at the First Conference on Cognition Research of the Israeli Society for Cognitive Psychology. Akko, 10–12 February.

Gawron, Jean Marc, 2002. Two kinds of quantizers in DP. Handout of talk at the Linguistic Society of America Annual Meeting, San Francisco, 3–6 January.

Geenhoven, Veerle van, 1998. *Semantic Incorporation and Indefinite Descriptions*. Stanford: CSLI Publications.

Ghaniabadi, Saeed, 2012. Plural marking beyond count nouns. In D. Massam (ed.), *Count and Mass across Language*, pp. 112–28. Oxford: Oxford University Press.

Gil, David, 2013. Numeral classifiers. In M. S. Dryer and M. Haspelmath (eds.), *The World Atlas of Language Structures Online*. Leipzig: Max Planck Institute for Evolutionary Anthropology. http://wals.info/chapter/55, Accessed on 31 March 2015.

Gillon, Brendan, 1992. Towards a common semantics for English count and mass nouns. *Linguistics and Philosophy* 15, 6, 597–640.

Greenberg, Joseph, 1974. *Language Typology: A Historical and Analytic Overview*. Berlin: de Gruyter.

Grestenberger, Laura, 2015. Number marking in German measure phrases and the structure of pseudo-partitives. *Journal of Comparative Germanic Linguistics* 18, 2, 93–138.

Grimm, Scott, 2014. Individuating the abstract. In U. Etxeberria, A. Fălăuş, A. Irurtzun and B. Leferman (eds.), *Proceedings of Sinn und Bedeutung 18*, pp. 182–200. Vitoria, Spain: University of the Basque Country.

    2015. Abstract nouns and countability. Paper presented at the 11th International Symposium of Cognition, Logic and Communication: 'Number: Cognitive, Semantic and Crosslinguistic Approaches'. University of Latvia, Riga, Latvia, December.

Grimm, Scott, and Beth Levin 2012. *Who has more furniture?* An exploration of the bases for comparison'. Paper presented at Mass/Count in Linguistics, Philosophy and Cognitive Science Conference. École Normale Supérieure, Paris, France, 20–21 December. Slides downloadable at: http://web.stanford.edu/~bclevin/paris12mcslides.pdf.

Grosu, Alexander, and Fred Landman, 1998. Strange relatives of the third kind. *Natural Language Semantics* 6, 2, 125–70.

Hammarström, Harald, 2010. Rarities in numeral systems. In J. Wohlgemuth and M. Cysouw (eds.), *Rethinking Universals: How Rarities Affect Linguistic Theory*, pp. 11–60. Berlin: de Gruyter.

Hanke, Thomas, 2010. Additional rarities in the typology of numerals. In J. Wohlgemuth and M. Cysouw (eds.), *Rethinking Universals: How Rarities Affect Linguistic Theory*, pp. 61–89. Berlin: de Gruyter.

He, Chuansheng, and Yan Jiang, 2011. Type shifting, Chinese hen+N structure, and implications for semantic parameters. *Lingua* 121, 5, 698–986.

Heim, Irene, 1982. The Semantics of Definite and Indefinite NPs. Unpublished Ph.D. dissertation, University of Massachusetts, Amherst.

1987. Where does the definiteness restriction apply? Evidence from the definiteness of variables. In A. ter Meulen and E. Reuland (eds.), *The Representation of (In)definiteness*, pp. 21–42. Cambridge, MA: MIT Press.

Higginbotham, James, 1987. Indefiniteness and predication. In A. ter Meulen and E. Reuland (eds.), *The Representation of (In)definiteness*, pp. 43–70. Cambridge, MA: MIT Press.

Hofweber, Thomas, 2005. Number determiners, numbers, and arithmetic. *The Philosophical Review* 114, 2, 179–225.

Horn, Laurence R., 1972. The Semantics of Logical Operators in English. Unpublished Ph.D. dissertation, UCLA.

1989. *A Natural History of Negation*. Chicago: University of Chicago Press.

Hsieh, Miao-Ling, 2008. *The Internal Structure of Noun Phrases in Chinese*. Taipei: Crane Publishers.

Huang, Yi Ting, Elisabeth Spelke and Jesse Snedeker, 2013. What exactly do numbers mean? *Language Learning and Development* 9, 2, 105–29.

Huntley-Fenner, Gavin, Susan Carey and Andrea Solimando, 2002. Objects are individuals but stuff doesn't count: perceived rigidity and cohesiveness influence infants' representations of small groups of discrete entities. *Cognition* 85, 203–21.

Hurford, James R., 1987. *Language and Number: The Emergence of a Cognitive System*. Oxford: Wiley-Blackwell.

Hyde, Daniel C., 2011. Two systems of non-symbolic numerical cognition. *Frontiers in Human Neuroscience* 5. http://dx.doi.org/10.3389/fnhum.2011.00150.

Hyde, Daniel C., and Elisabeth Spelke, 2011. Neural signatures of number processing in human infants: evidence for two core systems underlying numerical cognition. *Developmental Science* 14, 2, 360–71.

Ionin, Tania, and Ora Matushansky, 2006. The composition of complex cardinals. *Journal of Semantics* 23, 315–60.

Jackendoff, Ray, 1977. *X-bar Syntax: A Study of Phrase Structure*, Linguistic Inquiry Monograph 2. Cambridge, MA: MIT Press.

1991. Parts and boundaries. *Cognition* 41, 1, 9–45.

Jiang, Li, 2008. Monotonicity and measure phrases in Chinese. Paper presented at the 11th International Symposium of Chinese Language and Linguistics. Taiwan, 23–25 May.

Kadmon, Nirit, 1987. On Unique and Non-unique Reference and Asymmetric Quantification. Unpublished Ph.D. dissertation, University of Massachusetts, Amherst.

1990. Uniqueness. *Linguistics and Philosophy* 13, 3, 273–324.

Kamp, Hans, 1975. Two theories about adjectives. In E. Keenan (ed.), *Formal Semantics of Natural Language*, pp. 123–55. Cambridge: Cambridge University Press.

1981. A theory of truth and semantic representation. In J. Groenendijk, Th. Janssen and M. Stokhof (eds.), *Formal Methods in the Study of Language*, Volume I, pp. 277–322. Amsterdam: Mathematic Centre. Reprinted in P. Portner and B. H. Partee (eds.), 2002. *Formal Semantics*, pp. 189–222. Oxford: Wiley-Blackwell. And reprinted in K. von Heusinger and A. ter Meulen (eds.), 2013. *The Dynamics of Meaning and Interpretation: Selected Papers of Hans Kamp*, pp. 329–69. Leiden: Brill.

Kamp, Hans, and Uwe Reyle, 1993. *From Discourse to Logic: Introduction to Modeltheoretic Semantics of Natural Language, Formal Logic and Discourse Representation Theory*. Berlin: Springer (Kluwer).

Kaufman, E. L., M. W. Lord, T. W. Reese and J. Volkmann, 1949. The discrimination of visual number. *American Journal of Psychology* 62, 4, 498–525.

Keenan, Ed, and Jonathan Stavi, 1986. A semantic characterization of natural language determiners. *Linguistics and Philosophy* 9, 3, 253–326.

Keenan, Edward L., and Leonard M. Faltz, 2012. *Boolean Semantics for Natural Language*. Berlin: Springer.

Kennedy, Christopher, and Louise McNally, 1999. From event structure to scale structure: degree modification in deverbal adjectives. *Proceedings of Semantics and Linguistic Theory* 9, 163–80.

Khrizman, Keren, 2015. Russian as a (non)-classifier language. Paper presented at the 11th International Symposium of Cognition, Logic and Communication: 'Number: Cognitive, Semantic and Crosslinguistic Approaches'. University of Latvia, Riga, Latvia, December.

2016. Numerous Issues in the Semantics of Russian Numeral Constructions. Unpublished Ph.D. dissertation, Bar-Ilan University, Ramat Gan.

Khrizman, Keren, and Susan Rothstein, 2015. Russian approximative inversion as a measure construction. In G. Zybatow, P. Biskup, M. Guhl, C. Hurtig, O. Mueller-Reichau and M. Yastrebova (eds.),

Slavic Grammar from a Formal Perspective. The 10th Anniversary FDSL Conference, Leipzig 2013, Linguistik International 35, pp. 259–72. Frankfurt am Main: Peter Lang Edition.

Khrizman, Keren, Fred Landman, Suzi Lima, Susan Rothstein and Brigitta R. Schvarcz, 2015. Portion readings are count readings, not measure readings. *Proceedings of the 20th Amsterdam Colloquium.* http://semantic sarchive.net/Archive/mVkOTk2N/AC2015-proceedings.pdf.

Koptjevskaja-Tamm, Maria, 2001. 'A piece of the cake' and 'a cup of tea': partitive and pseudo-partitive nominal constructions in the Circum-Baltic languages. In Ö. Dahl and M. Koptjevskaja-Tamm (eds.), *Circum-Baltic Languages*, Volume II: *Grammar and Typology*, pp. 523–68. Amsterdam: John Benjamins.

2009. 'A lot of grammar with a good portion of lexicon': towards a typology of partitive and pseudo-partitive nominal constructions. In J. Helmbrecht, Y. Nishina, Y. Shin, S. Skopeteas and E. Verhoeven (eds.), *Form and Function in Language Research: Papers in Honour of Christian Lehmann*, pp. 329–46. Berlin: de Gruyter.

Krifka, Manfred, 1989. Nominal reference, temporal constitution and quantification in event semantics. In R. Bartsch, J. van Benthem and P. von Emde Boas (eds.), *Semantics and Contextual Expression*, pp. 75–115. Dordrecht: Foris.

1990. Four thousand ships passed through the lock: object-induced measure functions on events. *Linguistics and Philosophy* 13, 5, 487–520.

1992. Thematic relations as links between nominal reference and temporal constitution. In I. A. Sag and A. Szabolcsi (ed.), *Lexical Matters*, pp. 29–52. Stanford: Center for the Study of Language and Information.

1995. Common nouns: a contrastive analysis of English and Chinese. In G. N. Carlson and F. J. Pelletier (eds.), *The Generic Book*, pp. 398–411. Chicago: University of Chicago Press.

2009. Approximate interpretations of number words: a case for strategic communication. In E. Hinrichs and J. Nerbonne (eds.), *Theory and Evidence in Semantics*, pp 109–32. Stanford: CSLI Publications.

Kulkarni, Ritwik, Susan Rothstein and Alessandro Treves, 2013. A statistical investigation into the crosslinguistic distribution of mass and count nouns: morphosyntactic and semantic perspectives. *Biolinguistics* 7, 132–68.

Kulkarni, Ritwik, Alessandro Treves and Susan Rothstein, in press. Can mass-count syntax be derived from semantics? In F. Moltmann (ed.), *Mass and Count in Linguistics, Philosophy, and Cognitive Science.* Amsterdam: John Benjamins.

Landman, Fred, 1991. *Structures for Semantics.* Berlin: Springer (Kluwer).

1995. Plurality. In S. Lappin (ed.), *Handbook of Contemporary Semantics*, 1st edn, pp. 425–57. London: Wiley-Blackwell.

2000. *Events and Plurality*. Berlin: Springer (Kluwer).

2003. Predicate–argument mismatches and the adjectival theory of indefinites. In M. Coene and Y. d'Hulst (eds.), *From NP to DP: Volume 1*, pp. 211–37. Amsterdam: John Benjamins.

2004. *Indefinites and the Type of Sets*. Oxford: Wiley-Blackwell.

2011a. Count nouns, mass nouns, neat nouns, mess nouns. In *The Baltic International Yearbook of Cognition, Logic and Communication*, Volume VI. http://newprairiepress.org/biyclc/vol6/iss1/12.

2011b. Boolean pragmatics. In J. van der Does and C. Dutlih Novaes (eds.), 'This is not a Festschrift': A Festpage for Martin Stokhof. www.vddoes .net/Martin/articles/Fred.pdf.

2015. Lectures on Iceberg Semantics for Mass and Count Nouns. Unpublished manuscript, Tel Aviv University and Tübingen University.

2016. Iceberg semantics for count nouns and mass nouns: the evidence from portions. In S. Rothstein and J. Šķilters (eds.), *The Baltic International Yearbook of Cognition, Logic and Communication*, Volume XI: *Number: Cognitive, Semantic and Crosslinguistic Approaches*. Kansas: New Prairie Press. http://dx.doi.org/10.4148/1944-3676.1107 (Online publication.)

Landman, Fred, and Susan Rothstein, 2010. Incremental homogeneity in the semantics of aspectual for-phrases. In M. R. Hovav, E. Doron and I. Sichel (eds.), *Syntax, Lexical Semantics and Event Structure*, pp. 229–51. Oxford: Oxford University Press.

Lasersohn, Peter, 1999. Pragmatic halos. *Language* 75, 3, 522–51.

Lehrer, Adrienne, 1986. English classifier constructions. *Lingua* 68, 2, 109–48.

Levinson, Steven C., 1983. *Pragmatics*. Cambridge: Cambridge University Press.

2000. *Presumptive Meanings: The Theory of Generalized Conversational Implicature*. Cambridge, MA: MIT Press.

Li, XuPing, 2011. On the Semantics of Classifiers in Chinese. Unpublished Ph.D. dissertation, Bar-Ilan University, Ramat Gan.

2013. *Numeral Classifiers in Chinese: the Syntax–Semantics Interface*. New York: Mouton de Gruyter.

Li, XuPing, and Walter Bisang, 2012. Classifiers in Sinitic languages: from individuation to definiteness-marking. *Lingua* 122, 4, 335–55.

Li, XuPing, and Susan Rothstein, 2012. Measure readings of Mandarin classifier phrases and the particle de. *Language and Linguistics* 13, 4, 693–741.

Lima, Suzi, 2010. About the count-mass distinction in Yudja: a description. In Beth Rogers and Anita Szakay (eds.), *Proceedings of the Fifteenth Workshop on Structure and Constituency in Languages of the Americas*, pp. 157–64. Vancouver: UBCWPL.

2012. Numerals and the universal packager in Yudja (Tupi). In E. Bogal-Allbritten (ed.), *Proceedings of Semantics of Under-Represented Languages in the Americas 6*. Amherst: GLSA Publications.

2014. The Grammar of Individuation and Counting. Ph.D. dissertation, University of Massachusetts, Amherst.

Lima, Suzi, Peggy Li and Jesse Snedeker, 2014. Acquiring the denotation of object-denoting nouns in a language without partitives. Poster presented at Boston University Conference on Language Development 39. 7-9 November.

Link, Godehard, 1983. The logical analysis of plurals and mass terms: a lattice-theoretical approach. In R. Bauerle, C. Schwartze and A. von Stechow (eds.), *Meaning, Use and the Interpretation of Language*, pp. 302-23. Berlin: Mouton de Gruyter.

1984. Hydras: on the logic of relative clause constructions with multiple heads. In F. Landman and F. Veltman (eds.), *Varieties of Formal Semantics*, pp. 245-57. Dordrecht: Foris.

Lipton, James, 1993. *An Exaltation of Larks: The Ultimate Edition*. Middlesex: Penguin Books.

Lü, Shu-Xiang (吕叔湘), 1980/1999. *Xiandai Hanyu Babai Ci. [Eight Hundred Characters in Modern Chinese]*. Beijing: Commercial Press. (In Chinese.)

Lyons, John, 1977. *Semantics*, Volume II. Cambridge: Cambridge University Press.

Mathieu, Eric, 2012. On the mass/count distinction in Ojibwe. In Diane Massam (ed.), *Count and Mass across Languages*, pp. 172-98. Oxford: Oxford University Press.

Mel'čuk, I., 1985. *Poverxnostnyj Sintaksis Russkix čislovyx Vyraženij*, Wiener Slawistischer Almanach Sonderband 16. Vienna: Institut fur Slavistic der Universitat Wien.

Mithun, Marianne, 1988. Lexical categories and the evolution of number marking. In M. Hammond and M. Noonan (eds.), *Theoretical Morphology*, pp. 211-34. New York: Academic Press.

Mittwoch, Anita, 1988. Aspects of English aspect: on the interaction of perfect, progressive and durational phrases. *Linguistics and Philosophy* 11, 2, 203-54.

Moshavi, Adina, and Susan Rothstein, in press. Indefinite numerical construct phrases in Biblical Hebrew. *Journal of Semitic Studies*.

Müller, Anna, Luciana Storto and Coutinho Thiago, 2006. Number and the mass/count distinction in Karitiana. In A. Fujimori and M. A. Reis Silva (eds.), *Proceedings of the Eleventh Workshop on Structure and Constituency in Languages of the Americas*, pp. 122-35. Vancouver: UBC Working Papers in Linguistics.

Partee, Barbara H., 2008. Negation, intensionality, and aspect: interaction with NP semantics. In S. Rothstein (ed.), *Theoretical and Crosslinguistic Approaches to the Semantics of Aspect*, pp. 291-317. Amsterdam: John Benjamins.

Partee, Barbara H., and Vladimir Borschev, 2012. Sortal, relational, and functional interpretations of nouns and Russian container constructions. *Journal of Semantics* 29, 4, 445-86.

Paul, Waltraud, in press. The insubordinate subordinator 'de' in Mandarin Chinese. To appear in S.-W. Tang (ed.), *The Attributive Particle in Chinese*, Frontiers in Chinese Linguistics Series. Beijing: Peking University Press.

Peano, Giuseppe, 1889. *Arithmetices principia: nova methodo*. Turin: Fratres Bocca. Translated as The principles of arithmetic, presented by a new method. In J. van Heijenoort (ed.), 1967. *From Frege to Gödel: A Source Book in Mathematical Logic*, pp. 83-97. Cambridge, MA: Harvard University Press.

Pelletier, Francis Jeffry, 1975. Non-singular reference: some preliminaries. *Philosophia* 5, 4, 451-65.

(ed.) 1979. *Mass Terms: Some Philosophical Problems*. Berlin: Springer (Reidel).

2012. Lexical Nouns are both +MASS and +COUNT but they are neither +MASS nor +COUNT. In D. Massam (ed.), *Count and Mass across Languages*, pp. 9-26. Oxford: Oxford University Press.

Peyraube, Alain, 1999. On the modal auxiliaries of possibility in Classical Chinese. In H. Samuel Wang, Feng-fu Tsao and Chin-fa Lien (eds.), *Selected Papers from the Fifth International Conference on Chinese Linguistics*, pp. 27-52. Taipei: The Crane Publishing Co.

Pires de Oliveira, Roberta, and Susan Rothstein, 2011. Bare singular noun phrases are mass in Brazilian Portuguese. *Lingua* 121, 2153-75.

2013. Bare singular objects in Brazilian Portuguese: perfectivity, telicity and kinds. In J. Kabatek and A. Wall (eds.), *New Perspectives on Bare Noun Phrases in Romance and Beyond*, Studies in Language Companion Series 141, pp. 89-222. Amsterdam: John Benjamins.

Ritter, Elizabeth, 1988. A head movement approach to construct state phrases. *Linguistics* 26, 909-29.

1991. Two functional categories in noun phrases: evidence from Modern Hebrew. In S. Rothstein (ed.), *Perspectives on Phrase Structure*, Syntax and Semantics 25, pp. 37-62. New York: Academic Press.

Rothstein, Susan, 1999. Fine-grained structure in the eventuality domain: the semantics of predicative adjective phrases and be. *Natural Language Semantics* 7, 4, 347-420.

2000. Domain selection in relative clauses. Paper presented at the Workshop on the Syntax and Semantics of Relative Clauses. Tel Aviv University. June.

2001. *Predicates and their Subjects*. Berlin: Springer (Kluwer).

2004. *Structuring Events: a Study in the Semantics of Lexical Aspect*. Oxford: Blackwell.

2009. Individuating and measure readings of classifier constructions: evidence from Modern Hebrew. *Brill's Annual of Afroasiatic Languages and Linguistics* 1, 106-45.

2010. Counting, measuring and the mass count distinction. *Journal of Semantics* 27, 3, 343-97.

2011. Counting, measuring and the semantics of classifiers. *The Baltic International Yearbook of Cognition, Logic and Communication*, Volume VI. http://newprairiepress.org/biyclc/vol6/iss1/15.

2012. Numericals: counting, measuring and classifying. In A. Aguilar-Guevara, A. Chernilovskaya and R. Nouwen (eds.), *Proceedings of Sinn und Bedeutung 16*, pp. 527–43. Cambridge, MA: MIT Working Papers in Linguistics.

2013a. A Fregean semantics for number words. In Maria Aloni, Michael Franke and Floris Roelofsen (eds.), *Proceedings of the 19th Amsterdam Colloquium*, pp. 179–86. www.illc.uva.nl/AC/AC2013/uploaded_files/inlineitem/23_Rothstein.pdf.

2013b. Counting, measuring and the mass/count distinction. Paper presented at the Düsseldorf Workshop on Countability, September.

2013c Acrosslinguistic perspective on bare nominals: Modern Hebrew and Brazilian Portuguese. In J. Kabatek and A. Wall (eds.), *New Perspective on Base Noun Phrases in Romance and Beyond*, Studies in Language Companion series 141.

2016a. Counting and Measuring: a theoretical and crosslinguistic account. In S. Rothstein and J. Šķilters (eds.), *The Baltic International Yearbook of Cognition, Logic and Communication*, Volume XI: *Number: Cognitive, Semantic and Crosslinguistic Approaches*. Kansas: New Prairie Press. http://dx.doi.org/10.4148/1944-3676.1106 [Online publication]

2016b. Counting, measuring and approximation. Paper presented at the Second Düsseldorf Workshop on Countability. June.

Rothstein, Susan, and Roberta Pires de Oliveira, in press. *Comparatives in Brazilian Portuguese: counting and measuring*. In F. Moltmann (ed.), *Mass and Count in Linguistics, Philosophy, and Cognitive Science*, Amsterdam: John Benjamins.

Rothstein, Susan, and Alessandro Treves, 2010. Computational constraints on compositional interpretation: refocusing the debate on language universals. *Lingua* 120, 12, 2717–22.

Rotstein, Carmen, and Yoad Winter, 2004. Total adjectives vs. partial adjectives: scale structure and higher-order modifiers. *Natural Language Semantics* 12, 3, 259–88.

Schmitt, Cristina, and Alan Munn, 1999. Against the nominal mapping parameter: bare nouns in Brazilian Portuguese. In H. Mako (ed.), *Proceedings of the North East Linguistic Society 29: University of Delaware*, pp. 339–54. Delaware: University of Delaware.

2002. Bare nouns and the morphosyntax of number. In P. Tamanji, M. Hirotani and N. Hall (eds.), *Current Issues in Romance Languages: Selected Papers from the 29th Linguistic Symposium on Romance Languages (LSRL), Ann Arbor, 8–11 April 1999*, pp. 225–39. Amherst, MA: GLSA Publications.

Schvarcz, Brigitta R., 2014. The Hungarians Who Say -nyi: Issues in Counting and Measuring in Hungarian. Unpublished MA thesis, Bar-Ilan University, Ramat Gan.

in press. Classifier constructions in Hungarian and the semantics of the suffix *-nyi*. To appear in A. Liptak and H. van der Hulst (eds.), *Approaches to Hungarian 15*. Amsterdam: John Benjamins.

Schvarcz, Brigitta R., and Susan Rothstein, in press. Hungarian classifier constructions and the mass/count distinction. To appear in A. Liptak and H. van der Hulst (eds.), *Approaches to Hungarian 15*. Amsterdam: John Benjamins.

Schwarzschild, Roger, 2006. The role of dimensions in the syntax of noun phrases. *Syntax* 9, 1, 67–110.

2011. Stubborn distributivity, multiparticipant nouns and the count/mass distinction. In S. Lima, K. Mullin and B. Smith (eds.), *Proceedings of the 39th Meeting of the North East Linguistic Society*, pp. 661–78. Amherst: GLSA.

Selkirk, Elisabeth O., 1977. Some remarks on noun phrase structure. In P. W. Culicover, T. Wasow and A. Akmajian (eds.), *Formal Syntax*, pp. 285–316. New York: Academic Press.

Sharvy, Richard, 1978. Maybe English has no count nouns: notes on Chinese semantics. An essay in metaphysics and linguistics. *Studies in Language* 2, 3, 345–65.

Siloni, Tal, 2001. Construct States at the PF interface. In Pierre Pica (ed.), *Linguistic Variation Yearbook 1*, pp. 229–66. Amsterdam: John Benjamins.

Soja, Nancy N., Susan Carey and Elisabeth Spelke, 1991. Ontological categories guide young children's inductions of word meaning: object terms and substance terms. *Cognition* 38, 2, 179–211.

Srinivasan, Mahesh, Eleanor Chestnut, Peggy Li and David Barner, 2013. Sortal concepts and pragmatic inference in children's early quantification of objects. *Cognitive Psychology* 66, 3, 302–26.

Sybesma, Rint, 2007. Běifāng fāngyán hé Yuèyǔ zhōng míngcí de kěshǔbiāojì [Markers of countability on the noun in Mandarin and Cantonese]. *Yǔyánxué lùncōng* 35, 234–45.

Tai, James H.-Y., and Wang Lianqing, 1990. A semantic study of the classifier tiao. *Journal of the Chinese Language Teachers Association* 25, 35–56.

Tang, Chih-Chen Jane, 1990. Chinese Phrase Structure and the Extended X-bar theory. Unpublished Ph.D. dissertation. Cornell University, Ithaca.

2005. Nouns or classifiers: a non-movement analysis of classifiers in Chinese. *Language and Linguistics* 6, 3, 431–72.

Tsoulas, George, 2006. Plurality of mass nouns and the grammar of number. Handout from talk presented at Generative Linguistics in the Old World 2006. Barcelona, 6–8 April.

Varzi, Achille C., 2007. Spatial reasoning and ontology: parts, wholes, and locations. In M. Aiello, I. Pratt-Hartmann, and J. F. A. K. van Benthem (eds.), *Handbook of Spatial Logics*, pp. 945–1038. Berlin: Springer (Kluwer).

Wągiel, Marcin, 2015. Sums and groups: semantic analysis of Polish numerals. In Gerhild Zybatow, Petr Biskup, Marcel Guhl, Claudia Hurtig, Olav Mueller-Reichau and Maria Yastrebova (eds.), *Slavic Grammar from a Formal Perspective: The 10th Anniversary FDSL Conference, Leipzig 2013*, pp. 495–514. Frankfurt am Main: Peter Lang.

Watters, John Roberts, 1981. A phonology and morphology of Ejagham – with notes on dialectal variation. Unpublished Ph.D. dissertation, UCLA.

Wiese, Heike, 2003. *Numbers, Language and the Human Mind*. Cambridge: Cambridge University Press.

Wilhelm, Andrea, 2008. Bare nouns and number in Dëne Sųłiné. *Natural Language Semantics* 16, 39–68.

Wilkinson, Karina, 1995. The semantics of the common noun *kind*. In G. N. Carlson and F. J. Pelletier (eds.), *The Generic Book*, pp. 383–97. Chicago: University of Chicago Press.

Wiltschko, Martina, 2008. The syntax of non-inflectional plural marking. *Natural Language and Linguistic Theory* 26, 3, 639–94.

Yadroff, Michael, and Loren Billings, 1998. The syntax of approximative inversion in Russian (and the general architecture of nominal expressions). In Željko Bošković, Steven Franks and William Snyder (eds.), *Proceedings of Formal Approaches to Slavic Linguistics 6: The Connecticut Meeting 1997*, pp. 319–38. Ann Arbor, MI: Michigan Slavic Publications.

Yang, Rong, 2001. Common Nouns, Classifiers, and Quantification in Chinese. Unpublished Ph.D. dissertation, Rutgers University, New Jersey.

Yip, Chak-Lam, 2008. Complicating the oversimplification: Chinese numeral classifiers and true measures. In M. K. M. Chan and H. Kang (eds.), *Proceedings of the 20th North American Conference on Chinese Linguistics*, pp. 285–95. Columbus: The Ohio State University.

Zaroukian, Erin, 2011. Divergent approximators. In I. Reich, E. Horch and D. Pauly (eds.), *Proceedings of Sinn und Bedeutung 15*, pp. 677–90. Saarbrücken: Universaar – Saarland University Press.

Language Index

General Index

abundance plurals, 167
accumulation entailments, 241, 242, 243, 244, 245, 246, 247
additivity, 15, 231, 233, 234, 240, 241, 244, 248
agreement
  gender, 44, 61, 189, 190
  number, 15, 27, 34, 37, 48, 52, 54, 140, 169, 227
Aikhenvald, Alexandra, 150
Akmajian, Adrian, 214, 227
Alexiadou, Artemis, 149
Allan, Keith, 194, 195
Approximate Inversion, 140
approximation, 134, 135, 140, 141, 145
approximative construction, 39, 40, 48, 140
approximative interpretation, 45, 47, 48, 139
argument position, 17, 21, 22, 23, 25, 28, 66, 147
Ariel, Mira, 22
arithmetic, 7, 11, 12, 13, 135, 230
at least reading, 21–5, 41
atom, 90, 92, 93, 94, 142, 171, 181, 191, 211
  contextual, 108, 112
  natural, 109, 110, 112, 118, 132, 145, 154, 192
  semantic, 90, 108, 109, 110, 111, 112, 132, 137, 145, 163, 192, 208
  stable, 7, 94, 95, 96, 98, 99, 102
attributive measure predicates, 239, 248

Bach, Emmon, 181
Bale, Alan C., 103, 117, 119, 120, 121, 122, 132, 150, 183

bare noun, 148, 149, 152, 154, 155, 162, 163, 164, 165, 171, 175, 185, 186, 187, 212, 239
bare numeral, 43, 199
bare singular, 14, 49, 88, 101, 125, 126, 127, 128, 147, 149, 163, 186, 188, 207, 211, 254
Barner, David, 8, 86, 87, 88, 117, 118, 119, 120, 121, 122, 124, 129, 132, 137, 174, 176, 183
Barnes, Julian, 60
Barwise, Jon, 16, 25, 43
Benassi, Raíssa, 187, 190
Beviláqua, Kayron, 187, 190
Billings, Lorn, 140
Bisang, Walter, 150, 152, 154, 156, 203
Boolean algebra, 117, 248, 249
  complete, 108, 248
  atomic, 20, 109, 248
Borer, Hagit, 61, 62, 65, 114, 115, 122, 182, 183, 184, 188
Borges, Jorge Luis, 12, 13
Borschev, Vladimir, 50, 56, 74, 75, 80, 209, 219, 220, 221, 222
Bunt, Harry, 181

cardinal phrase, 19
cardinality, 12, 24, 30, 31, 33, 40, 42, 48, 105, 120, 122, 124, 125, 128, 131, 132–41, 142, 144, 168, 175, 241
cardinality function, 17, 20, 30
Carey, Susan, 84
Carlson, Gregory N., 20, 140, 147, 148, 160, 174
Casati, Roberto, 174, 217, 218
case
  genitive, 45, 74, 236
  instrumental, 74